SHELLEY'S
MAJOR
POETRY:

THE FABRIC OF
A VISION

AFTER occupations, he must needs be led to forms of knowledge, to behold, in turn, the beauty of the sciences, and, gazing at the realm, now vast, of beauty, no longer will he, like a menial, cleave to the individual form . . . to the beauty of . . . some one pursuit, living in a wretched slavery and talking tattle; no, turned about towards the vast sea of beauty, and contemplating it, he will give birth to manifold and beautiful discourse of lofty import, and concepts born in boundless love of wisdom; till there, with powers implanted and augmented, he has the vision of one single science, the science of that beauty I go on to.

—DIOTIMA, IN PLATO's *Symposium*

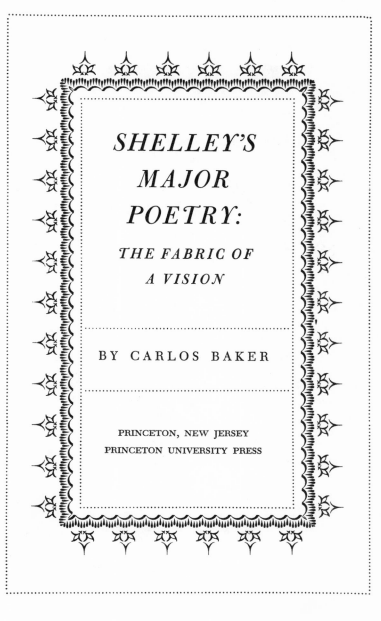

SHELLEY'S MAJOR POETRY:

THE FABRIC OF A VISION

BY CARLOS BAKER

PRINCETON, NEW JERSEY
PRINCETON UNIVERSITY PRESS

Copyright, 1948, by Princeton University Press
LCC 48-7103
ISBN 0-691-01284-9

First Princeton Paperback Printing, 1966
Third Printing, 1973

Printed in the United States of America
by Princeton University Press, Princeton, New Jersey

TO MY WIFE

PREFATORY NOTE

Although this note cannot repay, it can at least acknowledge, with the utmost gratitude, the kindness of those many friends and colleagues to whom I have turned for assistance during the long period of this book's preparation. Dr. Charles W. Kennedy and Professor Donald A. Stauffer both read the whole manuscript, and their patient wisdom, like that of Professor Charles G. Osgood at an earlier stage of the work, has been of inestimable value both to me and to what is here written. I have also to thank, for assistance of various kinds, Professors W. J. Oates, G. E. Duckworth, M. O. Young, Torsten Petersson, F. L. Jones, A. H. Macdonald, W. A. Ringler, and G. H. Gerould. My debt to Shelley scholars, past and present, is indicated throughout the book in the form of footnotes. I wish finally to record my sense of continuing obligation to three former colleagues with whom some phases of this work were discussed: the late Professors A. E. Hinds, D. F. Bowers, and H. H. Hudson.

Princeton University   C.B.
Princeton, N.J.

CONTENTS

SHELLEY'S
MAJOR
POETRY:

THE FABRIC OF
A VISION

INTRODUCTION

Thus much, Sir, I have briefly over-run, to direct your understanding to the well-head of the history, that from thence gathering the whole intention, ye may as in a handfull grip all the discourse, which otherwise may happily seem tedious and confused.—SPENSER TO RALEIGH

· I ·

THE purpose of this book is to examine and interpret Shelley's major poetry of the single decade of his mature writing-career, 1812-1822; to discuss the major problems which he encountered as a practicing poet; and to provide a careful critical survey of his developing thought as it bears upon and is reflected in the individual poems.

No book devoted exclusively to the full range of Shelley's major poetry has been undertaken since the Victorian period. Biographies of the poet have been frequent, and nearly all of them have had something to say about the poems. But even a critical biography throws the emphasis towards the outer circumstances of the life and consequently away from the inward circumstances of the poetry, and in all biographies of whatever category the poetry tends to receive serious attention only where it seems to shed light either on Shelley's development as a thinker, or on his nonliterary activity and opinions. The emphasis in the present volume is the other way round. Outward biographical circumstances have a place in it only as they help to explain what Shelley was trying to accomplish, and how he came by his philosophic convictions. A great many scholars and critics have examined, often with the utmost brilliance and penetration, a number of the problems here considered, and some valuable studies of individual poems have been published. Yet no one for a long time has made an attempt to live the inner life of these poems from one end to the other and to set down the record of his experience. That is what has been attempted in this book.

What has been done here is grounded on an empirical critical method from which a priori judgments and preconceptions have been excluded as rigorously as possible. The method of presentation has been kept as simple and regular as the materials and the groupings would allow. From time to time, where such discussion is relevant, the beginning of a chapter or section has been devoted to an exploration and summarization of various aspects of Shelley's theory of poetry. In general, though not invariably, the concluding numbered section of each chapter is given over to an account of the development of Shelley's philosophical ideas. The body of each chapter is about the poetry itself—what happens in it, what it means, and how well it succeeds. The simple theory behind this method is that if a reader knows what Shelley was trying to do, watches it done, and finally sees the place of the poem in the development of Shelley's art and thought, he will be able to return to any one of the poems with a fuller awareness of its significance in the whole pattern of Shelley's work, and a refreshed appreciation of its merits or demerits. Taken as a whole, the poems are extremely various both in form and in purpose. They consist of moral allegories and eclogues, a pseudo-epic and other examples of narrative poetry (a kind in which Shelley did not excel), lyrical dramas in the "ideal mode," semidramatic conversation pieces, a blank verse tragedy, a hortatory tract, some satire, an elegy, and many odes and other forms. In the face of such variety, some classification is convenient, has been adopted, and will be explained. Yet each of the poems in this assorted calendar offers its particular problems of analysis and interpretation, and each is here made the subject of an essay in which the attempt has been to show both what is unique about it, and what it has in common with other major—or minor—poems in the canon. When the total body of the poems is thus examined, a consistent and traceable pattern emerges in the fabric of Shelley's vision. The broad aim of the present book is to make that pattern clearer than it has ever been before, and to show by what conjurations and what mighty or lesser magic it was, in the first instance, laid down. For Shelley's strength, which is also the measure of his weakness as an artist, consists more in the qualities of vision and insight than in the accepted disciplines of poetry. Though his medium was poetic, and often succeeds as such, his laws were those of the philosopher, the psychologist, the seer, and the prophet, and it is to these laws rather than those of his chosen medium that he primarily conforms, both by preference and by inner constitution.

· II ·

The plan of this book is roughly chronological, providing a close study of the seventeen most important long poems, beginning with *Queen Mab*, written in 1812-1813 when the twenty-year-old poet stood on the threshold of maturity, and ending with *The Triumph of Life*, which Shelley left unfinished when he died a month short of his thirtieth birthday. The juvenile poems are here rejected without compunction as the products of what Shelley himself called a distempered and unoriginal vision, but other minor poems are considered where relevant. Part One is a consideration of the poems of Shelley's apprenticeship, 1812-1817. None of them has intrinsic importance as a work of art, yet all of them require attention. The first five years of Shelley's life as a maturing poet were devoted to the exploration and establishment of themes, ideas, images, and symbols which he was to engage with greater success in the last half of his single decade of "granted power." This was also the period when he was searching, with a bewildering eclecticism, for an ethic and a metaphysic which would be satisfying to his idealistic cast of mind and suitable for poetic exploitation. As Shelley's questing and questioning mind gradually emerged from the pseudo-gothic, pseudo-materialistic background in which it was nurtured, he began slowly to discover the modes in which he was to write and the principles by which he was to live. The section of the book on the apprenticeship has the over-all title, Necessity, because this section is an attempt to show what Necessity meant to Shelley both as a philosophical and psychological concept. In *Queen Mab* Necessity means a cosmic power whose rule is absolute both in the material and in the moral world, but a power which will inevitably, though by slow degrees, produce social, institutional, and even climatic changes leading to a world-situation like that described by the poet-prophet Isaiah. In *Alastor*, Necessity appears in the Wordsworthian invocation as the beneficent Nature-spirit, but it is another kind of necessity which stands at the center of the poem: the imperious psychological necessity of love, which is represented by the visionary maiden of Shelley's first nympholeptic myth. At this time originates the psyche-epipsyche concept which, when it has been clarified in Shelley's thought and purged of its physiological attributes, becomes the basic myth for all his best later work in "ideal" poetry. *The Revolt of Islam*, while putting this concept into operation through the characters of Laon and Cythna, involves at bottom a reexamination of the necessitarian law of *Queen Mab*. The ruling vision in *The Revolt* is still derivative, made over from a Zoroastrian myth which Shelley owed to Peacock. But the conclusion, which does not precisely coincide with the mythological assumptions, is that good and evil are inextricably mingled in the organization of the cosmos, and that Necessity is an amoral force on which men cannot afford to depend. The task of world-reform is now seen to fall upon the shoulders of wise, just, and virtuous moral leaders, the one small group to whom the lengthy and even disheartening task of guiding human society towards the historical millennium can be safely entrusted. In this essentially abortive "epic" appears Shelley's most forthright early profession of faith in the individual will as a directive force in human history. *The Revolt* marks the end of Shelley's literary apprenticeship to the eighteenth-century moral allegorists and to the method and manner of Southey's Orientalist romances.

Part Two, in which Shelley is shown to be seriously grappling with the problem of evil, begins with *Prometheus Unbound*, the first great poem in the canon as well as Shelley's first successful attempt to synthesize the ideas which he had handled (separately or confusedly) in the works of his apprentice period. Like *Alastor*, the *Prometheus* is a poem about a situation in the human mind. It is presented in a nonhistorical context because, although it has a bearing on every moment of man's existence, the situation has no history. Like *Alastor*, too, and like *The Revolt* (though much more subtly and satisfactorily), the *Prometheus* utilizes the psyche-epipsyche concept. Like *The Revolt* it places the responsibility for ridding the cosmos of evil squarely in the hands of virtuous and thoughtful leaders. The real philosophical advance here is the development of the idea that evil is largely, though not by any means entirely, the result of spiritual blindness, and that if man were able, by an act of willed spiritual self-reform, to overcome at some great

hour his inheritance of hate and superstition, there would be almost
no limits to what he could think and do. The real literary advance
in the *Prometheus Unbound* is Shelley's discovery of a device—the
careful remodeling and remotivation of traditional myth—which
he was to employ in a variety of ways in nearly all of his remaining
poems.

From the fourth chapter onwards, for reasons of order, illumina-
tion, and convenience, those poems which belong together are
considered in groups, although within and among these groups a
rough chronological sequence is maintained. The first is a group
of conversation poems centered on the problem of evil in a historical context. *Rosalind and Helen*, a sentimental piece which
Shelley did not like, presents the idea that true love without marriage is far better than marriage without love. Shelley draws an
overdramatized contrast between a marriage made in Hell and an
extramarital union made, or at least justified, in Heaven. *Julian and
Maddalo* is noteworthy for two reasons: the argument on free will
and destiny which takes place between Julian (Shelley) and Maddalo (Byron); and the story of the madness of the poet Tasso (a
story much disguised in the poem) which serves as the *exemplum*
of the argument. *The Cenci*, which is included among the conversation poems both for convenience and for ideological reasons,
provides a useful key to and demonstration of Shelley's concept of
tragedy, and is otherwise worth attention not only because it is a
sound play, but also because of Shelley's careful analysis of human
character, his study of changing states of mind, and his preoccupation with the corrupting forces which imperil the integrity and
force the hand of the virtuous individual in human society.

The next group consists of a number of poems whose orientation
is primarily, though not exclusively, political. All of them center on
the idea that liberty, whether considered as individual integrity
and dignity or as a political condition, can be bought only at the
price of a constant, preferably bloodless, struggle against those re-
actionary forces which in Shelley's view were opposing, inhibiting,
and frequently stifling, political reorganization in England and on
the continent during the late Regency period. As the conversation
poems, in the two instances that matter, had examined evil in a
socio-historical milieu, so the political poems examine evil in a
modern historical situation. Of particular importance here are

Shelley's attempt to reach the masses by the development of a poetic *lingua communis*; his desire to organize liberal elements into a strong united front; the reflection in several of the poems of the political attitudes of Leigh Hunt's *Examiner*; the dangers of prosecution for libel which were evidently chiefly responsible for preventing the dissemination in Shelley's lifetime of his most forthright political poems; the experiments with political satire in *Peter Bell the Third* and *Oedipus Tyrannus*; Shelley's sorrowful consideration of Wordsworth's apostasy from social liberalism; Shelley's views on bloodless revolution; his use of Biblical and Greek mythology as the groundwork of his poems; his tribute to the place of Greece in the development of western civilization; and his return in *Hellas*, the last political poem, to the idealistic mode which is his most characteristic means of expression.

Part Three, which is called, in a phrase of Goethe's, "The Spirit's Splendor," begins by examining in detail a group of poems for which Shelley's term was "visionary rhymes." These are intellectual play-poems or experiments with serious overtones. In various ways they consider the problem, which Shelley had dealt with in *Peter Bell the Third*, and which bulked large as a theme in his poetry from 1820 until his death, namely, the predicament of the gentle and acutely sensitive mind in a materialistic environment. This is one of the themes of *The Sensitive Plant* and it is the implied theme of the *Letter to Maria Gisborne*. The corollary theme of *The Sensitive Plant* is the failure in the organ of man's spiritual insight to remain in visual contact with the divine idea of love and beauty, with the result that an inward venomous corruption spreads through his spiritual life. The *Letter to Maria Gisborne* involves a different emphasis, centering on the compensations which partially repay the finely organized intellect which is obliged to live in the worldly life. The chief compensation proposed is the possibility of living a genuinely philosophic life in the midst of a small coterie of true friends, which is often, as William James asserts, the idealist's small-scale substitute for a large-scale millennium. In the third visionary rhyme, *The Witch of Atlas*, Shelley again enters the suprahistorical dimension to evolve, out of many literary experiences, a playful myth about his "witch": the divine Idea which had for so long bewitched his imagination. The Witch's visitations to the minds of men are a symbolic representation of the fleeting visits of the consciousness of intellectual beauty and love. But the Witch is seen half-humorously as if, through long familiarity with his vision of supernal power, Shelley now felt almost at home with it. Despite the playful manner of the *Letter* and *The Witch*, however, the tone of the visionary poems is more gloomy than cheerful. As the year 1820 waned into autumn, Shelley's youthful optimism, long under assault, had finally given place to a kind of pessimism. This was not by any means wholly quietistic or defeatist. Yet Shelley was becoming less and less sanguine about the possibility of immediate social progress, and more and more concerned with two aims which were ultimately the same: to remain in permanent touch with his cosmic vision, and to preserve his artistic integrity and his moral convictions against the incursions of a spiritless, careless, yet predatory social world. He did not any longer believe that human rationality was a positive guarantor of progressive moral achievement, nor was he so certain as he had formerly been that the forceful enunciation of the law of love would result in its universal acceptance. Indeed, what he saw as the fate of the ethic of Jesus Christ seemed to indicate the contrary. But he continued to believe in the efficacy of his vision, immediately for himself and many of his greater predecessors among the thinkers of the western world, and ultimately for the benefit of civilized man. In all his gloom there was no basic distrust of what Mr. Niebuhr calls "the tension of faith and hope in which all moral action is grounded."

The most remarkable group in this concluding section of the book is the last, comprising the great idealistic poems, *Epipsychidion* and *Adonais*, and the great idealistic essay, *A Defence of Poetry*. Here, in the first half of 1821, occurs Shelley's final correlation, clarification, and synthesis of his philosophic ideas. This synthesis is presented with reference to a symbolic scheme of deep complexity. As in several of the earlier poems, the underlying theme has to do with the poet's relation to human society, to his inmost self, and to supernal power. In both these poems Shelley seeks to represent symbolically his views on the interrelation of vision and art. *Epipsychidion*, the "idealized history" of Shelley's "life and feelings" offers an account, in a scheme based on Dante's *Vita Nuova, Convito*, and *Paradiso*, of the discovery, loss, and rediscovery of the supreme vision. The marriage symbol with which the poem closes is a way of imagining that the informing spirit of the cosmic scheme has entered into a permanent union with the creative mind, so that the poet, like those who drink from the crystal cup of the Witch of Atlas, lives thenceforward as if some control mightier than life were in him. The same vision reappears in *Adonais* under a different set of symbols, though here, because the poem is an elegy for a dead artist, the primary stress falls upon the malignity and callousness of a society which does not acknowledge its rightful legislators, the philosophical and psychological poets, the generals of the armies of the mind without whose ministrations chaos is come again—and again. *The Triumph of Life*, that exceedingly beautiful and important poem which marked the close of Shelley's career and serves as epilogue to the present book, presents another view of the same important subject: the impingement of the mundane and the meretricious upon the higher life of the soul.

The following book is long. Yet no thoroughgoing study of the large and various body of Shelley's work could have been made in a much briefer compass. By following Shelley's development through a ten-year period, with reasonably full attention to his more important sources, his moral and esthetic beliefs and aims, his changing philosophical and psychological convictions, and his most persistent poetic themes, it has been possible to provide revised interpretations of *Alastor, Prometheus Unbound, The Sensitive Plant, The Witch of Atlas, Epipsychidion, Adonais*, and *The Triumph of Life*; and also to throw new light on the eighteenth-century literary and philosophical background of *Queen Mab*, on the origins and conduct of the mythological scheme which underlies *The Revolt of Islam* and strongly affected the *Prometheus*, on the identity of the Maniac in *Julian and Maddalo*, on the motivation of the leading characters in *The Cenci*, and on the relationship of Shelley's political poems to the social background of the late Regency period. The hope is that a new and sharper portrait of the artist as a young man will emerge from these pages.

· III ·

THE argument which this book develops is that Shelley was primarily a philosophical and psychological poet with a strong if unorthodox ethical bias, an almost single-minded devotion to a set of esthetic ideals which he felt to be of the greatest utility to the inner life of man and to the progress of society, a conviction that in origin and effect the world's greatest poetry has been inspirational and in the best sense "visionary," and a belief, often enough reiterated to be taken as Shelleyan gospel, that the world's leading poets are great not so much because they have been artists as because they have been "philosophers of the very loftiest power." At any point in his mature career, Shelley would have been prepared to defend with eloquence, determination, and a mass of historical documentation culled from his extraordinarily wide reading, any or all of these biases, devotions, and convictions —because they were the very life-blood of his own effort as a writer.

Shelley's reputation has been distinguished by what may be called its regular variability. He has been praised as a resolute foe of political oppression, a prophet of far-off social events, an optimistic and altruistic idealist, a deliverer with a message of brotherly love, a noble rhetorician, a reviver of Platonism in a materialistic age, a romantic individualist, and a Newton among poets. He has been attacked as a falsetto screamer, a sentimental Narcissus, a dream-ridden escapist, an immoral free-love cultist with a highly inflammable nature, and, particularly in the present age, as the weakling author of the lyric called "The Indian Serenade." The remarkable aspect of these labels is that they regularly reappear: none of them is peculiar to any one age, although "The Indian Serenade" used to be liked, and understood, better than it is today. Shelley was praised or blamed in his own time for nearly all these virtues and faults, and each succeeding generation has had the battle to fight over again. There is hardly a poet in the history of English literature who has been the victim of so many attacks and so many defenses. No permanent peace is likely, nor is any single interpretation of the man or his work likely to gain universal acceptance. If all the lovers and haters of Shelley are not extremists, a sufficient number of hardy perennials is born into each generation to keep the colors flying. To achieve a balanced and judicious estimate of the only really important aspect of Shelley, his career as writer, in the midst of these periodic jostlings and fluctuations, one needs, above all, to understand his premises, his aims, and his achievements, and to keep as clear as may be from the two extremes. For of all the romantic poets Shelley has been taken for what, primarily, he was not, and praise or blame has been showered on him for what, only secondarily, he was.

What Shelley was has been either dimly comprehended or separately and atomistically demonstrated: a sensitive and profoundly serious philosophical and psychological poet, the author of three or four poems which, judged according to their own and some other laws, are great, and of large numbers of experimental, exploratory, and only partially successful poems in which he tried to employ and develop symbols of a sufficient magnitude and tensile strength to absorb the inner stress he laid upon them. The anthologies have tended to reprint numbers of little lyrics which Shelley never cared to print in his own lifetime and which were most often by-products of his main effort, sometimes ignoring the poems on which he spent his greatest care, or again, on the assumption that he was primarily a lyric poet, lifting shorter songs from the longer works and exhibiting them alone and out of context, a device which is excused by the space-limits of anthology-makers but which seems like trying to give an audience the central idea of *The Tempest* by quoting, without further comment, the song "Full Fathom Five."

It is a limited and partial, and therefore misrepresentative view of Shelley which sees him only as Ariel, floating down or exuberantly diving through waves of moonlit song, raising in the spirit those tempests of emotion which, though meaningless, are exceedingly beautiful. The lazy-mindedness of such a view consists in the failure to work back of the Arielism of Shelley into the stringently self-disciplined ethical and metaphysical thinker who employed the lyric as servant to his own particular brand of white magic. For Shelley, like Prospero in the mantle of invisibility, or like the poet in his own lyric, "The Skylark," was often hidden in the very light of his own thought: a manipulator of large conceptions whose fundamental operations no one quite understood. Often he rose like Ariel to sport among the clouds or coast upon the western wind or ascend as near as could be to the sun; it was at such times that he produced his most harmonious music, a music elicited by his ecstatic delight in moving swiftly among the timeless objects of his thought. Behind the ascensions of Ariel, however, there lay always the directive brain of Prospero, author of all the visions, wielder of the power.

A clear majority of Shelley's poems belong to the classification of inspirational literature, a kind somewhat out of critical fashion in the present age but not therefore to be ignored. The structural method on which most of his lyrics and longer poems have been built is characteristic of inspirational literature: an ascension from the quiet exposition of the opening stanzas to a kind of bursting climax at which the internal pressure apparently becomes too great to be any longer withheld. From what it is possible to learn of Shelley's writing habits, it would not appear that in the act of composition he paid more than cursory attention to the final order of the subdivisions of his poems. But in the arrangement of what he had written (as in *Adonais*, where nearly every one of the really memorable stanzas comes in the last third of the poem) Shelley seems intentionally to have placed the most inspired and potentially inspiring passages near the end of acts or scenes in order to emphasize the ascensional structure. Even if one doubts that this order was intentional, the fact remains that it was the characteristic order in Shelley's poetry.

Shelley placed great value on such passages, and believed that they were not the result of what he called labor and study. "The toil and the delay recommended by critics," said he, could mean only that one must make careful observation of his inspired moments, and fill up "the spaces between their suggestions by the intertexture of conventional expressions." In *Adonais*, which Shelley called a highly wrought piece of art, the intertexture of conventional expressions (derived from Milton, Bion, and Moschus) comes chiefly in the first two-thirds of the poem, and the product of Shelley's "inspired moments" appears at the end. Perhaps Shelley's main effort as poet consisted in the attempt not to bridge but to close the gaps between his inspired moments, and thus to eliminate the need of "conventional" expressions. In this effort he was no more successful than most poets of his stamp, and he was led by his experience to complain of the "limitedness of the poetical faculty itself." But he rarely stopped trying, being constituted as he was, to remove the limits and to make the inspired moment a permanent condition.

Keats once sought to persuade Shelley that "an artist must serve

Mammon." Shelley must be "more of an artist, and load every rift" of his subject with ore. Keats was thinking of Spenser's Cave of Mammon in the *Faerie Queene*, within whose rough vault

> the ragged breaches hong
> Embost with massy gold of glorious gift,
> And with rich metall loaded every rift.

Shelley's work from about 1820 onwards shows that he was making some such attempt as Keats advised, so that in time his thinking on the art of poetry might have led him, not to devalue the importance of inspiration, but to pay greater attention to the importance of "toil and delay." The real and heart-breaking toil in Shelley was expended upon the working-out of the vision which lay behind his greatest poems, and in the development of symbols which could bear the burden he placed upon them. Under the surface of *Epipsychidion* and *Adonais* lies a tremendously complex substructure of symbolism, and when one has explored some of its reaches he knows where Shelley's hardest effort was expended. If the fabric of the poetry is full of "ragged breaches"—syntactic disorders, obscurities, images carelessly thrown down or so changeable and various that they are scarcely caught before they are bewilderingly superseded by others—it is partly because he was more deeply concerned with perception and conception than with expression.

Yet Shelley has not been taken seriously as a philosophical poet, and one often gathers from the remarks of his critics, whether inimical or worshipful, that his philosophy does not matter. Yet it does matter—and vitally so—because it is always either the central matter of his poetry, or the frame of reference in terms of which his poetry has been written. That is the chief reason why the present book contains an account, made as precise as possible for each of the periods of his career, of his philosophical development, and of the subtle or sweeping changes which took place in his reading of the world. Shelley has not been taken seriously as a moralist, on the grounds that anyone who abandoned his first wife and ran off with another woman is scarcely to be trusted as an ethical teacher. Yet this foolish and certainly reprehensible act, committed before Shelley had succeeded in the difficult process of growing up emotionally, was paid for a dozen times over, and is pertinent to the problem of Shelley's worth as an ethical teacher only in the fact that his knowledge of human beings and of the human situation was clearly deepened and broadened as a result of his unfortunate experiences. Shelley has not been taken seriously as a psychological poet because it has not been generally understood that one of his major attempts was to present, by the use of a particular kind of symbolic language, his analyses of certain states of mind known to, but not often consciously recognized by, the thinking part of humankind.

Because the fundamentals of his poetic effort have been obscured—through careless or unsympathetic reading, through blind and breathless adulation, through the not inconsiderable difficulty of a great part of the major poetry, or through the fact that his spectacularly "romantic" life has tended to overshadow his achievement as a writer—Shelley has remained, in the century and a quarter since his death, a figure much talked about but seldom seen in his true light. Many of his biographers have sought to read his poetry as if it were literal or nearly literal autobiography, a mistake which this book seeks to adjust and to correct. Shelley is sometimes "autobiographical" in the very particularized sense that he uses his poetry as the vehicle for analysis of states of mind in which he has been interested. With the greatest rarity he will write of his own physical experience, as in the opening section of *Julian and Maddalo.* But in the main he is far more "objective" than has generally been believed, and the literalistic reading of his poetry will not hit the point, as many of the chapters in the present volume show.

Shelley was in fact one of the most literary poets who ever lived, and his poetry displays a striking combination of objective philosophical and psychological interests and a heavy dependence on antecedent literatures. His preoccupation with states of mind leads him to search for a special language through which they can be dramatically projected, and he arrives at a symbolic literary language developed from many traditional sources and refashioned into a mode of expression peculiarly his own. He once complained that when he tried to speak to other men in the language of poetry, they misunderstood him, as if he had been a visitor to an unknown country. Yet the explorer of Shelley's sources can nearly always trace his semiprivate language back to its origins, and its origins are almost invariably found, not in the events of his life, but in the events of his reading. With the help of earlier source-hunters, and through an extensive independent study of Shelley's reading, it has been possible in the present volume to discover the origins of most of his symbolic figures, to use that knowledge in the interpretation of the poems, and thus to provide a topographical map of Shelley's realms of gold.

If the study of Shelley's poetry is not necessarily a means of grace, the study of his source books is one of the means to an education. Among the important matters in the following pages are the proofs of Shelley's indebtedness to, and his imaginative reworking of, Greek literature (Plato, Aeschylus, Sophocles), Renaissance literature (Dante, Petrarch, Spenser, Shakespeare, and Milton), and the poetry of his own day (Wordsworth, Coleridge, Byron, and Keats). Though it is outside the scope of this book to provide an exhaustive study of Shelley's use of his forebears and his contemporaries, enough is included to show in broad outline, yet with necessary emphases, Shelley's direct relationship to the great tradition of western letters.

The definition of what Shelley was can be clarified by attention to what, primarily, he was not. He was not primarily an epic poet, though the internal dimensions of his four best poems, *Prometheus Unbound, Epipsychidion, Adonais*, and *The Triumph of Life*, are of an epic magnitude. He was not primarily a dramatic poet. Deeply interested in the analysis of character, and particularly of what he calls "the most interesting situations of the human mind," he read, admired, and imitated Shakespeare, Calderon, and Goethe. He wrote one tragedy, *The Cenci*, which with some editorial revision and directorial reemphasis, could be made into a highly effective stage-play. But he recognized in himself a deficiency in strictly literary architectonics, and he had not, as the first-line modern dramatist must have, a fundamental interest in the projection of character through action. He was not primarily a lyric poet. Though he was often most eloquent and memorable in the lyric mode, his greatest effort was expended on the arrangement, clarification, and development of his vision rather than on the hymning of it. He was not primarily a craftsman in the sense of being interested deeply in and unremittingly devoted to the finer details of structure and texture. On rare occasions, chiefly in the latter part of his life, he develops controlling metaphors whose logical complexities and multiple ramifications show that he took sometimes the craftsman-philosopher's delight in that process of verbal and ideological intensification on which modern criticism rightly, though sometimes too exclusively, insists. But his characteristic texture is loosely woven of many strings, as if he hoped that through the veil of language his readers might discern the complex and many-faceted vision on which, rather than on verbal patternings, his texture was based.

Secondarily, of course, Shelley was all these kinds of poet at one time or another in his writing life. The variety of his experimental work is one of the most remarkable aspects of his brief career. But whatever the form he essayed, the fundamental dynamic of his writing remained the same. He belongs primarily to the class of psychological and philosophical poets which he describes in the peroration to his *Defence of Poetry*. He sought, first, "to measure the circumference and sound the depths of human nature with a comprehensive and all-penetrating spirit." He attempted, in the second place, to be the "hierophant" or philosophic interpreter of the great vision of supernal beauty and love—a vision which he knew to be "unapprehended" by the majority of men and only "approximated" in perception and expression by the poet himself, yet a vision absolutely necessary to the moral progress and mental well-being of the benighted world of men. Knowledge of the circumference and the depths of human nature led in Shelley's view to knowledge of self. Knowledge of the great vision meant knowledge of the moral law of love. To these two concepts, self-knowledge and knowledge of what he thought of as God, his career as poet was dedicated.

To understand Shelley's means, one may look to his ends. He began, at one end, as a didactic allegorical poet and ended by writing symbolic mythological poetry of an impressively high order. He began as an imitator of eighteenth-century forms, and the early work is full of obvious creaking machines which served him as the vehicles for a materialistic, necessitarian ideology and a black-and-white ethic. He ended as the formulator of an idealistic vision by which he measured the mundane world and found it wanting, but a vision whose very complexity and many-sidedness indicate that he had come to a kind of answer, as tentative as all such answers must be, to the perennial ethical and metaphysical problems. When he began to find himself as a poet, somewhere in the latter part of 1818, he entered the line that begins with Dante and continues through Milton and Blake. As ultimately developed and refined, his vision employs traditional symbols in an unconventional fashion for the ethical end of man's redemption and salvation. If Shelley's vision is less firmly grounded and detailed than Dante's, less Hebraically majestic than Milton's, and less spectacular than Blake's, it is somewhat easier than Dante's to grasp in its totality, less heavily weighted with theology than Milton's, and less insistently arbitrary than Blake's. Shelley's place as philosophic poet may be defined in terms of the myth-makers of classical, Renaissance and modern times. His place as a psychological poet is beside Wordsworth and Keats. Like them he took self-knowledge as the key to the understanding of man, and like them he came, by tortuous ways, to an understanding of man's place in the cosmic scheme. A century and a quarter of readers have not been wrong in asserting the indubitable charm of Shelley's Arielism; the error has lain in supposing that he had nothing else to offer. This book is intended to introduce and to explain Ariel's master, Prospero.

PART ONE:

NECESSITY

I

THE NECESSITY OF REFORM:
QUEEN MAB

To me the wonder is . . . that the poets present and past
are no better—not that I mean to depreciate them; but
every one can see that they are a crowd of imitators, and
will imitate best and most easily the life in which they
have been brought up; while that which is beyond the
range of man's education he finds hard to carry out in
action, and still harder adequately to represent in language. —SOCRATES, IN THE *Timaeus*

These are my empire, for to me is given
The wonders of the human world to keep,
And fancy's thin creations to endow
With manner, being, and reality.

—SHELLEY, IN *Queen Mab*

· I ·

"POETRY," as Shelley observed in his preface to *Prometheus Unbound*, "is a mimetic art. It creates, but it creates by combination
and representation." From the earliest chaotic scribblings of his
schooldays, Shelley's writing was mimetic, and his juvenile work
in fiction and in verse is a dependable, and on the whole depress-
ing, index to the kinds of reading which attracted him when his
intellectual horizons were limited, his taste undiscerning, his tech-
nical skills undeveloped, his critical opinions unformed, and his
ignorance, like that of most boys his age, woeful. If a man is
known by the company he keeps, a young poet is known by the
models he rejects, and Shelley succeeded only very slowly in tear-
ing down the idols of his youth.

But by 1812 a kind of order had begun to emerge from the gothic chaos of the juvenilia, and the date may fairly be taken as the commencement of his creative life. In the beginning was the word—of William Godwin. Shelley's twentieth year, when he began *Queen Mab*, saw him entering on the career of social and moral reform which sporadically engaged his attention during the single decade of his maturity. He therefore turned for counsel, as was perfectly natural, to the ablest radical thinker he knew, the author of *Political Justice*.

"I will publish nothing," he told Godwin, "that shall not conduce to virtue." The question was how one could best set about the task of equipping oneself to lead men into the paths of righteousness. "Guide thou and direct me. . . . To you I owe the inestimable boon of granted power, of arising from the state of intellectual sickliness and lethargy into which I was plunged two years ago, and of which *St. Irvyne* and *Zastrozzi* were the distempered, although unoriginal visions."[1] No philosopher, least of all William Godwin, could disregard so eloquent a plea, and he summed up his prescription for the improvement of mankind in five words: "Discussion, reading, enquiry, perpetual communication."[2] Shelley's inquiry should be directed towards the study of history; the scope of his reading should be enlarged to include the great writers of the English Renaissance. History was, after all, the best means of "becoming acquainted with whatever of noble, useful, generous and admirable human nature is capable of designing and performing." As for Shelley's taste in poetry, it was false. He loved the "perpetual sparkle and glittering" of authors like Darwin, Southey, Scott, and Campbell, and chose to ignore all the rest.[3] Shelley's response to these suggestions was reasonably encouraging. Despite his youthful hatred of the subject he almost immediately placed an order for the "most standard and reputable histories" of Greece, Rome, England, Scotland, America, India, and Brazil, remarking to his bookseller that anyone who expected to become a "mender of antiquated abuses" must devote his days and nights to the study of the past. His reaction to Godwin's literary suggestions was less enthusiastic. Although his mentor had assured him that "our elder

---

[1] *Letters*, VIII, 280, 287.

[2] C. K. Paul, *William Godwin: His Friends and Contemporaries* (Boston, 1876), II, pp. 203-204.

[3] F. K. Brown, *The Life of William Godwin* (New York, 1926), pp. 274-275.

writers" had lived in a time when "every author thought," and when "every line was pregnant with sense," Shelley's conversion to the great works of the past was slow. Among the poets he ordered in cheap editions one could find the names of Shakespeare and Spenser. But equally conspicuous, not because Godwin recommended but because he depreciated them, were the names of Southey and Erasmus Darwin.[4]

Since *Queen Mab* was finished and transcribed at too early a date (February 19, 1813)[5] to have felt the full benefits of Godwin's counsel, one may fairly describe it in the very words with which Shelley had characterized his earlier efforts in prose: it is a distempered and unoriginal vision, mediocre as verse, and something less than mediocre as history. Yet because it provides a kind of groundplan for his subsequent development, it will be useful to examine this highly mimetic production, in order to determine as precisely as possible the state of Shelley's mind and art at the beginning of his career as a serious poet who believed in the necessity of reform.

· II ·

IN contriving a literary vehicle for his radical ideas, Shelley made use of a considerable amount of second-hand lumber, on which the stamp of the eighteenth century was prominent. This is hardly surprising. He had been born in that century and nurtured as a child upon its literature, and in adopting the manner of his immediate predecessors and his elder contemporaries he was merely following a pattern common to young writers in his own and other times.[6] To one critic the mixture of "mincing eighteenth-century verse" and "revolutionary war-cries" seems almost to be a contradiction in terms.[7] Yet this mixture was common enough, both in Shelley's time and in the preceding age. *Queen Mab* is a somewhat belated example of the eighteenth-century moral allegory, a genre which had attained great popularity among the Augustan and post-Augustan imitators of Spenser, and of which specimens were still appearing in Shelley's lifetime.[8]

---

[4] *Letters*, IX, 33-36.   [5] *Ibid.*, 47.

[6] Dobell so describes Shelley's manner in *Queen Mab*. See the preface to the Shelley Society's facsimile reprint of *Alastor* (1886), p. xii.

[7] O. W. Campbell, *Shelley and the Unromantics* (London, 1924), p. 114.

[8] For an extensive list of these imitations of Spenser, see H. E. Cory, *PMLA* 26

Spenser had long stood as model for anyone who undertook an allegory. So Leigh Hunt asserted in 1802, citing West's *Education* and Thomson's *Castle of Indolence* as notable examples.[9] Among the other collateral descendants of *The Faerie Queene* and first cousins to *Queen Mab* were such moral disquisitions as William Thompson's *Sickness*, a poem in five books one of which is called *The Palace of Disease*; Thomas Denton's *House of Superstition*; W. J. Mickle's *The Concubine*; Sir William Jones's *Palace of Fortune* (a clear imitation of Pope's *Temple of Fame*); Hunt's own *Palace of Pleasure*; and Erasmus Darwin's *Temple of Nature*. The experience of reading some of these might have been painful to Spenser; it was evidently not so with the youthful Shelley.

Although Shelley has chosen to particularize his characters in *Queen Mab*, he is clearly thinking throughout in allegorical terms.[10] It is only because the central figures in the poem are called by unusual proper names that their kinship with typical allegorical figures has been concealed. The Queen, for example, is the usual hierophant, the revealer of wonderful secrets. The spirit of the heroine, Ianthe, is the virtuous soul, for whose edification the veil of false propaganda is ripped away and the underlying truth made plain. That fool "whom courtiers nickname monarch" is the personification of political tyranny, while Ahasuerus, in spite of his particularized name and his associations with Shelley's juvenile writing, is the spiritual essence of all those infidels who have been crushed under the heel of the Christian Church.[11] Were it not for its new nomenclature and its more ambitious scope, *Queen Mab*

(1911), 51-91, and Traugott Böhme, "Spenser's Literarisches Nachleben bis zu Shelley," *Palaestra* 93 (Berlin, 1911), 125-220. A discussion of the incidence of the Spenserian stanza in the eighteenth century has been written by E. P. Morton, *MP* 10 (1913), 265-291. The more prominent parodies of Spenser are mentioned by R. P. Bond, *English Burlesque Poetry 1700-1750* (Cambridge, Mass., 1932), p. 271.

[9] Leigh Hunt, *Juvenilia* (London, 1802), pp. 153-154. The dates of these poems are scattered through the eighteenth and early nineteenth centuries. Although blank verse and heroic couplets appear now and again, the Spenserian stanza predominates.

[10] Besides the dialogue between Vice and Falsehood in the notes to the poem, one may note personified abstractions like Time the Conqueror (IX, 23, 138-139), Selfishness (V, 22, 187, 249), and Falsehood (V, 197; VI, 48). Böhme (*op. cit.*, 295-296) regards these figures as Spenserian. Ultimately they probably are, but they occur too frequently among Spenser's imitators to make it necessary to suppose that Shelley went directly to Spenser for them.

[11] On the connection between Shelley's Ahasuerus and Milton's Satan, see Appendix I.

would long ago have taken its place in literary history—perhaps under some such name as *The Palace of Nature*—with all those other palaces, castles, temples, and houses of Fame, Pleasure, Indolence, Nature, Disease, and Superstition which had been strewn across the literary landscape by Shelley's predecessors.

Most of these poems share an easily recognizable pattern, in which the poet or his muse, or some male or female protagonist without literary pretensions, dreams that he enters a palace alone or under the guidance of a goddess or a sage. He may walk, fly, or ride in a magical conveyance to some spot from which he is able to take a long look at human difficulties, and to learn a lesson by means of allegorical personages. As soon as the moral is driven home, the chastened or enlightened visitor returns to earth, although the author is sometimes so intent upon his teaching that his central figure is left, so to speak, up in the air.

The general outline of Shelley's poem runs true to form. Queen Mab, an omniscient spirit, descends in a magic car to the bedside of a sleeping maiden called Ianthe. Disengaging the girl's soul from her body, which continues in sleep, Mab conducts the fellow-spirit to a magnificent sky-palace from whose battlements they look down upon the little globe of the earth while Mab elucidates the secrets of past, present, and future time. The only speakers besides the queen and the soul are two figures called up by Mab's wand, representing the chief *bêtes noires* of the poem: the evils of temporal power and religious tyranny. Having assured the soul that in the future such evils will be removed, Mab sends Ianthe thoughtfully home again. Nearly every creaking cog in the machinery of Shelley's poem was borrowed from the stock-pile of the moral allegories of the eighteenth century.[12]

Most of the institutions and crimes attacked in *Queen Mab* had received similar treatment in allegories or moral epistles written several decades before Shelley's birth. Three examples will suffice.

[12] Shelley agrees, for example, with Jones and Darwin in using women as central characters. Mab's hierophantic powers are shared by Volney's Genius and Darwin's Nature-spirit. Ianthe is chosen for her virtue and sincerity. The detail is duplicated in Volney, Darwin, and Jones. The ancestor of Mab's car can be found in Jones, and several times over in Southey's *Thalaba* and *Kehama*, where people are always being carried off in magic chariots. Descriptions of palaces much like Mab's may be found in Pope, Southey, Jones, Darwin, Hunt, and Spenser. The little spot of earth, visible to the distant observer, is a convenient piece of stage property in Pope, Volney, Thomson, and probably others.

Shelley holds "custom" responsible for the continuation of political despotisms. The unconquered powers of precedent and custom interpose, says he, between a king and virtue—a problem to which he returned at the end of his life when he began to write the historical tragedy, *Charles the First*.[13] West's *Education* describes a battle in which a knight overthrows the giant Custom, whom he subsequently releases.[14] Again, Shelley attacks venality, cupidity, and selfishness as the enemies of love.[15] The burden of Mickle's *The Concubine* is that love is sold in the interests of sensuality and cupidity, a thesis which is proved by the example of Sir Martyn, whose affair with a milkmaid gives her the opportunity to transfer his patrimony to her own name, while Martyn is led by Dissipation to the Cave of Discontent. A rough parallel to Shelley's attack on priesthood and institutionalized Christianity may be found in Denton's *House of Superstition*, where the poet depicts past and present evils in Christianity, foreseeing, like Shelley, a time when Truth will usher in the millenary year. Other parallelisms of idea and imagery could be presented, but these few will perhaps suffice to show that *Queen Mab* is similar in nearly every particular to the moral allegories of the preceding age.

As a young poet learning the fundamentals of his craft, Shelley borrowed what he chose to borrow with little compunction. His indebtedness to his peers among the early Georgian poets is apparent in the frequency with which echoes of Gray's *Elegy* and Thom-

---

[13] *Queen Mab*, III, 98.

[14] The genius of Britain later gives the knight advice in which Shelley would have concurred. Since he mourns the "prevalence of custom lewd and vain," the knight must nourish his love of piety and truth, and use all his manly zeal "the present to reclaim, the future race improve." (*Education*, I, lxxxii) Even in the midst of the allegedly self-satisfied Age of Reason, the necessity of reform was recognized in many quarters. Shelley's view of the necessity of reform follows a good eighteenth-century principle.

[15] Shelley may also have known the work of William Thompson. One of Mab's diatribes against war and religious persecution (VI, 113-119) tells of the fanatical butchering of "millions": "Innocent babes writhed on thy stubborn spear." Thompson's *Sickness* (1745) angrily opposes the mass murder of human beings, and points out that a monk invented gunpowder. Courageous in his guilt, says Thompson, man has often "smiled at the infant writhing on his spear" (V, 89-90). Ianthe is the name of Thompson's heroine. Shelley may have borrowed the name from Thompson, or Ovid, *Metamorphoses*, IX, 715 *et passim*; or Hesiod, *Theogony*, 349; or Homeric Hymns, II, 418; or Landor's *Simonidea* (1806). Byron's stanzas to Ianthe (Lady Charlotte Harley) which appear in modern editions of *Childe Harold*, were written in 1812, but remained unprinted until 1814, when they appeared as dedicatory verses to the seventh edition of Cantos I and II.

son's *Seasons* rise to the lips of his learned fairy queen. He had long
known Gray and as a school exercise had once turned into toler-
able Latin the epitaph from the *Elegy*. At one point in Canto v, he
is clearly thinking of the famous quatrain in which Gray blames
"chill penury" for repressing village Hampdens and for rendering
potential Miltons mute and inglorious.[16] According to Shelley, the
"iron rod of penury" yet compels

> Her wretched slave to bow the knee to wealth,
> And poison, with unprofitable toil,
> A life too void of solace to confirm
> The very chains that bind him to his doom. . . .
>
> How many a rustic Milton has passed by,
> Stifling the speechless longings of his heart
> In unremitting drudgery and care!
> How many a vulgar Cato has compelled
> His energies, no longer tameless then,
> To mould a pin or fabricate a nail!
> How many a Newton, to whose passive ken
> Those mighty spheres that gem infinity
> Were only specks of tinsel fixed in heaven
> To light the midnights of his native town!

To the cursory eye such passages look like a form of plagiarism,
not only of ideas but even of stylistic devices like the "how [full]
many a" construction which Gray uses so effectively in the original.
But anyone who has looked carefully into Shelley's sources both
early and late must conclude that a kind of imaginative act always
took place between the recollection and the re-expression. Shelley
displayed a singular capacity for projecting himself imaginatively
into the literature he admired, and his reading became for him a
part of his actual experience, like any other emotional or intellectual adventure which arose from his contact with flesh-and-blood
people. The maiden in *Alastor* is borrowed from a novel by Lady

---

[16] *Queen Mab*, v, 127-131; 138-147. Shelley's sister Hellen said that as a child
Shelley repeated verbatim, after a single reading, Gray's lines on Walpole's aquatic
cat (Hogg, *Life*, I, 9). Medwin (*Life*, 1847, I, 48) mentions the Latinized epitaph,
which may now be found among Shelley's juvenilia. Halliday, a fellow Etonian,
mentions Shelley's fondness for the *Elegy* (Hogg, *Life*, I, 43). Shelley quoted the
"full many a flower" passage to Godwin (*Letters*, VIII, 243. Jan. 16, 1812). Reminiscences of Gray in Shelley's early work have been observed by F. J. Glasheen,
MLN 56 (1931), 192-195.

Morgan. But Shelley falls in love with her even more unreservedly than he would have done if she had been a tangible creature, and when she reappears in his poem she has become, to all intents and purposes, his own. In *The Revolt of Islam*, Laon and Cythna originate mainly from Shelley's reading in Southey and Peacock, but Shelley has pumped them full of his own enthusiasms, reoriented them in terms of his own ethic, and clothed them in his own rhetoric. The record of Shelley's borrowings from other poets is the record of his own intense imaginative reactions to people or landscapes or striking situations which he encountered in his reading. From *The Ancient Mariner*, for example, he picked up the suggestion of a paradise at the South Pole; this suggestion was combined with one from Peacock, set forth in imagery derived from *Kubla Khan*, and used rather obviously in the mythological conclusion of *The Revolt of Islam*. By the time of *The Witch of Atlas*, when Shelley employed the idea again, it had been assimilated to his private mythology, developed imaginatively, and merged with many other ideas until it became his own, owing nothing but its inception to Coleridge. In a cruder way, the same sort of psychological reaction to a passage in the *Elegy* led to its reappearance in the quoted passage from *Queen Mab*.

What evidently caught Shelley's eye in the *Elegy* was not so much the idea of original genius as the picture of the village Hampden withstanding the little tyrant of his native town. He seems to have been struck in much the same way by a graphic account of life among the eskimos within the Arctic circle which he found in Thomson's *Winter*. According to Thomson, the sunless gloom of the polar regions renders man so gross that he is no better than an animal. Shelley was interested, not because of the idea of the ignoble savage, but because Thomson painted a portrait which the imagination could not resist.[17]

· III ·

THE ideology of *Queen Mab*, as distinct from the allegorical frame-

---

[17] Compare *Queen Mab*, VIII, 145-155 and *Winter*, 936-946. Echoes of the *Seasons* are frequent in *Queen Mab*. Cf. Shelley's description of a shipwreck (IV, 19-33) which closely resembles *Summer* (980-1000). A list of verbal echoes would include *glittering spires* (*QM*, IV, 11; *Spring*, 523); *bitterness of soul* (*QM*, V, 245; *Spring*, 288); *insect tribes* (*QM*, IV, 131; *Spring*, 60).

work which encloses it, represents Shelley's first major attempt to clarify his antipathies and to synthesize in poetry his ethical, political, and metaphysical views. The synthesis is hardly successful because at this date Shelley had not discovered an all-embracing formula under which his often mutually contradictory convictions could be arranged. A study of his letters and other pronouncements during the period 1810-1813 shows that emotionally he was drawn towards a kind of pantheism, though intellectually he liked to regard himself as an agnostic. The title of his college pamphlet should have been *The Necessity of Agnosticism* rather than *The Necessity of Atheism*, for the argument developed there is not that God does not exist, but rather that no proofs of his existence thus far adduced will stand up under rational scrutiny. Moreover, Shelley's use of the term *atheism* is always rather narrow; he means that he does not believe in the Old Testament God of Wrath. Like Godwin, Shelley placed primary trust in reason; like Godwin, too, he was more or less committed to a deterministic view of the cosmos, for he had picked up from Godwin, Hume, and Holbach the doctrine of necessity. From Godwin, and possibly also from Hume and Condorcet he had derived his belief in man's perfectibility, although neither of his mentors would have followed Shelley into the utopian dream of a future golden age (largely modeled on Pope's *Messiah*) which he includes in *Queen Mab*. Shelley thought of "man preterit" as sinful, but would not accept the doctrine of original sin, and was reasonably certain that in due course, after certain fundamental socio-political reforms had occurred, man's socially induced tendency to sinfulness would be overcome. A consideration of the total pattern of these beliefs indicates that Shelley's philosophical "position" at the time of *Queen Mab* was an unsuccessful emulsion of anti-Christian, pantheistic, deistic, materialistic, and necessitarian principles.

Shelley's anti-Christian prejudice entered his thinking early and remained to the end. It was not so much that he disliked the ethical thought of Jesus Christ, which as a youth he had not understood, though he came later to a profound admiration for it. It was rather that in his opinion the whole teaching of Christianity had been utterly perverted and falsified by successive generations of theologians. At the time of *Queen Mab*, however, he was subsisting on borrowed thinking and emotional prejudice masquerading as irrefutable logic. Hatred of oppression was a fixed idea with him from his school days onward, and by 1810 when he went into residence during the Michaelmas term at Oxford, he had decided that the Christian church was the most oppressive of social institutions. His case against Christianity, somewhat intensified by his belief that the failure of his love affair with Harriet Grove had been immediately caused by that young lady's fear and distrust of his anti-Christian opinions, was enunciated sometimes in the phraseology of a callow fanatic, and sometimes in the cool accents of an eighteenth-century schoolboy rationalist. By December of 1810, his fulminations had reached the point at which he wished he were "the Anti-Christ" in order to "crush the Demon."[18] From January to June, 1811, he devoted much time and effort to an attempt to show by logical argumentation what he felt to be the basic difficulties with the Christian position: that the existence of God could not be proved; that Christian dogma required an entirely irrational acceptance of scriptural testimony, including miracles and prophecies; that, historically speaking, Christianity had sanctioned "murder, war, and intolerance," and that the institution of the Christian church had conspicuously failed to produce happiness among men. His rationalist approach forbade belief in the divinity of Jesus Christ. On Jesus' value as ethical teacher he blew hot and cold. "Let this horrid Galilean rule the *canaille*," he desperately cries at one point. "I give them up."[19] Again, in more temperate terms, he asserts that the Christian system "can do no harm, and is indeed highly requisite for the vulgar" if one could retain its "virtuous precepts," qualify its "selfish dogmas," and lop off "all the disgusting excrescences."[20] Even by the time of *Queen Mab*, where he makes an attempt to draw together all his accusations against Christianity, his views on the character of Jesus Christ have not yet solidified. In the notes he speaks of Jesus as one of "those true heroes who have died in the glorious martyrdom of liberty, and have braved torture, contempt, and poverty in the cause of suffering humanity." Then in a footnote to this note he records his more recent suspicion that "Jesus was an ambitious man who aspired to the throne of Judea!"

[18] *Shelley at Oxford*, ed. W. S. Scott (London, 1943), p. 16.
[19] *Ibid.*, p. 27. April 24, 1811.
[20] *Ibid.*, p. 29. April 26, 1811. Cf. *Letters*, VIII, 285. Feb. 27, 1812. Cf. Voltaire's remark: "Religion for the masses, Philosophy for the classes."

Shelley's rejection of revealed religion and Christian theology led him to search for a central religious position which would be acceptable to both his reason and his feelings and this he evidently found in a kind of pantheism. At Oxford he had defined the Deity as "the Soul of the Universe, the intelligent and necessarily beneficent activating principle,"[21] but would not call this Deity by the name *God*, on the grounds that this substantive had too many associations with the wrathful Jehovah of the Old Testament, and with the anthropomorphic Being of those whom Shelley undemocratically called the "canaille." But while he sought to detect and expose "the impudent and inconsistent falsehoods of priest-craft," he was ardently wishing "to be profoundly convinced of the existence of a Deity," and was exclaiming, "Oh, that this Deity were the soul of the universe, the spirit of universal, imperishable love! Indeed I believe it is. . . ."[22] After his expulsion from Oxford in March, 1811, he told his father that the *Necessity of Atheism* pamphlet was undertaken not through "profligacy," but with the serious intent of discovering whether some "proofs of an existing Deity" could not be got from men who professed religious beliefs.[23] In June of that year he assured Miss Hitchener that he would indeed sooner admit than doubt the actuality of a Deity defined as "the existing power of existence" or "the essence of the universe."[24] When he repeated these sentiments to Southey the following January, and proposed to call Deity "the mass of infinite intelligence," Southey agreed that the definition was a good one, but said that by such a definition Shelley was "not an Atheist but a Pantheist."[25]

In the third place, Shelley's opposition to revealed religion had led him to embrace certain deistic principles: a desire to simplify the articles of ancient faith, a refusal to accept miracles and prophecies, a hatred of superstition, a pronounced anti-ecclesiastical prejudice, and a tendency to give more weight to Christian ethics than to Christian metaphysics. In May, 1811, he found himself at odds with Leigh Hunt's brand of deism, which involved "high veneration" for a Deity who was, however, "neither omnipotent, om-

---

[21] *Ibid.*, p. 16.
[22] *Letters*, VIII, 43-44. Shelley's career as thinker was devoted to the gradual ordering, testing, strengthening, and deepening of this belief.
[23] *Ibid.*, 59.   [24] *Ibid.*, 101-103.   [25] *Ibid.*, 227 and 232.

nipresent, nor identical . . . by no means perfect, but composed of good and evil, like man." This Shelley called "a damnable heresy from reason." But the views of Southey, who did not believe the Evangelists were inspired, rejected the Trinity, and thought that "Jesus Christ stood precisely in the same relation to God as himself," represented, Shelley said, a superlatively clear "definition of a Deist."[26] On these points, at least, Shelley was in agreement with Southey.

In May, 1811, Shelley asserted that he had once been "an enthusiastic Deist," but had rejected natural religion "from reason."[27] If this statement may be trusted, the likeliest date for his deistic period is probably the winter of 1810, when to Shelley's professed amusement, his mother feared that he was making "a deistical coterie" of his little sisters.[28] But Shelley's deism was probably in the main the result of his opposition to revealed religion. His basic personal inclination was towards pantheism. He had all along been conducting an ardent search for a "God" in whom he could believe, had repeatedly defined Deity as the soul or essence of the universe, and had finally been labeled "pantheist" for his pains by Southey. That Southey's term was not far off center is indicated by a letter Shelley sent Hogg December 8, 1810, in the period (if the above conjectural date be allowed) when he fancied himself a deist. "I may not be able to adduce proofs, but I think that the leaf of a tree, the meanest insect on which we trample, are in themselves arguments more conclusive than any which can be adduced that some vast intellect animates Infinity. . . . I confess that I think Pope's 'all are but parts of one tremendous whole' something more than Poetry; it has ever been my favourite theory."[29] The line of Pope's which Shelley quotes (or rather misquotes) marks the opening of the famous passage near the close of Epistle i of *An Essay on Man*, where Pope memorably summarizes a pantheistic conception of the universe.[30] Various apostrophes to the spirit of Nature in Queen Mab reflect, though seldom with close verbal echoing, certain passages, including these pantheistic lines, from the *Essay on Man*.[31]

After the hierophant Mab, in what might be legitimately de-

---

[26] *Ibid.*, 223.   [27] *Ibid.*, 89.   [28] *Ibid.*, 39. Cf. *Ibid.*, 23. Dec. 20, 1810.
[29] *Shelley at Oxford*, p. 16.   [30] *Essay on Man*, i, 267-280.
[31] Cf., for example, Pope, i, 87-88 and Shelley, vi, 216-217.

scribed as Shelley's own essay on man, has exposed the horrors of man's predicament both as they have obtained in the past and as they exist in the present, she unveils the future to Ianthe's contemplation. The eighth and ninth cantos are occupied with a vision of the new Golden Age, such as Shelley was to describe again in a number of later poems.[32] At this period Shelley was deeply interested in the notion that there might be a close connection between man's spiritual well-being and his dietary habits and climatic environment.[33] Among the blessings of his Golden Age will be the complete absence of disease, a condition achieved largely through everybody's having learned to follow the ascetic eating habits of which Shelley was at this early date a confirmed exponent. But Shelley's vision is derived mainly from Pope's *Messiah*, where the prophet Isaiah, "rapt into future times" like Ianthe, observes a complete change in the climate of the earth, which has become a continuous temperate zone, and where the temperateness is reflected in a wonderful cessation of bloodthirstiness among the predatory beasts.[34]

Although at first glance the doctrines of materialism and necessitarianism would seem to have little connection with such utopian dreams, Necessity has a prominent place in the substructure of Shelley's poem, and in the notes he seems to have accepted, for the time being, certain of the leading doctrines of the French materialists. Shelley derived his ideas on Necessity from Godwin's *Political Justice*, and from two books which profoundly influenced Godwin's thought: the *Système de la Nature* of the scandalously eminent French atheist, materialist, and necessitarian, Baron Holbach; and David Hume's *An Inquiry Concerning Human Understanding*.[35] The inception of Shelley's interest in skeptical thought cannot be dated with absolute certainty, but if Hogg's memory can be trusted, a fairly likely date would be the latter months of

[32] *Prometheus Unbound, The Witch of Atlas, Hellas*, for example.

[33] See I. J. Kapstein, *PMLA* 52 (1937), 238-243, on this point.

[34] Cf., for example, *Messiah*, 67-84, and *Queen Mab*, viii, 70-87.

[35] Professor F. B. Evans in "Shelley, Godwin, Hume, and the Doctrine of Necessity," *SP* 37 (1940), 632-640, proves that Godwin borrowed both ideas and illustrations from Hume's *Inquiry*, and that Shelley, in preparing his note on Necessity, must have had both Godwin and Hume before him. Professor Evans has ignored the third major source-book, that of Holbach. Yet about a quarter of the space in the notes to *Queen Mab* is devoted either to direct quotation from Holbach or to remarks by Shelley which evidently owe their origin to a reading of the Frenchman.

1810. Hogg notes Shelley's early interest in Locke and Hume, and adds that he and his friend also read "certain popular French works, that treat of man, for the most part in a mixed method, metaphysically, morally, and politically." Hogg offers an explanation as to why Shelley should have become so enthusiastic over "the sceptical philosophy, a system so uncongenial with a fervid and imaginative genius." Shelley loved disputation, and found the skeptical position well adapted to defensive warfare; he loved excitement and change, and to such persons "destruction, so that it be on a grand scale, may sometimes prove hardly less inspiring than creation." Finally, as Hogg rather superciliously sums it up, Shelley was very young, and "the philosopher who declares that he knows nothing, and that nothing can be known, will readily find followers among the young, for they are sensible that they possess the requisite qualifications for entering his school, and are as far advanced in the science of ignorance as their master." Hogg's animadversions would have us assume that "French" ideas were never very close to Shelley's heart, but were assumed, like a dirty toga, for the immediate purposes of disputation.[36]

But if that was true of Shelley while he was still at Oxford, it was emphatically not true in the summer of 1812, when he read (there is no indication that it was a rereading) Holbach's *Système*. Like Godwin's, Holbach's theory of knowledge followed that of Locke and Hume. The dependable instruments to knowledge are sense impressions and reason: that is, knowledge is reasoned experience. Sense impressions reach us from the phenomenal world, which is reduced in definition to the concept of matter in motion. Man, though a highly organized and complex entity, is only one of many forms of matter, and is governed by the same laws which govern the material universe. Ideas of personal immortality, freedom of choice, or of the existence of a supernal immaterial Being are the result of wishful thinking. The individual is motivated by utilitarian self-interest, the familiar seek-pleasure-avoid-pain strategy. Ethical science, completely secularized and rejecting all appeals to a higher law, must persuade men that it is

---

[36] Hogg, *Life*, i, 99-102. Shelley thought of himself as a skeptic in December, 1812. Cf. the letters to Hogg and to Hookham, both of date Dec. 3 (*Letters*, ix, 27, 29). "I certainly am a very resolved republican (if the word applies) and a determined sceptic." "I am an infidel and a democrat."

to their interest to live virtuously; political science must devise penalties for those who have not been otherwise persuaded of the utility of the virtuous life.[37]

When Shelley finished reading Holbach about June 3, 1812, he wrote Godwin that it was a "work of uncommon powers." Repeating this judgment on July 29, he qualified it by admitting that the book was "too obnoxious to accusations of sensuality and selfishness" but otherwise he could not see why "the loftiest disinterestedness" was not compatible with "the strictest materialism."[38] Though he was unwilling to agree with Holbach that utilitarian self-interest could serve as the basis of ethics, he has tacitly accepted Holbach's theory of knowledge, and the assumption that the universe is reducible to the concept of matter in motion. Further, he would agree with Holbach's anti-Christian fulminations. What seems to have impressed him most, however, was the possible connection between his idea of Deity as "the mass of infinite intelligence" and Holbach's necessitarian doctrine, which, it will be remembered, was also strongly enunciated in Godwin. The materialistic aspect of Holbach's thought continued to exert a hold over Shelley at least through the year 1813, if we may assume that the views of Eusebes in *A Refutation of Deism* (in print early in 1814) are also those of Shelley. "The system of the Universe," says Eusebes, "is upheld solely by physical powers. The necessity of matter is the ruler of the world." And again, "The laws of motion and the properties of matter suffice to account for every phenomenon, or combination of phenomena exhibited in the universe."[39] By 1815, however, Shelley had rejected materialism with the comment that it is "a seducing system to young and superficial minds. . . . I was discontented with such a view of things as it afforded; man is a being of high aspirations, 'looking both before and after,' whose 'thoughts wander through eternity,' disclaiming alliance with transience and decay."[40] But if Shelley rejected materialism,

---

[37] On Holbach, see M. P. Cushing, *Baron d'Holbach: A Study of Eighteenth Century Radicalism in France* (New York, 1914) and W. H. Wickwar, *Baron d'Holbach; a Prelude to the French Revolution* (London, 1935). The Catholic case against Holbach, who was a very disturbing influence, is well set forth in R. R. Palmer, *Catholics and Unbelievers in Eighteenth Century France* (Princeton, New Jersey, 1939), pp. 188-191 and 214-218.

[38] *Letters,* VIII, 332 and IX, 11.   [39] *Prose,* VI, 49-50.

[40] *Prose,* VI, 194. Even at this date Shelley allows for the possibility of some sort of free will. He suggests (*Letters,* VIII, 202. Nov. 24, 1811) that Nature might turn

he clung, though with increasing unwillingness, to necessitarianism, which colors his thinking even as late as *Prometheus Unbound*, although by that time it has receded considerably in importance, while the idea of the power and priority of the mind has usurped the prominent position formerly occupied in Shelley's thought by necessitarianism.

Shelley resolves both his problem and his poem by supposing that, in due time, there is in store for man, through the workings of natural law, a future golden age. This resolution has no counterpart in Godwin or in Holbach's rather gloomy work, but Godwin would have been readier than Holbach to concur in Queen Mab's parting admonition to Ianthe:

> Yet, human Spirit! bravely hold thy course,
> Let virtue teach thee firmly to pursue
> The gradual paths of an aspiring change:
> For birth and life and death, and that strange state
> Before the naked soul has found its home,
> All tend to perfect happiness, and urge
> The restless wheels of being on their way.

It is extremely difficult to make philosophical sense of the congeries of impressions and ideas which stirred Shelley's mind and his emotions at this period. Eradication of evil seemed possible to him. "That which appears to be a taint of our nature," he said "is in effect the result of unnatural political institutions,"[41] and good will naturally ensue upon the elimination of outworn political and religious establishments. This is, of course, a version of the common anti-institutional bias of late eighteenth-century French and English radicalism, from Rousseau to Godwin. His determination is imbued with a Condorcet-like faith in the inevitability of progress, and he likes to imagine widespread future changes in the physical condition of the world, which will result in better health

---

out, under the microscope, to be "a mass of organized animation," and that "free will must give energy to this infinite mass of being," whatever this may mean or however it may be done. In February, 1812, he said that Time conquers all but the "fixed and virtuous will." *Letters*, viii, 271. The conclusion would seem to be that in the period 1810-1815 Shelley was trying out all the metaphysical and ethical theories which he had encountered in Godwin, Locke, Hume, Holbach, Spinoza, and dozens of others on both sides of the Channel, and, without benefit of formal philosophical training, was trying to reduce them to some kind of order.

[41] *Letters*, viii, 228.

and well-being for humankind. On the question of free will, Shelley appears to think that the human mind is at least partially subject to what we should now call psychological determinism; but he cannot rest content without adding that if the mind's eye can penetrate the fog of superstition, it can discover the path of true virtue, and he who sees it will inevitably follow it, whatever his blind companions may do. Shelley uses reason as far as it will take him; but he never hesitates to make the leap of intuition. He cannot deny the existence of matter, and in talking of Berkeley he is as adamant in his opposition to "immateriality" as Dr. Johnson kicking a stone. Yet his whole emotional being yearns away from a strictly materialistic view of the cosmos, and finds solace in envisioning a future golden age.

The synthetic poem that results when Shelley attempts to pull these ideas and visions together is certainly imperfect, but Shelley does a better job with it than one would have supposed possible. It is indeed a remarkable feature of *Queen Mab* that Shelley was able to bring so many ostensibly contradictory notions within the compass of a single poem without their seeming more completely immiscible than they do to the cursory reader. In general, however, his strategy is fairly straightforward. By the use of his allegorical framework and the device of surveying past, present, and future from a suprahistorical plane, he achieves a certain unity and a sense of forward movement. His ideological argument includes a historical survey of human misery and crime; a series of allegations against superstition and Christian dogma as the sources of much of that misery and criminality; a pseudo-deistic rejection of the concept of God as an anthropomorphic Being, and as the type of vengeful ruler who must be propitiated by sacrifice, prayer, and genuflexion; and a pantheistic argument for the existence of a Nature-Spirit, Shelley's substitute for the traditional Christian deity. Finally he indulges the optimistic, progressivistic, and in one sense idealistic supposition that at a future date the normal operations of the Nature-Spirit will have produced widespread climatic changes in the world, and that these changes (owing to psycho-physical connections) will be reflected in the realm of morals and general human welfare, man having long since eliminated disease by abandoning carnivorous and embracing herbivorous habits, and having long since rid himself, by the exercise of sweet reason, of the superstitions and bigotries, the institutions and customs by which his progress had been, in past ages, abnormally inhibited.

In thus summarizing the argument of *Queen Mab,* which is chiefly concerned with the perennial metaphysical questions as they appear to a radical young enthusiast, it has been necessary to underemphasize some other ideas which are to be found in the poem: echoes of Spinoza; scientific crumbs picked up from encyclopedists like Laplace, Bailly, Cuvier, and others; views on marriage and love from Godwin, Mary Wollstonecraft, and Lawrence's *Empire of the Nairs.* A more extended consideration of these multiple influences would, however, simply go to show what should by now have become sufficiently apparent, that in ideology and intent, as in structure and imagery, *Queen Mab* derives from the most characteristic modes of eighteenth-century thought and expression.

Queen Mab has found few defenders. One of the few, Mr. Bernard Shaw, told the Shelley Society in 1886 that he found it to be a "perfectly original poem on a great subject."[42] Unless we allow that an attempted synthesis of ideas widely held at a given historical period constitutes originality, the first part of Mr. Shaw's remark is at least questionable, while the second part looks to the analytic eye like the faint praise of a man whose tongue is in his cheek. The cumulus of literature and philosophy and history which assisted in the evolution of Shelley's first major poem was neither very deep nor very wide. The limitations of Shelley's learning, and the comparative brevity of his literary experience, are everywhere apparent in *Queen Mab.*

A revised version of the first part of *Queen Mab* was included in the *Alastor* volume of February, 1816, where it was called *The Daemon of the World.* The revision was confined to the first two (chiefly descriptive) cantos of the original poem, and seems decidedly innocuous by comparison.[43] But the original poem saw no wide circulation until 1821, when it appeared in a pirated edition, and when Shelley applied to Chancery for an injunction to restrain

[42] Meeting of April 14, 1886. Shaw's remarks appear in abbreviated form in the *Notebook of the Shelley Society* (1888), p. 31. *Shelley Soc. Public,* first series, No. 2.

[43] Shelley also included in the *Alastor* volume a 32-line section from *Queen Mab* (vi, 72-104). The original lines were directed against the "prolific fiend," religion. Shelley now modified it slightly and called it "superstition."

the sale of the book. Now, privately at least, he was ready to call *Queen Mab* "villainous trash," and to describe it as "a poem written by me when very young, in the most furious style, with long notes against Jesus Christ, God the Father, and the king, and the Bishops, and marriage, and the Devil knows what."[44] Many of Shelley's critics would heartily agree with this characterization of the poem.

But Shelley's open letter to the editor of *The Examiner* on his reasons for wishing to suppress the pirated edition contains a much more judicious estimate of the poem: "I have not seen [*Queen Mab*] for several years; I doubt not but that it is perfectly worthless in point of literary composition; and that in all that concerns moral and political speculation, as well as in the subtler discriminations of metaphysical and religious doctrine, it is still more crude and immature. I am a devoted enemy to religious, political, and domestic oppression; and I regret this publication, not so much from literary vanity, as because I fear it is better fitted to injure than to serve the cause of freedom."[45]

If the success of *Queen Mab* as a work of art is not marked, the poem is nevertheless of importance as a first, imitative, experimental step towards the finest work of Shelley's maturity. It shows the inception of the formula and the faith which inform his best work up to the middle of 1819. The formula is one of contrast: the world as it is over against the world as it ought to be. The faith is that the great gap between the two worlds can be closed. At this early date, Shelley believed that the reform of political institutions and the elimination of religious superstitions would effect the changes he desired. Accordingly he preached the necessity of reform. By 1817 he had become convinced of the necessity of leadership by the wise and the just; in *The Revolt of Islam* he presented a *beau idéal* of revolution to show how two fearless challengers of political and ecclesiastical authority succeeded, though only temporarily, in breaking the power of the opposition. Since the world was not yet ready to live according to the moral law of love, Laon and Cythna went down to martyrdom. By 1819, though his faith in the proper kind of leadership had not at all diminished, Shelley had reached the conclusion that evil was essentially (though not wholly) a deficiency of spiritual vision; his first great poem, *Prometheus*

---

[44] *Letters*, x, 278.   [45] *Ibid*., 280.

Unbound, was written to show men what kind of world they had within their own skulls, and what kind of world they might have if their deficiency of vision were overcome. Throughout his life, Shelley's appreciation of the power and pervasiveness of evil steadily deepened, though at every step he carefully outlined his views on the means of combating it. He concluded that the universal human tragedy was moral deformity, not innate, but induced by the conspiracy of society against the integrity of its individual members. When he was drowned in July, 1822, he had been reflecting upon the greatest tragedy of all, namely, that the world's leading thinkers, the only leaders whom men ought to be able to trust, had all of them, with the exception of a "sacred few," eventually succumbed to the blandishments, temptations, and corruptions of mundane life. *Queen Mab* and *The Triumph of Life* were separated by an interval of ten years. To the poetry of that decade we may now go on.

2

THE NECESSITY OF LOVE: *ALASTOR*
AND THE EPIPSYCHE

> She disappear'd, and left me dark, I wak'd
> To find her, or for ever to deplore
> Her loss, and other pleasures all abjure.
> —ADAM, IN *Paradise Lost*

> Egeria! sweet creation of some heart
> Which found no mortal resting-place so fair
> As thine ideal breast; whate'er thou art
> Or wert—a young Aurora of the air,
> The nympholepsy of some fond despair;
> Or, it might be, a beauty of the earth,
> Who found a more than common votary there
> Too much adoring; whatsoe'er thy birth,
> Thou wert a beautiful thought, and softly bodied forth.
> —BYRON, IN *Childe Harold's Pilgrimage*

> Pray, are you yet cured of your Nympholepsy? 'Tis a
> sweet disease: but one as obstinate and dangerous as any.
> —SHELLEY TO PEACOCK, AUGUST 1818

· I ·

THE concept of a strictly materialistic necessity, with which Shelley had dealt as vigorously as he knew how in *Queen Mab*, was a sufficiently poetical subject, as Shelley's admired Lucretius had proved in *De Rerum Natura*. Yet the stress on natural law, however fundamental in the life of man, tended to de-emphasize another law of which Shelley had become deeply though imperfectly conscious in the period between 1813 and 1815. This was the law of love, and in composing *Alastor* Shelley was attempting to dramatize a conflict of allegiance between what might be called the law for thing (natural law) and the law for man (the law of love). The general failure to see that this is the purpose of Shelley's second major work has resulted in a misapprehension of its meaning; and though Shelley and Mary both insisted that the poem ought to be considered didactic rather than merely descriptive-narrative, readers have regularly found difficulty in deciding what lesson was intended.[1]

The problem has been to account for an apparent discrepancy between the poem and a sentence or two in the preface. The second paragraph of the prefatory remarks implies that a curse-motif is at work in the poem; yet neither the first paragraph nor the poem itself will support the implication.[2]

Medwin, Dowden, Peacock, and Peck have all passed over this problem as if it did not exist.[3] But it has bothered Mrs. Campbell, who notices that "in the preface the youth is condemned: in the poem he is glorified";[4] her opinion is echoed by White, who says that "no one who had not read the Preface would suppose that the author intended the poem as a criticism of him";[5] and Havens, after an extensive study of the poem, has concluded that *Alastor* is "not a unity, does not produce a single impression, and was not the offspring of a single dominating purpose."[6] Dissenters from this position have included Stovall, who regards as untenable Mrs. Campbell's view that "Shelley, in his preface, misinterprets his own poem"; and Hoffman, who believes that Havens is wrong, and that "we must not abandon the attempt to discover minute con-

---

[1] Shelley's contemporary reviewers damned the poem for its obscurity. See N. I. White, *The Unextinguished Hearth* (Durham, N.C., 1938), pp. 105-116. Victorian critics still found it obscure, but admired its noble language; better a "dreamy mysticism" than Queen Mab's subversive propaganda. See F. C. Mason, *A Study in Shelley Criticism* (Mercersburg, Pa., 1937), pp. 109-110, 112, 120, 147.

[2] Peacock assisted in confounding the confusion.

[3] Thomas Medwin, *The Life of Percy Bysshe Shelley*, ed. H. Buxton-Forman (London, 1913), pp. 138-140. T. L. Peacock, *Memoirs of Shelley*, in *Works*, Halliford ed., VIII, 100. E. Dowden, *The Life of Percy Bysshe Shelley* (London, 1886), I, 531-533. W. E. Peck, *Shelley, His Life and Work* (Boston, Mass., 1927), I, 422-431.

[4] O. W. Campbell, *Shelley and the Unromantics* (London, 1924), p. 188.

[5] N. I. White, *Portrait of Shelley* (New York, 1945), p. 192.

[6] R. D. Havens, *PMLA* 45 (1930), 1098-1115.

nections between it [the poem] and the Preface, for the Preface makes us aware that a meaning was intended."[7]

The real point at issue would seem to be this: when Shelley wrote the poem, did he mean it to be the story of a peerless youth's quest for the ideal maiden of his dreams, or did he mean to imply that the youth was in some way culpable, and that the quest was a punishment? All the evidence points to the probability that the poem was originally intended to be what the poem itself and the first paragraph of Shelley's preface indicate—the story of a youth who took natural philosophy as his province, and was happy enough until he suddenly awoke to the thought that he needed sympathetic association with an ideal. Having united into a single idealized but pleasantly voluptuous image all of the wonderful, wise, and beautiful ideas known to him, he became passionately attached to his creation. When she vanished, his disappointment at not being able to find her again was too great for his sensitive spirit. He descended "to an untimely grave." This quest-motif is really the central motif in the poem.

The first paragraph of the preface contains nothing that would suggest an avenging spirit of solitude. In the poem itself Professor Havens has noticed two passages which seem to show that in writing the poem Shelley had in mind the curse-motif. Yet neither of them is necessarily involved with the avenging *alastor* theme. The first has to do with the origin of the vision. The preface says that the poet "images to himself the Being whom he loves," neither stating nor implying that this being has been sent to punish him, or that any supernatural agency beyond the poet's own imagination is involved, or even that the poet has been really culpable in his neglect of love. The poem (203-205) states that the vision was sent by "the spirit of sweet human love" to a youth who had hitherto spurned her "choicest gifts." In terms of the curse-motif, these

[7] Floyd Stovall, *Desire and Restraint in Shelley* (Durham, N.C., 1931), p. 150, note 21. H. L. Hoffman, *An Odyssey of the Soul* (New York, 1933), p. 3. Carl Grabo, *The Magic Plant* (Chapel Hill, N.C., 1936), p. 174, does his best to bring together the poem and the preface. Other studies of the poem include that of Mueschke and Griggs, *PMLA* 49 (1934), 229-245, which argues that Wordsworth is the prototype of Shelley's poet, an argument effectively answered by Marcel Kessel, *PMLA* 51 (1936), 302-310. There appear to be good grounds for the belief of F. L. Jones, *PMLA* 49 (1934), 969-971, that *Alastor* is to some extent foreshadowed in Shelley's early novel, *St. Irvyne*. Cf. also the article by A. E. Dubois, *JEGP* 35 (1936), pp. 530-545, which answers Havens.

words would suggest that the vision was sent for punitive purposes. But if the poem were written in ignorance of the *alastor*
theme, the lines would mean simply that the youth, long preoccupied with philosophical considerations, suddenly awoke to the notion that he had been neglecting love.

The second passage has been generally misunderstood. The
problem hinges on the interpretation of the phrase "fair fiend"
(297). Professor Havens believes that the words refer to the visionary maiden.[8] But they seem rather to refer to the enigmatic figure
of death, whom the poet regards as a kind of *ignis fatuus.* In the
preceding lines, the youth has watched a swan fly back to its mate.
He thinks of its flight as a symbol of his own desire to rejoin the
vanished maiden of his dream—a desire which leads him seriously
to consider the notion of suicide. Why should he continue to waste
his powers on an unresponsive earth when those powers would
evoke sympathetic response from his dream-maiden in some other
world? But can he safely trust death? May not death be just as
false to him as was sleep in snatching away and keeping "most
relentlessly" her precious charge? He seems to see death with a
mocking smile dangling before him a shadowy lure.

> Startled by his own thoughts, he looked around.
> There was no fair fiend near him, not a sight
> Or sound of awe but in his own deep mind. . . .

The figure of death, which for a moment he seemed to see, was
only a phantasm conjured up from the depths of his imagination,
a fiend who looked fair because he half promised reunion with
the lady.

We have seen that the first paragraph of the preface has nothing
to do with the curse-motif. We now discover that in the poem itself the only two passages that might suggest a curse-motif are
perfectly amenable to other interpretations. The poem—aside from
the title and the second paragraph of the preface—can without
difficulty be regarded as the quest-poem whose argument is given
in the first prefatory paragraph.

Much of the prevailing confusion about the meaning of the
poem can be traced to Peacock's generally misunderstood explanation of the title, and to the second or final paragraph of the pref-

8 R. D. Havens, *op. cit.,* p. 1105.

ace, which looks very much like an ex post facto attempt by Shelley to moralize his song and to justify Peacock's nomenclature. Peacock suggested the title, very likely after the poem was finished. Shelley, says his learned friend, was "at a loss for a title, and I proposed that which he adopted: Alastor, or the Spirit of Solitude. The Greek word *Alastor* is an evil genius. . . . The poem treated the spirit of solitude as a spirit of evil. I mention the true meaning of the word because many have supposed *Alastor* to be the name of the hero."[9]

Peacock's explanation, while it enlightened those who had mistakenly supposed that the poet had a name, also helped to obscure Shelley's intention, for it implied that a curse-motif was prominently at work in the poem, and one could thereby infer that the visionary maiden was sent to the poet on a kind of punitive expedition. In this interpretation, of course, the poet was punished for having ignored the demands of human sympathy.

But Shelley's poem does not represent "solitude" as "evil." The word *solitude* occurs only three times in the whole piece, and in only one of these (line 414) could it possibly be construed as having evil significance. We are told that the poet longed to deck his hair with flowers. "But on his heart its solitude returned/ And he forebore." Here again we encounter ambiguity, for the lines may mean simply that the feeling of solitude (*i.e.*, empty loneliness in the absence of his beloved) returned to grip the poet's heart and to dissuade him from lingering over the flowers. The explanation immediately follows: his vivid remembrance of the maiden's charms still exercised too powerful an influence over his mind to let him interrupt his search for her, even though his ill-kempt hair was by this date badly in need of embellishment.

The Greek idea of an avenging spirit would not therefore appear to have been in Shelley's mind during the composition of the poem. "At a loss for a title," he accepted Peacock's rather esoteric suggestion. It then became his task to explain the poem in terms of the new title without the need of revising the text itself. The second paragraph of the preface contains the attempted explanation.

The pertinent sentences are the second and ninth. Sentence two reads: "The Poet's self-centered seclusion was avenged by the furies of an irresistible passion pursuing him to a speedy ruin."

---

[9] *Memoirs of Shelley* in *Works of Thomas Love Peacock*, Halliford ed., VIII, 100.

Sentence nine expands the idea: "Among those who attempt to exist without human sympathy, the pure and tender-hearted perish through the intensity and passion of their search after its communities, when the vacancy of their spirit suddenly makes itself felt." The first of these sentences clearly asserts Peacock's *alastor* idea. The poet was "self-centered" in his "seclusion" and the "furies of an irresistible passion" drove him to ruin. But in the second sentence the poet is called (at least by implication) "pure and tender-hearted," and he perishes, not through the ministrations of vengeful furies, but by "the intensity and passion" of his search after human sympathy. The two sentences do not cohere: the self-centered poet of the first could hardly be the "tender-hearted" creature alluded to in the second. One might guess—though it is only a guess—that Shelley inserted the sentence about the "furies of an irresistible passion" in order to justify Peacock's title. Nowhere else in the preface, and nowhere in the poem, is the curse-motif visible.

Hoffman thinks that the "idea of Solitude as an avenging genius" is the central theme of *Alastor*. But he significantly adds that Shelley did not have the classical conception of *alastor* in mind when he composed the poem. Instead, according to Hoffman, he was thinking of Wordsworthian solitude as set forth in the picture of the Solitary in *The Excursion*. "It was not," he says, "until Peacock supplied the Greek word that Shelley saw how admirably it fitted the idea he had already worked out."[10] It might be urged rather that the Greek word did *not* fit the idea Shelley had worked out; but it had a sufficient connection with his main theme so that he seized upon it. In seizing upon it, however, he unfortunately threw the emphasis away from his primary theme: the conflict in a sensitive individual between allegiance to a kind of materialism and allegiance to a kind of idealism.

The real driving force in the poem is love, which obtains a complete hold over the intellect, imagination, and senses of the protagonist. According to Shelley's preface, "the intellectual faculties, the imagination, and the functions of the sense have their respective requisitions on the sympathy of corresponding powers in other human beings. The Poet is represented as uniting these

[10] H. L. Hoffman, *An Odyssey of the Soul: Shelley's Alastor* (New York, 1933), p. 53.

requisitions and attaching them to a single image." When that image appears in the form of a maiden, the poet responds on all levels.

Seated beside him, talking solemnly of "knowledge and truth and virtue," the maiden at first evokes intellectual response in the poet, for these are the "thoughts most dear to him." Soon the young lady, herself a poet, turns to the subject of poesy, and, in a voice partly stifled by sobs, raises "wild numbers" as she fingers her "strange harp." Poetry, the language of the imagination, is also familiar ground to a youth long since acquainted with all "great or good or lovely" things which the "sacred past in truth or fable consecrates." Presently, however, it is time for the "functions of the sense." Rising suddenly and impatiently to her feet, the maiden gives every indication of a desire to embrace the poet. Uninitiated though he is in the arts of courtship, the youth responds to her rather obvious mating signals. With that "frantic gesture and short breathless cry" not uncommon in early Shelley heroines, the maiden has just "folded his frame in her dissolving arms" when the now thoroughly erotic vision ends, dark sleep floods in, and the youth awakes into a dismal loneliness. His intellect, his imagination, and his senses have all established bonds with corresponding powers in the maiden, or to put the matter simply, he is in love. Thereafter his every effort is directed towards reunion with the dream-maiden, failing which he wastes away to death.

The poem is an attempt to show, more or less symbolically, the intensity of one highly sensitive being's search for the "communities" of sympathy. The curse-motif is in the title and the preface alone. The erotic vision leading to a passionate quest was originally, and remained finally, the real central motif of Shelley's poem.

· II ·

STOPFORD BROOKE long ago observed a fundamental dichotomy in Shelley's poetry which now becomes pertinent. Shelley, says Brooke, lived in two worlds. "One was the world of Mankind and its hopes, the other was the world of his own heart. His poetic life was an alternate changing from one of these worlds to the other. He passed from poetry written for the sake of mankind, to poetry written for his own sake and to express himself; from the Shelley who was inspired by moral aims and wrote in the hope of a regeneration of the world, to that other Shelley who, inspired only by his own ideas and regrets, wrote without any ethical end, and absolutely apart from humanity."[11] Brooke states his idea too mechanically and applies it too rigidly. His picture of a Shelley who walks across the stage singing of mankind, disappears into the wings, reappears singing of himself, and disappears once more only to reappear singing of mankind, and so on, has too many overtones of the quick-change artist of vaudeville. But the insight is not without value, and its psychological implications have been developed at some length by Stovall in his *Desire and Restraint in Shelley*, a very searching study of the opposition of altruistic and egoistic strains in Shelley's nature.[12] Brooke, Stovall, and their followers are all in substantial agreement that *Alastor* is an egoistic poem in which Shelley was seeking to express himself, to give an account, as Hoffman calls it, of the odyssey of a soul very like his own.[13]

While it is unlikely that Shelley could have written *Alastor* without benefit of introspection, and while the portrait of the wandering poet inevitably suggests an idealized and somewhat sentimentalized Shelley, it is possible to push the egocentric argument too far. One need not suppose that the poem is basically autobiographical any more than one need imagine that Hamlet was intended as an idealized portrait of Shakespeare himself. Although an argument might be made to show that the *Alastor* poet is really T. J. Hogg in disguise, and although an argument has been presented to show that Shelley had Wordsworth in mind when he wrote the poem, neither of these arguments is any more impressive than the view that Hamlet is meant for Sir Philip Sidney, the perfect soldier-scholar-courtier of the Elizabethan age. Instead of trying to paint an idealized picture of anyone (himself included), Shelley meant, as the first paragraph of his preface indicates, to describe, in an objective parabolical fashion, a state of mind which he had observed both in himself and in Hogg during the period 1811-1815.[14]

11 Stopford A. Brooke, *Poems from Shelley* (London, 1880), preface, pp. xi-xii.
12 See esp. Chapter xii, and elsewhere *passim*.
13 H. L. Hoffman, *op. cit.*, see esp. p. 3.
14 Hoffman states (*op. cit.*, p. 10) that the poem is a "metaphorical representation of a mental state."

Shelley was acquainted with that phenomenon of some impressionable minds in which the lover builds up in his consciousness an ideal of a woman. The real woman, whom he clothes with the light that never was on sea or land, has little resemblance to the ideal. Shelley's own affair with Harriet Grove in 1810-1811 provided one example: he had painfully observed the discrepancy between the Harriet of his fond dreams, and the Harriet who was so afraid of his iconoclasm that she quickly married a mere "clod." At this same time he had tried, with a peculiar combination of sentimental and experimental motives, to build up in Hogg's mind an ideal image of his sister, Elizabeth Shelley. He wished to see Hogg and Elizabeth united outside the marriage tie. By the summer of 1811 Elizabeth had withdrawn in much the same manner as Harriet Grove, and for similar reasons, chiefly a fear of the opinions of her elders. On June 2, the *deus ex machina* of Field Place explained to his presumably bewildered friend how the delusion about Elizabeth had arisen: "You loved a being, an idea in your own mind. You concreted this abstract of perfection. . . . The being, whom that name signified, was by no means worthy of this. . . . You loved a being; the being, whom you loved, is not what she was; consequently, as love appertains to mind, and not body, she exists no longer."[15]

Two weeks later he all but admitted that he had built up an idea of Elizabeth's perfection in Hogg's mind to see how his friend would react. "I knew what an unstable, deceitfull thing Love is; but still did I wish to involve you in the pleasing delusion."[16] In short, there were two events in 1811 which served to acquaint Shelley with the tendency in the youthful and imaginative male mind to concrete abstracts of perfection, to love an idea. At the same time Shelley realized that this tendency did not necessarily require the activating agency of flesh and blood. For someone like himself a literary heroine would serve. When he read Lady Morgan's novel, *The Missionary*, he became ecstatic over the "divine Luxima." "What a pity," he cried, "that we cannot incorporate

---

[15] *Letters*, viii, 98.

[16] *Shelley at Oxford*, p. 40. June 16, 1811. When Hogg printed this letter in his *Life* of Shelley, he changed the pronoun *you* to *myself* in order to cover up the real situation.

these creations of fancy; the very thoughts of them thrill the soul."[17]

Between 1811 and the composition of *Alastor* in 1815, these early experiences were duplicated several times over. Shelley had (and variously embraced) other opportunities to involve himself in what he had called the "pleasing delusion." The foci were Harriet Westbrook, Elizabeth Hitchener, Cornelia Turner and her mother Mrs. Boinville, and in 1814, Mary Godwin. Shelley's emotional instability was marked during the early months of 1811. He was in a state of constant emotional turmoil from this time until after the climactic elopement with Mary in the summer of 1814. With each of the women the pattern was repeated until he met Mary: attraction, approach, involvement in the "pleasing delusion," and finally detachment or retreat. The determination to elope with Mary cost Shelley a great mental struggle, and only after the decision had been made, after the union had in fact been effected, did his emotions gradually settle back towards something approximating calm. Other excitants followed. Apparently the affair between Hogg and Mary in the early months of 1815 was the result of another attempt by Shelley to involve Hogg in the "pleasing delusion." Hogg was now sufficiently experienced to approach Mary only with considerable caution, so that his involvement was not especially spectacular.[18] But the mere existence of such a liaison must have been enough to keep the participants and the onlooker in an unusually active emotional state, which the premature birth and early death of Mary's child did nothing to mollify. Therefore the summer and early autumn of 1815, which saw the composition of *Alastor*, was the first period of reasonably complete emotional calm in four years' time. The point to be stressed here is that the psychological phenomenon which Shelley had early observed in Hogg recurred often enough in his own experience during the next four years so that he could call it, as he did in the preface to *Alastor*, "one of the most interesting situations of the human mind."

Shelley's most extensive and searching statement about this recurrent mental situation occurs in a letter to Hogg written in

[17] *Letters*, viii, 117.
[18] An account of this affair occurs in White, *Shelley*, i, 391-393, 400-402. The pertinent letters are reprinted in R. M. Smith, *The Shelley Legend*, pp. 148-153.

August, 1815, about the time when, in calm of mind, all passion spent, he was beginning, or was about to begin, the composition of *Alastor*. The language here is so close to that used in the preface to the poem, and the theme he is discussing is so similar in its essentials to that of *Alastor*, that the paragraph ought probably be taken as a glossary to his intention. "It excites my wonder to consider the perverted energies of the human mind. That so much benevolence and talent, as the missionary who travelled with you seemed to possess, should be wasted in such profitless endeavours, nor serve to any other end than to expose its possessor to perpetual disappointments. Yet who is there that will not pursue phantoms, spend his choicest hours in hunting after dreams, and wake only to perceive his error and regret that Death is so near? One man there is, and he is a cold and calculating man, who knows better than to waste life; but who alas! cannot enjoy it. Even the men who hold dominion over nations fatigue themselves by the interminable pursuit of emptiest visions; the honour and power which they seek is enjoyed neither in acquirement, possession or retrospect; for what is the fame that attends the most skilful deceiver or destroyer? What the power which awakens not in its progression more wants than it can supply?"[19]

The mind is energetic in the pursuit of illusions. One may, like Hogg's benevolent and talented missionary, cherish hopes for the reformation of the world through the influence of Christian doctrine. His doom is perpetual disappointment in the failure of his hopes. One may, like the statesman, go in search of honor, power, and fame. He will enjoy these neither in the getting, holding, nor remembering. One may, like the cold realist, entertain no illusions; yet by the same token he cuts himself off from the enjoyment of life. The paradox is that the pursuit of phantoms is necessary to human happiness but inevitably productive of despair, while one who refuses to admit illusions to his thinking at the same time dries up the springs of joy in life. Shelley's preface to *Alastor* indicates that he would side with the missionary as against the cold calculator. The most quixotic dreamer is preferable, if he hurls himself at a vision with passionate intensity, to those who wither up in loveless lethargy.

[19] *Letters*, ix, 116. Aug., 1815.

There is a strong hint in Shelley's remarks of a type of ethical hedonism, not unknown among the sentimental writers of the eighteenth century: the implication that it is man's duty to seek love; he can thus avoid moral desuetude, even though disappointment and disillusion are likely to ensue upon his efforts. This view would go far towards explaining the essential paradox of *Alastor*, where a blameless youth, in pursuit of an impossible ideal, comes to grief because of the very intensity of his search after perfection. It would also explain why Shelley felt that the poem was "not barren of instruction to actual men," and why Mary Shelley asserted that "the poem ought rather to be considered didactic than narrative." Didactic it is, though not in the usual sense of explicit moral preachment, for its truths, to follow for a moment the language of Wordsworth, are not "individual and local, but general, and operative; not standing upon external testimony, but carried alive into the heart by passion"—which was always Shelley's way in poetry after the time of *Queen Mab*.

It would thus appear that Brooke's generalization, while it helps to categorize Shelley's poetry as a whole, does not really inhere in this poem. Ostensibly, *Alastor* is a poem "inspired only by [Shelley's] ideas and regrets," written "without any ethical end, and absolutely apart from humanity." One may also catch hints of self-justification in Shelley's admiration for an essentially Shelleyan hero. But the buried movements of the poem have an ethical end, and against Brooke's belief that in works like *Alastor* Shelley stood apart from humanity one ought to place Shelley's own statement about his poem, which he called "my first serious attempt to interest the best feelings of the human heart."

· III ·

Shelley's aim in *Alastor*, then, was to set forth as objectively as possible, and as an object lesson, a state of mind with which his own experiments and experiences had intimately acquainted him. The preoccupation with such problems has been distinguished as the "pan-erotic element" in Shelley.[20] At this stage of his career, however, he was only beginning to formulate the doctrine of love

[20] J. Kooistra, *English Studies* 4 (July, 1922), 171-176.

which came gradually to supersede the doctrine of necessity in his thinking.[21]

Although the work suffers from the conflict of motives under which it was written, *Alastor* was a key poem in Shelley's development as philosophical and psychological poet. For it was the first of the major poems to undertake an experiment with what may be called the psyche-epipsyche strategy, of which he was to make considerable use in the central story of *The Revolt of Islam*, which was to become one of the major interrelated themes in his first great poem, *Prometheus Unbound*, and which was to be used at the highest possible level in *Epipsychidion, Adonais,* and *The Triumph of Life*. The basic assumption of the psyche-epipsyche strategy may be found under explicit discussion in the *Symposium* and *Phaedrus* of Plato. Phaedrus himself calls it, in Lane Cooper's excellent rendering, "the emulous desire for what is fine," without which "it cannot be that either state or individual should accomplish any great and noble work."[22] Whether or not the mind is disciplined it wishes to possess that which it does not have. When the mind is reined in by discipline, its motivating or driving force (the eros of the *Symposium*) is directed towards the goal of what is fine: the good and the beautiful, or rather the best and the most beautiful. To put the matter in Shelleyan terms, the mind (psyche) imaginatively creates or envisions what it does not have (epipsyche), and then seeks to possess epipsyche, to move towards it as a goal. Therefore the psyche-epipsyche strategy in a nutshell is the evolution by the mind of an ideal pattern towards which it then aspires. Or, as Aristophanes puts the matter in the *Symposium* (in full awareness of its comic aspects): "Our species would be happy under these conditions, if every one achieved his love completely, and found his own true mate."[23]

Although the epipsyche terminology does not appear in Shelley until 1821, the notion of a search for a true mate, a complementary heroine for the Shelleyan hero, has been born by 1815 and is well developed by 1817. The relationship is always, at its highest level, a spiritual union. But it must be, as it were, supported from below

[21] See F. Stovall's valuable study of "Shelley's Doctrine of Love," *PMLA* 45 (March, 1930), 283-303.

[22] *Symposium*, p. 178. Lane Cooper, tr., *Plato: Phaedrus, Ion, Gorgias, and Symposium*, etc. (New York, 1938), p. 224.

[23] *Ibid.*, p. 240.

by other unifications. The Spanish word *simpatico* expresses the whole notion with some precision. It includes not merely an idea of voluntary sympathy and empathy; it has also a physiological aspect involving the sympathetic nervous system. The remarks which Shelley prefixed to *Alastor* specify a hierarchy of correspondences or levels of sympathy. As Shelley puts it there, the hero's "mind is at length suddenly awakened and thirsts for intercourse with an intelligence similar to itself. He images to himself the Being whom he loves. . . . The vision in which he embodies his own imaginations unites all of the wonderful or wise or beautiful, which the poet, the philosopher or the lover could depicture. The intellectual faculties, the imagination, the functions of sense have their respective requisitions on the sympathy of corresponding powers in other human beings. The Poet [-Hero] is represented as uniting these requisitions and attaching them to a single image. He seeks in vain for a prototype of his conception."

This is not the straight supernaturalism of Keats in *La Belle Dame* or *Lamia*; nor is it that form of neurasthenic fixation which Byron sums up in his phrase, "The nympholepsy of some fond [i.e. foolish] despair." Rather it is a form of idealism, with its roots in the romantic psychology of aspiration, and its branches extending up towards the "light that never was on sea or land." Shelleyan nympholepsy appears to signify the fulfillment or rounding out of the unfinished self. It is a version of that longing for completeness which has been a constant theme in world literature from Dante to Henry James, and usually ends, as in Shelley's later work, by taking on religious connotations.

A possible inception for the epipsyche notion in Shelley may be his early conviction that he was dependent for complete self-realization upon "women of character," whom he tended to look up to and to lean on rather more than the facts ever warranted. Shelley's consciousness of this dependence is well shown in his statements to Elizabeth Hitchener and Mary Godwin. He told the former, "You are as my better genius—the judge of my reasonings, the guide of my actions, the influencer of my usefulness."[24] And again, a few months later, "You are to my fancy as a thunder-riven pinnacle of rock, firm amid the rushing tempest and the boiling

[24] *Letters*, VIII, 206. Nov. 26, 1811.

surge."[25] In 1814, Miss Hitchener's place had been usurped by another female paragon. "Your thoughts alone," he told Mary, "can waken mine to energy; [my mind] without yours is dead and cold. . . . It seems as if you alone could shield me from impurity and vice. If I were absent from you long I should shudder with horror at myself. My understanding becomes undisciplined without you." Evidently Harriet had never been capable of performing this function. "I believe," says Shelley in the same letter, "I must become in Mary's hands what Harriet was in mine."[26] In the end, when all the evidence has been published, it will probably appear that the illusion of Mary's over-all superiority to Harriet, and the delusion that Mary was as superior to him as he was to Harriet, were prominent factors in Shelley's ultimate determination to leave his first wife and elope with Mary Godwin. But the biographical implications of Shelley's peculiar submissiveness to what he regarded as female superiority are less important for our purposes than the results as manifested in the poetry. The Shelleyan hero is very often somehow dependent upon the Shelleyan heroine. His spirit is often "girt round with weakness"; he is unable to cope with his environment effectively unless he is able to establish a connection with some epipsychological counterpart, through whom he is completed and strengthened, wakened to energy, shielded from impurity, disciplined, and directed. The pattern can be discerned in the Laon-Cythna relationship of *The Revolt of Islam*. In *Alastor*, the focus of these remarks, Shelley for the first time engages the theme. The separation of epipsyche from psyche produces death, whether actual or symbolic. The lamp is shattered, or at any rate is incapable of giving light because the energizing power is not there.

· IV ·

One who has observed Shelley's preoccupation with Necessity, and his enthusiastic espousal of the doctrine at the time of *Queen Mab*, is naturally curious to discover what has happened to the doctrine by 1815. Since *Alastor* is primarily a picture of a state of mind, one would expect that, if necessitarianism is involved at all, it would be most likely to appear in the form of psychological determinism. *Alastor* pictures a superior and exemplary young man

[25] *Ibid.*, 320. May 1, 1812.   [26] *Letters*, ix, 103. Oct. 28, 1814.

as subject to subliminal necessitarian drives: he cannot escape from pursuing an ideal, even though he may sometimes suspect that his ideal is an illusion, and never learn otherwise prior to death. In short, it may be fair to say that in accepting from Peacock the notion of *alastor* Shelley made certain reservations or perhaps alterations in the accepted view of the meaning of the term. Instead of regarding *alastor* as a spirit of evil he associated the word with a particular form of psychological determinism. The youthful poet of *Alastor* could not have chosen to act otherwise than he does act: The inevitability of his fate is indeed, as we have seen, the fundamental implication of the poem. Therefore a special kind of necessity is at work in the poem.

But the beautifully realized and majestic invocation to the poem recalls also the beneficent Daemon of the World as she appears in *Queen Mab*. In lines whose movement and texture are close to the caliber of Wordsworth, Shelley calls upon the "beloved brotherhood" of earth, ocean, and air, claiming a fraternal kinship with them which in turn presumes their and his common filial relationship to the "great mother." Shelley worships her with "natural piety," one of the several Wordsworthian phrases in the poem.[27] But the language in which he addresses the immanent spirit is strongly reminiscent of the "Necessity, thou mother of the world" phraseology for which he had caught the initial suggestion from Holbach.

> Mother of this unfathomable world!
> Favor my solemn song, for I have loved
> Thee ever, and thee only; I have watched
> Thy shadow, and the darkness of thy steps,
> And my heart ever gazes on the depth
> Of thy deep mysteries.

Although his mind's eye has never penetrated to the inmost sanctuary of the brooding maternal spirit, he is intuitively aware of an indwelling essence both in natural phenomena and the "deep heart

[27] Shelley quotes the *Excursion*, I, 503-505 at the end of his preface. Besides the phrase "natural piety" (from *My Heart Leaps Up*, 9) Woodberry notices "obstinate questionings" (26) and "too deep for tears" (713), both from the *Ode on Intimations of Immortality*, for which *My Heart Leaps Up* served as headnote. Shelley was evidently deeply struck by the great ode of Wordsworth, which affected his own great fragment, *The Triumph of Life*.

of man," and serenely awaits the harmonizing powers of this spirit which he supposes will inform his verses. Some of this language may be discounted for what it is, conventional invocation. The tone also seems mimetically Wordsworthian, made Shelley's only by adoption, like the reworking of Gray in *Queen Mab*. But in addressing the "Great Parent" he uses language so reminiscent of that of the sixth canto of his earlier poem as to make it fairly clear that the maternal Necessity of *Queen Mab* and the immanent nature-and-mind essence of *Alastor* may be roughly equated.[28]

The long elegiac conclusion contains one curious episode which points up the full significance of necessitarian doctrine in *Alastor*, and its relation to the Epipsyche theme. After the poet's miraculous voyage, he seeks out a natural sepulcher in which to compose himself for death, and he comes, along the way, to a dark well, into whose mirror-like waters he pauses to gaze, seeing his reflection

> as the human heart,
> Gazing in dreams over the gloomy grave,
> Sees its own treacherous likeness there.

As he watches, less acutely conscious of his own image than filled with an intense awareness which is subliminally focused on that image

> A Spirit seemed
> To stand beside him—clothed in no bright robes
> Of shadowy silver or enshrining light,
> Borrowed from aught the visible world affords
> Of grace, or majesty, or mystery;
> But undulating woods, and silent well,
> And leaping rivulet, and evening gloom
> Now deepening the dark shades, for speech assuming,
> Held commune with him, as if he and it
> Were all that was; only—when his regard
> Was raised by intense pensiveness—two eyes,

[28] Additional credence is lent to the equation of Necessity and the World-Mother of *Alastor* when it is recalled that Shelley rewrote parts of *Queen Mab* as *The Daemon of the World* and included it in the *Alastor* volume. At the other end, one notices a clear foreshadowing of *Hymn to Intellectual Beauty*, Stanza V, in *Alastor*, 23-28. Stovall, who does not, I think, take Shelleyan necessitarianism into sufficient account, makes the rest of the equation. *Desire and Restraint in Shelley*, p. 144.

Two starry eyes, hung in the gloom of thought,
And seemed with their serene and azure smiles
To beckon him.

Then, "obedient to the light/ That shone within his soul" he goes on.

Like the "fair fiend" passage discussed earlier in the chapter, this episode has been generally misinterpreted. Hoffman's reading of the lines may perhaps be taken as typical. He believes that the "Spirit" of line 479 is identical with the owner of the "two starry eyes." That is, the whole passage relates to the visionary maiden alone, except that she is now utterly without fleshly attributes, and has come to represent "the false lure of the soul's hope of survival beyond the grave."[29]

But this reading ignores the descriptive phrases applied to the "Spirit," phrases which make it plain that Shelley is alluding to Mother Nature, phenomenal nature, clothed in "undulating woods, and silent well/ And leaping rivulet, and evening gloom." The spirit with whom the poet holds communion is the Spirit of Nature, that "all-sufficing power," Necessity, "the mother of the world," which Shelley had celebrated in *Queen Mab*. For the poet is now in the very lap of nature, in the utter solitude of a mountain plateau where he is presently to die. He communes with that spirit as if it and he "were all that was." The "spirit" of line 479 is obviously not the visionary maiden. Hoffman's reading also ignores the crucial word *only* at line 488. When the poet's "regard" is "raised by intense pensiveness" (that is, when his imaginative powers are heightened by the very intensity of his concentration upon natural objects),[30] he sees "two starry eyes hung in the gloom of thought." He has at first considered the nature-spirit as if he and it were all that was—*only*, in the deep intensity of his communings, he becomes aware of the "two starry eyes" of the visionary maiden which beckon him onward in his quest.

It has been necessary to undertake this *explication de texte* in order to show that Shelley is not here speaking only of the visionary maiden. He intends rather to represent two visions in conflict. One is the vision of a beneficent nature-spirit with which the poet

---

[29] Hoffman, *op. cit.*, pp. 48-49.
[30] Wordsworth often observed a similar psychological phenomenon in his own experience. See the incident of the hooting owls in "There was a boy."

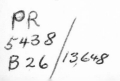

communes until that vision is superseded by a second vision. The "two starry eyes" of course symbolize the maiden he has loved and lost. The upshot of the matter is that the second vision draws him away from the consolations of inward calm which are tacitly offered by the first vision.

It may be asked what this very interesting episode signifies in the interpretation of the poem. The answer is simple enough: to commune in solitude with the spirit of nature will not suffice; man needs love. The poet of *Alastor*, driven on by his Faustian curiosity, had explored in solitude the world of phenomenal nature, attempting (though apparently not consciously) "to exist without human sympathy." But there was that in him which made such an existence impossible. He conceived an epipsyche whose sympathetic community with him was absolute, and in the end perished through the intensity of his search after an absolute he could not find again, either in the flesh or elsewhere.

Shelley inadvertently made the best commentary on his poem some three years later when, fresh from translating the *Symposium*, he was engaged in writing an essay on the arts and manners of the Athenians. The archetype of one's love, said he, "for ever exists in the mind, which selects among those who resemble it that which most resembles it; and instinctively fills up the interstices of the imperfect image." Even in his most savage state, Shelley goes on, man is a social being. Civilization only quickens and enhances his sociality, producing a desire for "sympathies still more intimate and complete." Thence arises "that profound and complicated sentiment, which we call love, which is rather the universal thirst for a communion not merely of the senses, but of our whole nature, intellectual, imaginative, and sensitive, and which, when individualised, becomes an imperious necessity, only to be satisfied by the complete or partial, actual or supposed, fulfillment of its claims."[31]

The precision with which these remarks bear on *Alastor* should be at once apparent. Man is not by nature a creature of solitude; he is a social being. The more civilized he is, the more he thirsts for communion of his whole nature with that of another. When his sentiment is individualized, it becomes an imperious necessity, and can be satisfied only by the fulfillment of its claims—whether par-

[31] *Prose*, vii, 228.

tially, through sensual connections, or totally, through a communion involving one's whole nature.

The spirit of solitude therefore stands in opposition to what is human. The poet of *Alastor* is humanized (though also done to death) by the "imperious necessity" of love. The essential conflict is set forth in the crucial episode which we have examined in detail. The spirit of nature is the spirit of solitude; the poet is half in love with Necessity, the beneficent but inhuman law of the natural world. But his greater need, the need which draws him on with an intensity so great that it wastes and kills his body, is the unrequited need for human sympathy. In a very real sense the conflict in *Alastor* may be described as the love of necessity *versus* the necessity of love.

The principle of love gradually came to occupy the central position in Shelley's thought. Towards the end of his life he gathered up in terms of the concept all his deepest convictions about the aspiration and inspiration of the creative mind, about the immortality of thought, and about the reservoir of divine power which is available to all creatures according to their respective degrees of sensitivity, integrity, high seriousness, and perseverance. The process by which Shelley achieved this clarification of his vision was, however, gradual. As analyzed in *Alastor* and other documents of the 1815 period, love is a necessary concomitant of and motivating force in the individual mind, but it has not yet been purged of its fleshly attributes, nor has it passed beyond the sphere of imperious individual need. By 1817-1818, in *The Revolt of Islam* and *Prometheus Unbound*, love has broadened in Shelley's thought to an ethical principle: "the sole law which should govern the moral world." In the first of these poems love is still, in one of its aspects, an irresistible force making for the union of man and woman. But in both poems, and particularly in the *Prometheus*, love is seen also as the most important socializing, civilizing, and restorative power available to man. This development is symbolically represented in the transfiguration of Asia. By 1821, love has undergone an apotheosis in Shelley's thinking and has become merged with the metaphysical concept of the "One"—that supreme power from which all that is good is born, and to which all that is best aspires to return.

3

THE NECESSITY OF LEADERSHIP:
THE REVOLT OF ISLAM

Knowledge is power; it is in the hands of a few, who employ it to mislead the many, for their own selfish purposes. . . . What if it were in the hands of a few who should employ it to lead the many? What if it were universal, and the multitude were enlightened? No. The many must always be in leading-strings; but let them have wise and honest conductors. A few to think and many to act; that is the only basis of perfect society.
—MR. SCYTHROP (SHELLEY) IN *Nightmare Abbey*

And ever from that hour upon me lay
The burden of this hope, and night or day
In vision or in dream, clove to my breast. . . .
These hopes found words through which my spirit sought
To weave a bondage of such sympathy
As might create some response to the thought
Which ruled me now.
—LAON, IN *The Revolt of Islam*

· I ·

THE record of Shelley's development as poet is the story of a struggle to realize in images a vision which in a measure resisted adequate realization. Most poets engage in some such struggle: it is partly a problem of comprehension, and partly one of expression. For Shelley these problems were complicated by his inability to decide between two essentially opposed points of view as to what kind of poetry he was best suited to write. He greatly wished to write poetry based on the sympathetic observation of human beings engaged in significant action. He had, on the other hand, a strong predilection for the construction of abstract metaphysical systems, and his works constantly show his tendency (in part an inheritance from his eighteenth-century reading, but in part also the result of his continuous preoccupation with morals) to think in allegorical terms. His reconciliation of these two points of view, insofar as it was at all complete, was achieved through the use of mythology. An existing myth could often be adapted in such a way as to incorporate within it his current metaphysical theories. At the same time existing mythological personages, suitably re-modeled and remotivated, could serve as legitimate substitutes for idealized human beings.

At the philosophical level a similar dilemma existed. Early in his career Shelley was inclined to think of man as a mere historical animal, whose movements were inescapably conditioned if not completely fixed by external natural laws, by social and economic drives, and by subliminal determinants. Beside this view there was quite early another one which argued that man's greatest glory consists in his ability to transcend his physical and historical environment, to overcome his inheritance of social superstition, to establish a meaningful relationship with his fellows and with supernal power. The key to this ability was self-knowledge. Given such knowledge, man might be able to hasten or otherwise dominate the historical process; in any event, this was the position towards which he ought to aspire, for if his immediate defeat was probable, some kind of long-term moral victory was at least possible. This ethical idealism ultimately prevailed in Shelley's thought. As it grew stronger, his early faith in the inevitability of progress and his trust in the essential benignancy of external cosmic powers became weaker. Consequently his thought, though one would not always think so from a reading of his poetry, tended to become more and more humanistic, less and less naturalistic or theistic, until about 1821, when he evolved a metaphysic in which nature, man, and God (the "One") were unified.

To return now to the literary aspects of Shelley's development in the period 1816-1817, three interrelated questions arose in his mind which seemed to require settlement. These were: the question of didactic poetry—how far one was justified in mixing the moral and the esthetic aims; the question of communicating moral teaching by other than didactic means; and the question of "universalizing" narratives of human experience by the establishment of a metaphysical frame of reference. *The Revolt of Islam* provides an answer to these questions, and therefore serves as a useful index to the direction of Shelley's development.

Shelley professed to abhor, and after *Queen Mab* sought to avoid writing, straight didactic poetry. But he was all his life a didactic poet. The roots of the problem lay in his conviction that poetry is one of the most powerful moral forces at work in the world. Shelley's reforming instinct is a constant among variables. Where he varies is in his opinions as to how the power of the written word can best be invoked for the ultimate purpose of reform. Shelley's prefatory remarks to *The Revolt of Islam* make it plain that he was by this date trying to break loose from didactic poetry. "I have chosen," he says, "a story of human passion in its most universal character, diversified with moving and romantic adventure, and appealing . . . to the common sympathies of every human breast. I have made no attempt to recommend the motives which I would substitute for those at present governing mankind, by methodical and systematic argument. . . . The Poem therefore (with the exception of the first canto, which is purely introductory) is narrative, not didactic." *The Revolt* will not, like *Queen Mab*, seek to proselytize by building up an irrefutable logical pattern. It will teach by example rather than by precept. It is an illustrative fable in which human beings wrestle with powerful social forces and gain through martyrdom a moral victory. The hero and heroine, Laon and Cythna, represent "human passion in its most universal character" by typifying the indomitable human spirit which aspires after excellence and is devoted to the love of mankind. Othman represents the tyranny of man-made institutions and superstitions, the evil of established and unchecked power. But it would not appear that Shelley intended his "mere human" characters to be allegorical figures except, say, in the sense that Sydney Carton represents noble self-sacrifice, or Nora Helmer resurgent womanhood, or Sir Willoughby Patterne blind egotism, or Tennyson's Ulysses the unconquerable will to achieve.

Shelley's growing conviction that didacticism makes for poor art led him to ask how, without being obviously propagandistic, poetry can act to the improvement of men. The prefatory remarks to

The Revolt record Shelley's wish to "excite in the reader a gener-ous impulse, an ardent thirst for excellence" by communicating to him "the pleasure and the enthusiasm arising out of those images and feelings in the vivid presence of which within [the poet's] own mind consists at once his inspiration and his reward." The aim is to re-create in the reader feelings analogous to those which inspired the author, and thus to convert him to the author's way of thinking through activation of his imagination.

Shelley was, finally, intent upon giving his narrative a universal significance. Despite Mary's recommendations to the contrary, he was unable at this time to interest himself in a "mere human" story. To stop with a dramatization of the conflict between partic-ular social mores and individual rights in the manner, say, of Hen-rik Ibsen, would not satisfy his notion of the high aims of poetry. For a poet, as Shelley said in the *Defence*, "would do ill to embody his conceptions of right and wrong, which are usually those of his place and time, in his poetical creations, which participate in neither." A human predicament, to be worth serious consideration, must be seen in terms of some carefully worked out cosmological plan.

The Revolt of Islam is therefore intentionally designed as two poems, one within the other. The first presents human beings, the other supernatural forces under whose influence the human beings are supposed to act. The human story occupies most of the poem; the metaphysical section serves as the frame for the main romance, and is obviously meant to heighten and universalize the signifi-cance of the struggle in which, as members of human society, Laon and Cythna are engaged.

· II ·

SOME acquaintance with the origins of the mythological section of the poem is necessary to an understanding of the meaning both of *The Revolt of Islam* and of *Prometheus Unbound*, the greatly superior poem which followed it. *The Revolt* has been said to be the first major work in which Shelley used his "myth-creating fac-ulty."[1] Though he made it over according to his own standards and

[1] Traugott Böhme, "Spenser's Literarisches Nachleben bis zu Shelley," *Palaestra* 93 (Berlin, 1911), 298.

requirements, the myth of *The Revolt* was not original with Shelley. What Böhme resoundingly calls "der urewige, weltumspannende Widerstreit zwischen Gut und Böse, zwischen Licht und Finsternis"[2] in the first canto of the poem is actually a version of the Oromaze-Ahriman antithesis from Zoroastrian mythology. Later in his career Shelley habitually utilized pagan (chiefly classical) mythology as the groundwork of his poems. What he took was, however, always modified: he blurred the original outlines, extended and "modernized" the meaning, changed the philosophical implications, and often carried the myth along by the use of symbols foreign to the original mythological pattern. In this he resembles, among others, his peers, Spenser and Milton. Therefore, although his myth in *The Revolt* can be traced by devious stages back to Zoroaster, the alterations are frequent and important enough so that what Zarathustra spake is heard only contrapuntally.

Information on pagan religious cults, customs, ceremonies, and mythologies was generally available to romantic poets like Scott, Southey, Byron, Shelley, and Peacock. French and English ethnologists, religious historians, and comparative mythologists like Bryant, Dupuis, Hyde, Jones, Maurice, Moore, and Selden had published extraordinarily learned tomes on the origin and development of ancient religious cults, the interpretation of fable by astronomical computations and zodiacal manipulations, the correspondence among Persian, Indian, Egyptian, Phoenician, and Greek deities, and allied subjects—poking about, as Maurice said, in "the rubbish of pagan history," and coming up with odd treasures.[3]

The Revolt was only one of several poetic redactions of the Zoroastrian scheme among romantic writers. Southey, who had constituted himself the amateur anatomist of world mythology from India to Mexico, employed a watered-down version of Indo-Ira-

---

[2] *Idem.*

[3] For example: J. S. Bailly, *Lettres sur l'Origine des Sciences, et sur celle des peuples de l'Asie* (Paris, 1777); A. Banier, *La Mythologie et les Fables Expliquées par l'Histoire,* 3 vols. (Paris, 1738-1740); Jacob Bryant, *A New System, or an Analysis of Ancient Mythology,* 3 vols. (London, 1774-1776); C. Dupuis, *Memoire sur l'Origine des Constellations et sur l'Explication de le Fable* (Paris, 1781-1792); G. S. Faber, *A Dissertation on the Mysteries of the Cabiri,* 2 vols. (Oxford, 1803). Among prominent orientalist literature should be mentioned Thomas Hyde's *Historia Religionis Veterum Persarum,* Thomas Maurice's *Indian Antiquities,* Edward Moore's *Hindu Pantheon,* and the works of Sir William Jones, 6 vols. (London, 1799).

nian theology in *The Curse of Kehama* (1810). The Persian god of evil, Ahriman, puts in appearance as Arimanes, one of the dark spirits in Byron's *Manfred* (1817),[4] whose "heterogeneous mythological company" occasioned an amusing footnote in Peacock's *Nightmare Abbey* the year following. In 1825, Scott evolved a wild yarn for the early chapters of *The Talisman*, and afterwards had his Saracen chant (to the horror of the Crusader) a reputedly ancient hymn to Ahriman.

Except for Shelley, however, Thomas Love Peacock was the only English romantic writer to use the Zoroastrian scheme at all extensively, and his unfinished epic poem, *Ahrimanes*, is the primary source for much of the mythological background of *The Revolt of Islam*.[5] It is of some interest to know how Shelley and Peacock came to discover Oromaze and Ahriman or, at any rate, how the interest of the two poets came to be intensified.

The discovery or intensification of interest seems to have come about through the mythological enthusiasms of their mutual friend, John Frank Newton of London. Shelley was the first to meet him, on November 5 or 7, 1812—about a week before Shelley and his wife left for Tanyrallt, North Wales, where they spent the winter.[6] Newton had virtually cured an allergic asthma of many years' duration by following a vegetarian diet, and in 1811 had published a singular pamphlet, *The Return to Nature; or, A Defence of The Vegetable Regimen*, in which he supported his views not only by personal testimony, but also by the citation of classical authority.[7] In 1812 he had also contributed a series of learned papers to the miscellany columns of the *Monthly Magazine*, where he argued that evil and sickness entered the world along with cookery and animal food, and that a period of health and universal happiness would result from the restoration of a natural diet of distilled water, vegetables, fruits—and nuts.[8] When Peacock returned from Wales in late July or early August, 1813, Shelley in-

[4] White, *Life*, I, 714, note 46, suggests that Byron's use of Arimanes arose from a conversation with Shelley.

[5] A number of verbal parallels between Peacock's *Ahrimanes* and *The Revolt* are presented by K. N. Cameron, *MLQ* 3 (1942), 287-295.

[6] White, *Shelley*, I, 645, note 22.

[7] The pamphlet is rare. For a reprint see the London *Pamphleteer*, XIX, 497-530, and XX, 97-118, 411-428 (1821-1822).

[8] *Monthly Magazine* for February, 1812 (pp. 18-22); March (pp. 107-109); May (pp. 318-321); June (pp. 408-409); and July (pp. 509-510).

vited him to Bracknell, and introduced him to the Newtons. Mrs. Newton disliked Peacock, who struck her as a "cold scholar," but Newton and Peacock discovered that they could talk zodiacal theory and classical literature like old cronies.[9] Newton's ideas may well have been a topic of conversation between Shelley and Peacock in the late months of 1813, when the warm enthusiast and the cold scholar visited the Lake District and Scotland, returning to London at the end of the first week in December. Peacock's continued interest in Newton's classical authorities is shown by the fact that he began about this time to write an epic poem called "Ahrimanes." Although it was never finished, and survives only as a set of fragments in prose and verse, this was the poem which served to launch Shelley's *Revolt of Islam* several years later.

Newton, whose learning exceeded all bounds, professed to find authority for his vegetarian views in the "most ancient Zodiac, which was that of Dendera."[10] The Dendera Zodiac is noteworthy in that it effects a combination of Zoroastrian, Brahminical, and Greek theology. Of the two hemispheres which compose it, the upper is that of Oromaze, the principle of good, and the lower that of Ahrimanes, the principle of evil. Associated with Oromaze are "Uranus or Brahma the Creator, and Saturn or Veishnu the Preserver"; the Ahrimanic hemisphere contains the compartments of "Jupiter or Seva the Destroyer, and of Apollo or Krishna the Restorer." By sundry manipulations of his astrological machinery, Newton was able to argue for a connection between the Ahrimanic hemisphere and evil's entrance into the world through the practice of flesh-eating.

Upon such theorizing as this, Peacock based his abortive epic. Although he tacitly admits indebtedness to Newton and one or two others by naming the *Monthly Magazine* for the first half of 1812 as the source of some of his ideas in Version I of his poem, the "cold scholar" did not merely ape Newton's dogmas. Other footnotes appended to Version I indicate that he had read, among

[9] H. F. B. Brett-Smith and C. E. Jones, *Works of Thomas Love Peacock*, Halliford Edition, introduction, p. liv. See further, Hogg, *Life* (1858) II, 477. Peacock's editors have pointed out that Newton appears under at least two aliases in the novels: Mr. Toobad, the "Manichean Millenarian" of *Nightmare Abbey* (1818); and Mr. Ramsbottom, the zodiacal mythologist of *Crotchet Castle* (1831). See Peacock, *Works*, I, lxxxvii and cxlix.

[10] *Memoirs of Shelley* in Peacock, *Works*, VIII, 71-72.

the astronomical mythologists, Bryant's *Ancient Mythology* on Nimrod and Ahrimanes, Dupuis' discussion of "primogenial love" in the *Origine des Tous Les Cultes*, and Hyde's essay on Manicheism in *Historia Religionis Veterum Persarum*.[11]

Peacock's poem was begun not long after his return with the Shelleys to London in early December, 1813, and he seems to have abandoned it by "the middle of 1815 at latest." Thus he was sporadically occupied with the poem through the year 1814 and the early months of 1815,[12] and in the course of this period he had ample opportunity to discuss his progress with Shelley. Although his marital and extramarital affairs chiefly occupied Shelley's mind from the spring until the early autumn of 1814, he returned in September from his flight to the continent with Mary Godwin, and thereafter Peacock "often passed an evening" at Shelley's lodgings,[13] while on some occasions the creditor-hounded poet concealed himself at Peacock's.[14] In the summer of 1815 (roughly the time when Peacock was losing interest in "Ahrimanes") Shelley took a house at Bishopgate and Peacock, at nearby Marlow, was a frequent visitor. The visits continued during the "Attic" winter of 1815-1816, when with occasional assistance from Hogg, the friends followed an "exclusively Greek" course of study.[15] In January Shelley sent Murray the sheets for the *Alastor* volume, on which he had been at work since summer,[16] and about which he and Peacock had talked extensively. That the mysteries of the zodiac had been in their minds during these months of association is indicated by the passage in *Alastor* where the youth is said to have found ruined Ethiopian temples "where marble daemons watch the Zodiac's brazen mystery."[17] From the Vale of Chamounix,[18] during his second continental trip the following summer, Shelley told his friend that the desolating snows and palaces of death and frost on the summit of Mont Blanc and its neighbors seemed sculp-

---

[11] Peacock, *Works*, VII, 422-425. Peacock had almost certainly read Bryant and Dupuis in the winter of 1809-1810. See letters of Sept. 19, 1809 and Feb. 26, 1810 in *Works*, VIII, 176 and 180.

[12] Peacock, *Works*, VII, 516-518.   [13] *Ibid.*, VIII, 96.

[14] *Letters*, IX, 105.   [15] Peacock, *Works*, VIII, 99-100.

[16] *Letters*, IX, 125.   [17] *Alastor*, 118-119. Cf. White, *Shelley*, I, 657.

[18] *Letters*, IX, 186-187. While Peacock was Shelley's chief mentor on Zoroastrianism, Shelley could have found allusions to Oromaze and Ahriman in Barruel's *Mémoires*. See W. E. Peck, *PMLA* 36 (1921), 347-353. Another source may well have been Volney's *Ruins*, which Shelley had previously put to use in *Queen Mab*. See K. N. Cameron, *PMLA* 56 (1941), 175-206.

tured "by the unsparing hand of necessity," and that Peacock, who customarily asserted "the supremacy of Ahriman" might well imagine his evil spirit enthroned there, preparing avalanches, torrents, and thunders for the "first essays of his final usurpation." Newton's zodiacal theories, and Peacock's further readings in the subject, as well as Peacock's attempts to write an epic in which a pair of young lovers were seen against the mythological backdrop of Zoroastrianism, must have been a matter of common talk on those frequent occasions when Shelley and his friend were reading, studying, and conversing together.

Before he abandoned his poem, Peacock had prepared two versions, both consisting of a few Spenserian stanzas followed by detailed outlines in prose. The first version was to consist of two cantos. He finished sixteen stanzas of Canto I, and subjoined a full plan for the unversified remainder. Theological exposition comes first, and we are told that Necessity rules, through the successive delegation of power to four rival gods: El Oran the Creator, who first harmonized Chaos and produced Primordial Love; Oromaze the Preserver, who succeeded El Oran and preserved the best elements of his predecessor's reign; Ahrimanes the Destroyer, the present evil incumbent, who will rule until Mithra the Restorer establishes peace and harmony once more. Although Oromaze and his genii retired to the "south's impenetrable bowers" when Ahrimanes took over, some of the Preserver's votaries may still be found in sylvan areas. Two of these incorruptibles are the lovers Darassah and Kelasris, natives of an island in the Araxes; they have successfully resisted the temptations of the destroyer-god, and are guarded by the genii of Oromaze. The substance of the poem would have consisted in the harrowing adventures of the lovers, their pursuit by Ahrimanic daemons, and their flight to a Pacific island which is destroyed by a volcanic eruption. Given an opportunity to pay homage to Ahrimanes, they refuse, and are then assured by an Oromazian genius that they are worthy to be guests in the Preserver's southern domains, to which they accordingly sail in a small boat, assailed by Ahrimanic storms, but serenely confident of reaching the final haven.

Peacock's second version was an ambitious expansion of the earlier attempt. Of the intended twelve cantos, he was able to finish one of thirty stanzas, and about half (fourteen stanzas) of

Canto II. As before, he subjoined a careful prose argument for the unfinished cantos. Here Necessity is retained as supreme power, but the subsidiary agents are reduced from four to two: Oromaze and Ahrimanes. The completed first canto opens with Darassah by the moonlit sea, out of which arises a beautiful female genius. After explaining the current situation among the gods, she reveals herself as a votary of Ahrimanes. The complex development of the rest of the poem roughly follows that of the earlier version, but with the very major difference that Darassah yields to the temptations of the evil genius, becoming a tyrant, while Kelasris is finally discovered as an Oromazian sub-deity in disguise.[19]

· III ·

SHELLEY's letter to a prospective publisher of *The Revolt* stated that, except for the first canto and a part of the twelfth, he had written "a mere human story without the smallest intermixture of supernatural interference."[20] The statement is not quite true, but it is true that most of the "supernatural interference" occurs in Canto I and the last twenty-five stanzas of Canto XII. These parts, taken together, Shelley added, constituted "in some measure a distinct poem, though very necessary to the wholeness of the work"—distinct because they involved the supernatural, necessary because they provided a mythological framework for the "mere human story," giving it a cosmic significance comparable, though on a far lower scale, to that which Milton reached by setting the story of Adam and Eve against the background of heavenly strife.

Canto I begins when a youth, who serves as observer-narrator, ascends a high and sea-girt promontory to watch the dawn. A storm darkens the sky, but presently through a rift among the clouds the youth sees a tremendous aerial struggle going on between a snake and an eagle. After some minutes of fierce combat the snake falls vanquished into the sea, and the youth hurries from the promontory to the sandy beach, where he is astonished to discover a beautiful woman in whose bosom the talon-raked serpent contentedly coils. With the woman and the snake, the youth now embarks in a high-prowed boat of moonstone upon a "voyage di-

---

[19] Peacock, *Works*, VII, 265-286. See also *ibid.*, 513-518.
[20] *Letters*, IX, 250-251. Oct. 13, 1817.

vine and strange." The woman explains to her companion the nature of the struggle which they have just witnessed, and recounts her life story. The snake in her bosom is an incarnation of the spirit of good, with whom she long ago fell in love in a vision. Since the time when man first became a thinking being, there has been a constant struggle in progress between the spirit of good and the spirit of evil, one of whose forms is that of the victorious eagle. Good is only temporarily vanquished, says the woman. The war will be shortly renewed.

As she ends her narrative, the youth discovers that their craft has reached a magnificent temple in a mountain-walled bay. Within its dome the Great Departed occupy thrones, one of which, reared on a fiery pyramid, is vacant. As the youth watches entranced, the woman miraculously dissolves into a darkness which fills the temple; the only visible light comes from the eyes of the snake of Good, which move along the temple floor, mingle, and rise high until they gleam like a mighty planet, beneath which, as the lights come up, sits a radiant male form on the erstwhile vacant throne. This is the anthropomorphic manifestation of the spirit of good, who says that the youth is to be instructed with a "tale of Human Power." Two other forms, male and female, now stand forth; the youth learns that they are Laon and Cythna, who lived nobly and died gloriously in the war for the victory of Good.

This concludes the first canto. The rest of the poem, up to Canto xii, stanza xvii, details the adventures of Laon and Cythna until their death at the hands of the tyrannical Othman and an Iberian priest. The final twenty-five stanzas round out the mythological first canto by showing how, after their deaths, Laon and Cythna are magically transported in a boat of pearl to the "Temple of the Spirit" of Good, where they find perpetual haven, and where, at the conclusion of Canto i, we have discovered them as close associates of the good spirit.

The opening of *The Revolt* closely follows the opening of Peacock's second version. Shelley's first canto begins with early dawn, and Peacock's in the midst of a moonlit night; in Shelley the place is a high promontory by the sea, and in Peacock a lonely seashore; in Shelley the protagonist is a youth who has just awakened from "visions of despair," while in Peacock the musing, mourning and wakeful Darassah watches the sea and the moon as if they were "phantoms of a half-remembered dream." At sunset, after the snake and eagle have ended their battle, Shelley's youth sees a beautiful woman on the sand; Darassah watches a lovely "female form" rise out of the sea. The woman in Shelley has shadowy hair, pale lips, sweet eyes, speaks in a melodious silvery voice, and wears a "star-bright robe," while the woman in Peacock is dark, with pale cheeks, and radiant eyes, and a voice solemn as "music's vesper peal," and wears a sable veil inwoven with "flowers of living flame." Seeing that the youth is sorrowful, the woman in Shelley assures him that grief is wise, but that it was a "weak and vain" despair that led him there from sleep; he will learn something useful if he will come with her. The woman in Peacock's poem asks Darassah why he has foregone sleep, and advises him to "leave tears to slaves," for through her he can gain "power for weakness" if he follows his splendid destiny. Many of the rudiments of Shelley's mythological picture are therefore in Peacock.

But it was characteristic of Shelley from this time on to make significant modifications in his source-myths.[21] Important among these are the symbols of the snake, the eagle, the morning star, the red comet, and the antarctic paradise, many of them to be put to further use in Shelley's later poems. Although the symbolism is derived from a variety of sources—including Milton and Coleridge —it is consistently developed and applied, and gives the mythological section of *The Revolt* a kind of imaginative reality which Peacock's work does not share.

The snake and eagle symbols, like those of the morning star and the comet red as blood, are developed from a combination of literary and mythological traditions. Shelley's association of the serpent with the spirit of good shows his knowledge of the common Greek belief that the serpent was "an auspicious and favourable being" and of the use of the serpent as "an hieroglyphic of eternity"

---

[21] For example, other literary figures than Peacock's Aretina contributed to the portrait of the woman on the strand. The fourth chapter of Shelley's fragment, *The Assassins*, shows a girl child harboring a snake in her arms. See W. E. Peck, *Shelley*, II, 13, note. Böhme compares the woman by the sea in Spenser's *Ruines of Time* (8-12), Britomart mourning by her sea of grief (*Faerie Queene*, III, iv, 8), and Phaedria (*ibid.*, II, xii, 14). C. W. Lemmi, in *MLN* 50 (1935), 167-168, suggests the woman weeping over a dead dragon in Boiardo's *Orlando Innamorato*. The figure of Grief with a serpent in the original ninth canto of Southey's *Joan of Arc* is another possibility.

among the Egyptians.[22] The aerial combat between the snake and the eagle, which is not in Peacock, may have been derived from the *Iliad*, the *Aeneid*, the *Metamorphoses*, or the *Faerie Queene*, or possibly developed independently.[23] But it is presented largely in terms of *The Ancient Mariner*, as will presently appear. The spirit of good is represented also as Lucifer, the morning star. As his later essay, "On the Devil, and Devils," proves, Shelley was aware of the passage in his favorite prophet, Isaiah, about the demise of the Assyrian king. Isaiah compares that fall with the descent of Lucifer, the morning star, and the passage was connected by some of the Church Fathers with the fall of Satan in *Revelation*, a circumstance which accounts for the otherwise meaningless equation of Lucifer and Satan.[24] Having borrowed one emblem often associated with the devil, Shelley added the Lucifer emblem, for his spirit of good was in fact the bearer of light. Another passage in the same essay seems to explain the association of the spirit of evil with the red comet. Hell, wrote Shelley, is distributed "among the comets . . . a number of floating prisons of intense and inextinguishable fire."[25]

The development of the serpent and Lucifer symbols shows that Milton's epic was prominent in Shelley's mind; for the double metamorphosis of the Serpent of Good within the Temple of the Spirit at the end of the first canto of *The Revolt* is probably modeled on an incident in *Paradise Lost*. Referring to this episode in a review of *The Revolt*, Leigh Hunt commented: "A magic and obscure circumstance then takes place, the result of which is: that the woman and the serpent are seen no more, but that a cloud opens asunder and a bright and beautiful shape, which seems compounded of both, is beheld sitting on a throne—a circumstance apparently imitated from Milton."[26] Hunt does not further identify

[22] *Prose*, VII, 103. One of Shelley's many nicknames was "The Snake."

[23] *Iliad*, Bk. XII, is suggested by A. H. Gilbert, *MLN* 36 (1921), 505-506. This and the *Aeneid*, Bk. XI, are cited by Douglas Bush, *PQ* 13 (1934), 302. *Metamorphoses*, Bk. IV, is suggested by Peck, *Shelley*, I, 430. *The Faerie Queene*, I, v, 8 is noted by Böhme, *op. cit.*, 298, and again by Lemmi, *MLN* 50 (1935), 167-168.

[24] *Prose*, VII, 103. The Lucifer-symbol reappears in *The Masque of Anarchy* and *Adonais*.

[25] *Ibid.*, 101. Shelley quotes Byron's *Manfred*, I, i, "A wandering Hell in the eternal space," and may owe the notion to Byron. Some echo of the same idea may be found in the comet-symbol of *Epipsychidion*.

[26] *Examiner*, Feb. 1, Feb. 22, and March 1, 1818. Reprinted in White, *The Unextinguished Hearth*. See esp. p. 118.

the Miltonic passage, but he may have had in mind Satan's return to Pandemonium in Book x. Like the Serpent of Good in Shelley, Satan passes unseen through the assembled throng in his Plutonian hall and ascends his throne.

> Down a while
> He sate and round about him saw unseen:
> At last as from a cloud his fulgent head
> And shape Starr-bright appeer'd, or brighter, clad
> With what permissive glory since his fall
> Was left him. . . .

Shelley's description is fairly close:

> The cloud which rested on that cone of flame
> Was cloven; beneath the planet sate a Form,
> Fairer than tongue can speak or thought may frame,
> The radiance of whose limbs rose-like and warm
> Flowed forth, and did with softest light inform
> The shadowy dome, the sculptures and the state
> Of those assembled shapes—with clinging charm
> Sinking upon their hearts and mine. He sate
> Majestic yet most mild, calm yet compassionate.

As in Milton one sees a vast shadowy hall crowded with shapes; over the high throne in the middle hovers an apparently empty cloud, in the midst of which the assemblage becomes aware of a radiant and majestic form.[27]

Shelley's elaboration of Peacock's poem owes something also to Coleridge's *Ancient Mariner*. Thus, when the youth first observes the fighting serpent and eagle, they are far off:

> A speck, a cloud, a shape, approaching grew,
> Like a great ship in the sun's sinking sphere
> Beheld afar at sea, and swift it came anear.

[27] A few stanzas earlier Shelley had already echoed Milton, this time in the woman's story of the advent of evil into the world. The names of the Spirit of Evil are

> Legion, Death, Decay,
> Earthquake and Blight, and Want, and Madness pale,
> Winged and wan diseases, an array
> Numerous as leaves that strew the autumnal gale.

On the beach of the flaming sea of Hell, Milton's Satan called

> His legions, angel forms, who lay entranc'd
> Thick as autumnal leaves that strow the brooks
> In Vallombrosa. . . .

These lines are almost a plagiarism from Coleridge's account of the arrival of the skeleton ship:

> A speck, a mist, a shape, I wist!
> And still it neared and neared. . . .
> Almost upon the western wave
> Rested the broad bright Sun;
> When that strange shape drove suddenly
> Betwixt us and the Sun.

It was again by an association with *The Ancient Mariner* that Shelley developed Peacock's suggestion about the location of Oromaze's place of retirement. According to Peacock's prose argument (version 1), when Oromaze's reign was ended, "he retired with his genii to the extremities of the South, where he drew an impenetrable veil around the bowers of his repose. There the mariner glides over a boundless ocean, and seeks in vain the shores of the Southern world." The allusion to the "extremities of the South" and to the "mariner [who] glides over a boundless ocean," occurring together in Peacock's prose statement suggest not only that Peacock may have had Coleridge in mind when he framed his prose statement, but also that Shelley, reading Peacock, could hardly have missed the association with Coleridge. The Ancient Mariner's ship, by Coleridge's account, "was driven by storms to the cold country toward the South Pole" and subsequently "made her course to the tropical latitude of the Great Pacific Ocean." As Coleridge rendered this poetically, the Mariner's ship fled far to the south where "the ice was all around."

> And now there came both mist and snow
> And it grew wondrous cold:
> And ice, mast-high, came floating by,
> As green as emerald. . . .

Near the end of his voyage with the woman in the magical boat, Shelley's youth looks up to see that they are sailing swiftly and smoothly among

> Mountains of ice, like sapphire, piled on high,
> Hemming the horizon round. . . .

and observes that their boat has

> passed the ocean
> Which girds the pole, Nature's remotest reign. . . .

The "lawny islands" and "blosmy forests" with which the Temple
of the Spirit is surrounded suggest the "tropical latitude of the
great Pacific Ocean," though not, of course, the "hot and copper
sky" with which the Ancient Mariner is there rewarded for having
killed the albatross.[28]

Shelley used the end of Canto xii to round out his sustaining
myth by showing how, after their death at the stake, Laon and
Cythna reached the Temple of the Spirit. Like Canto i, this section of the poem takes the reader into a visionary realm, an extra-
historical paradise of everlasting peace and beauty such as Shelley
delighted to picture. The scenery with which Shelley renders his
vision palpable indicates beyond a doubt that he was thinking of
the domain of Kubla Khan. Xanadu contains "gardens bright with
sinuous rills," and "many an incense-bearing tree" among ancient
forests which enfold "sunny spots of greenery." There is also a
"deep romantic chasm" which slants "down the green hill athwart
a cedarn cover," where the river Alph flows, boiling up at one point
in a "mighty fountain," but also "meandering with a mazy motion"
down to the "caverns measureless to man." Laon and Cythna
awake on a river-bank covered with "star-bright flowers," and see,
around them "many a lawny mountain with incense-bearing forests and vast caves," mountains whose flanks slope down to "that
mighty fountain." When they embark, it is to follow the river "between a chasm of cedarn mountains riven" and thence "along the
wandering watery ways . . . a long and labyrinthine maze."[29]

How all this happened in Shelley's mind is one of the psychological mysteries about which one can only guess. But his refashioning of the basic mythological pattern which he found in Pea-

---

[28] Other echoes of Coleridge appear in *The Revolt*, Canto iii: thus in xviii, 5,
"the wan stars came forth" (cf. *Ancient Mariner*, 317: "the wan stars danced between"); and xxi, 5-6, where Laon is without water, reads, "The uprest/ Of the
third sun brought hunger" (cf. *Ancient Mariner*, 98, where "the glorious Sun up-
rist," but rendered the Mariner and his friends uncomfortably thirsty when by noon
they were becalmed). The second of these, and many other echoes of the *Ancient
Mariner* in Shelley are noticed by A. C. Bradley, *A Miscellany*, London, 1929, pp.
171-176. One of the abodes of Shelley's Witch of Atlas is a south polar paradise.

[29] These echoes have been noted by A. C. Bradley, *op. cit.*, pp. 175-176. Bradley
has not established their connection with Shelley's development of the myth.

cock is a genuine refashioning and not a mere embroidery or *décor* of shining images. As Peacock's scheme turns in his mind over a period of two or three years, the associations begin, and it is notice-able that they are all graphic; there is a continual accession of particulars. Thus the air-battle between the snake and the eagle, drawn perhaps from classical or renaissance sources, dramatically depicts the Good-and-evil opposition which Peacock, that "cold scholar" and indifferent poet, is content rather pedantically to ex-plain; even the air-battle must be made more graphic by drawing upon that memorable scene of the skeletal ship crossing the eye of the sun in *The Ancient Mariner*. The connection of the serpent with eternal and unvanquishable good has classical precedent; but it also recalls Milton's Satan, whose metamorphosis in Pandemo-nium provides Shelley with the "magical and obscure circum-stance" with which he ends Canto i. Moreover, the possibility of a closer relationship between human beings and supernal power, which is one of the constant themes in Shelley, is better repre-sented by his story of the love affair between a mortal maiden and the spirit of good than by Peacock's Aretina, an inferior deity in the service of Ahrimanes into whose thoughts the notions of love and aspiration towards the good never enter. Once Shelley has got hold of the two ideas from Peacock—that Oromaze is a benign guardian spirit and that his place of retirement is in the extremities of the southern world—he recalls the Ancient Mariner's adventure with the South Polar Spirit, and sends his miraculous voyagers through polar ice on their way to the Temple of the Spirit. But when he wishes to call up associations of richness, fertility, and that beauty which has some strangeness in it, to show the bright reward which awaits his martyred revolutionists in the world be-yond death, he sends them through the romantic dream-landscape of Xanadu. Böhme's adjective *weltumspannende* is well-chosen: Shelley's myth spans the world from the English Channel to Ant-arctica, from China to Egypt, and from Persia to Pandemonium.

· IV ·

To Shelley in the autumn of 1816 it appeared that the French Revolution furnished the "master-theme of the epoch in which we live," and he recommended it to Byron as a subject "involving pictures of all that is best qualified to interest and to instruct mankind."[30] The central story of *The Revolt of Islam* is Shelley's attempt to engage the master-theme of his epoch, but he engages it as a theme and not as a specific historical phenomenon. The setting is not France, but Argolis and Byzantium; Shelley is not writing history, but presenting what he calls a "beau idéal" of the French Revolution. The reasons behind this decision are set forth in his preface. The historical revolution was a manifestation of "a general state of feeling among civilized mankind, produced by a defect of correspondence between the knowledge existing in society and the improvement or gradual abolition of political institutions." Political institutional reform had not kept pace, as Shelley saw it, with the growth of human knowledge, and the revolution was an attempt to readjust the "defect of correspondence." Yet too much was expected of the French Revolution. "Can he who the day before was a trampled slave," asks Shelley, "suddenly become liberal-minded, forbearing, and independent?" Such a change requires hope, courage, and "the systematic efforts of generations of men of intellect and virtue." The failure to recognize this truth, as well as the wave of revulsion which followed the atrocities of the Reign of Terror and the reestablishment of successive tyrannies in France, had produced, Shelley observed, widespread misanthropy and despair. But in recent years "a slow, gradual, silent change" had been increasingly noticeable. Wishing to encourage the nascent hopes which he thought he saw around him, Shelley set out to depict, not the historical failure, but a picture of what might be: a revolution "produced by the influence of individual genius" and founded upon the ideal of love, the only law, said Shelley, "which should govern the moral world." Even in his idealized revolution, however, Shelley admits that the permanent overnight regeneration of mankind is impossible. When his individual geniuses, Laon and Cythna, die at the stake, they have achieved a victory, but it is only a moral victory. And this, for Shelley, is all that can now be expected. As far back as June, 1812, he had enthusiastically cried to Elizabeth Hitchener, "Let us shew that truth can conquer falsehood. . . . It is a glorious cause; martyrdom in such a cause were superior than [sic] victory in any other." If his master-theme was

[30] *Letters*, IX, 195, 199. His novel, *Hubert Cauvin* (begun January 1812) had tried the theme. See *Letters*, VIII, 231.

the moral revolution which can be effected at some future date by individual leadership, his supporting theme was human martyrdom in the cause of truth over falsehood.[31]

Shelley's martyrs, Laon and Cythna, have obvious prototypes in the lovers Darassah and Kelasris of the early version of Peacock's *Ahrimanes.* As usual, however, their portraits were modified with details borrowed from other sources, and there is a strong likelihood that both Peacock and Shelley ultimately derived their central characters from Thalaba and Oneiza in Southey's *Thalaba the Destroyer* (1801). That is, Shelley followed Peacock where it suited him, as Peacock had followed Southey. But Shelley knew *Thalaba* well enough to use ideas from that poem in conjunction with ideas obviously gained in the first instance from Peacock. Southey's heroine is abducted by ruffians and subjected to sexual indignities, from which she is rescued by Thalaba at the end of Book VI; Kelasris and Cythna are both put into seraglios, one by a Sultan, the other by the tyrant Othman. Shelley is of course following Peacock in making his heroine an earthly representative of the Oromazian spirit. Like Thalaba, Darassah and Laon have to endure imprisonment. All three poems unite the lovers in paradise. The point, which is that Shelley drew heavily on both Peacock and Southey, need not be labored further.

The turgidness of Shelley's central story is partly attributable to a similar quality in his immediate sources. But it may also arise from the fact that, with little previous experience in the mechanics of narrative verse, he was trying to weld into a single piece a whole series of episodes drawn from diverse secondary sources. Some of the adventures come from Spenser.[32] Old favorites like Volney's *Ruins of Empires*, Lady Morgan's *The Missionary*, and Lawrence's

[31] See *Letters,* VIII, 338, and IX, 251. For the rest, Shelley's rather wordy preface is being followed.

[32] Among Laon's adventures after his parting with Cythna is a seven-year residence with a hermit, whose origins have occasioned some debate. Mary identified him with Dr. Lind; Peck suggests the hermit in the Corsican novel, *Rinaldo Rinaldini.* A more likely source than either of these would be the hermit in the *Faerie Queene* (Bk. VI). The central episode of Canto V, where Laon finds Cythna enthroned among "female choirs" owes something to the Temple of Venus episode in the fourth book of Spenser. Böhme believes that the erotic reunion episode in Canto VI is derived from the adventures of Arthur in Spenser's first book. The greater part of Canto VII, where Othman gloats over his odalisque, is repulsed by the virtuous Cythna, and has her placed in a submarine dungeon, may remind Spenserians of Florimell in the fell clutch of Proteus in Spenser's third book.

Empire of the Nairs are sporadically drawn upon. In preparation for his account of the pestilence in Canto x, Shelley read Wilson's *City of the Plague*, Defoe's *Journal of the Plague Year*, and Brown's *Arthur Mervyn* and *Ormond*. Louvet's *Memoirs of the French Revolution*, of which one might have expected greater use to be made, appears to be connected only with the death-scene of Laon and Cythna in Canto XII.[33]

One unifying agent in the poem, however, is Shelley's consistently revolutionary point of view. There could have been no doubt in his mind as to the outcome of the kind of effort Laon and Cythna make. As early as 1812 he had thought of glorious martyrdom as the future of those who championed truth over falsehood in human society. By 1817, he had battered his own head too often against obdurate public opinion and caging social environment to have any remaining doubt that the wages of revolution is martyrdom.[34] It is, however, his conviction that social tyranny must be resisted which gives Shelley's poem an advantage over such works as *Thalaba* and *Ahrimanes*. Had Peacock's patience and interest enabled him to turn into Spenserian stanzas the prose outlines he prepared, the result would somewhat have resembled *Thalaba*, which is a run-of-the-mill adventure story, partly Gothic, partly Oriental-exotic, with little attempt to distinguish between the actual and the supernatural—a romance, in short, which has not even the advantage of a vertebral moral idea. Peacock's outlines have the defeatist tone of one who has not made up his mind that it is necessary to resist the chthonic forces represented by Ahrimanes, but he succeeds, nevertheless, in suggesting the outlines of the struggle and in making a rough alignment of the opposing forces. Although Shelley recognizes the probability of martyrdom, he is not defeatist. Completely convinced of the necessity for action, he throws his hero and heroine into the arena as leaders of resistance. The result is a struggle of white against black, and one is never in doubt as to where Shelley's sympathies are. His revolutionary convictions give his poem greater force and surer

[33] See W. E. Peck, *MLN* 40 (1925), 246-249 on the connection with Lawrence; and E. Sickels, *PMLA* 45 (1930), 1116-1128, on the part played by Wilson, Defoe, and Brown in the plague sequence. The structure of Canto XII, which describes the capture and execution of Laon and Cythna, follows closely the climactic moments at the end of Lady Morgan's novel, as Woodberry has shown in his notes to the poem.

[34] *Letters*, IX, 145 and 208-209.

direction in crucial episodes, and more over-all unity than can be found in either of his chief source-books.

The central agent of unification is the heroine, Cythna. She serves throughout the poem, even when she is not present, as a positive dynamic force, a kind of matrix of revolution, and is very obviously the apple of Shelley's revolutionary eye. By comparison, Laon is a mere shadow, a bearer of news, an observer and reporter, more acted upon than acting. The force of her personality and her capacity for leadership result in partial success for her campaign. She faces down Othman, enslaver and hater, and temporarily establishes emancipation and love. Laon, however, seems to ask for martyrdom. After the counter-attack has once more enthroned Othman, Laon appears in disguise with an offer to "betray Laon" if Cythna is granted amnesty and permission to emigrate to America. Securing the promise, he throws off his disguise, surrenders, and is condemned. At the stake Cythna joins him, though she need not have done so, as a token of her love and sympathy. Despite these altruistic histrionics, it is evident from the first that Laon is inviting just such a disaster as occurs, and one wonders whether Shelley, who repeatedly hurled himself against the phalanx of bourgeois morals, was not by his own conduct doing likewise.

Laon is a Shelleyesque hero, with a strong messianic complex which seeks to accomplish its mission through the force of words. "I will arise and waken the multitude," cries Laon at one point, and he henceforth carries "the burden of this hope," seeking

> To weave a bondage of such sympathy
> As might create some response to the thought
> Which ruled me now.

This ruling thought he invested "with the light of language," and wherever that light streamed "all bosoms made reply." His song, like a west wind bearing seeds[35]

> Peopled with thoughts the boundless universe,
> A mighty congregation, which were strong,
> Where'er they trod the darkness, to disperse
> The cloud of that unutterable curse
> Which clings upon mankind; all things became

[35] *Revolt*, ii, xv-xvi, and xxx. Cf. ix, xx-xxv, for a further anticipation of the "Ode to the West Wind" (1819) and also of the idea developed in *The Sensitive Plant*.

Slaves to my holy and heroic verse,
Earth, sea and sky, the planets, life and fame
And fate, or whate'er else binds the world's wondrous frame.

But if Laon is intended as Lucifer, bearer of light, his rays are disappointingly feeble and fitful in connection with the events described in *The Revolt*. The will to self-sacrifice is stronger than the will to survive and triumph, or at any rate to continue to fight the good fight. He does not seem to have heard the old maxim that a living dog is better than a dead lion, or to have paid due heed to Godwin's view of martyrdom: "I had rather convince men by my arguments than seduce them by my example. . . . Nor is it improbable . . . that long and persevering services may be more advantageous than brilliant and transitory ones."[36]

Shelley's sincere desire to fashion Laon and Cythna as flesh-and-blood enabled him to resist to a limited degree the temptation to see them as personified abstractions. But he calls Cythna at one point "the prophetess of Love."[37] He also alludes with great frequency to such capitalized ideals as Truth, Liberty, Virtue, Hope, and Joy—by which he apparently means the several aspects of the spirit of good—while their antitheses, Falsehood, Oppression, Slavery, Fear, and Grief, would stand for the various facets of the spirit of evil. The symbolism attaching to Cythna's child, while difficult to follow, suggests even more strongly than the foregoing that when the poem was in the process of construction Shelley was thinking in allegorical terms. Cythna bears the child during her incarceration in the submarine dungeon, and it is stolen away from her by the diver who brought her there. Later the child is discovered to be serving as the scorned companion of the temporarily vanquished tyrant, Othman. Just as her parents are executed, the child dies of the plague. And in the final episode she reappears, "a winged shape," as pilot of the magic boat in which Laon and Cythna are carried to the Temple of the Spirit. A possible clue to the significance of the child may be found in Canto II, stanza xiii: "Justice and Truth their winged child have found." If a connection between this otherwise inexplicable line and the denouement may legitimately be made, one might guess that Cythna represents

---

[36] *Political Justice*, Bk. IV, Ch. I, "Of Resistance."
[37] *Revolt*, IX, XX. For some further discussion of Cythna, and her literary antetypes, see Appendix II.

Justice, Laon Truth, and their winged child Freedom, a notion that would be supported by the fact that Othman, who represents Tyranny or Political Oppression, treats the child with scorn despite her attempts to enter into some sort of companionable relationship with him. A very much disguised allegorical armature may therefore be discerned in the main story of the poem. But unless Shelley was deceiving his prospective publisher, he finally decided against allegory and in favor of a "mere human story." The result is that we have in the poem as it stands only the shreds and patches of what might have been a closely woven allegorical fabric. This is not to be especially regretted, but only pointed to as evidence of Shelley's rather pathetic attempt to appeal through his poem to the sympathies of a large audience.

· V ·

THE most conspicuous change in Shelley's thinking between 1812-1813 and 1817 is the new emphasis placed upon the human will as a directive force in human history. A consideration of his essays "On Life" and "On the Punishment of Death" indicates that his theory of knowledge is still Lockean. He has rejected strict materialism as essentially negativistic and nihilistic. Man, considered as a being of high aspiration whose spirit is at war with nothingness and dissolution, cannot be explained in purely materialistic terms.[38] He likewise rejects fatalism in favor of what he calls "philosophic Necessity," a position which evidently allows for the power of the human will as one "active source of future events."[39] He defines God in much the same terms as formerly: "The vast sum of action and of thought which disposes and animates the universe."[40] But he does not explicitly equate this Being with Necessity. He is much less certain than he formerly was that evil may be extirpated by reforming or abolishing outworn social institutions. He refers to "that intertexture of good and evil with which Nature seems to have clothed every form of individual existence," and he is aware of the deep complexities of human life—"the accidents of disease, and temperament, and organization, and circumstance, together with the multitude of independent agencies which

[38] "On Life," *Prose*, VI, 194.
[39] "On the Punishment of Death," *Prose*, VI, 189, note.   [40] *Ibid.*, 186.

affect the opinions, the conduct, and the happiness of individuals, and produce determinations of the will, and modify the judgment."[41]

The Revolt is of course not intended as a reasoned statement of Shelley's philosophical position as of 1817, but the general shape of his thinking at that period can be discerned in the speeches of Cythna. Insofar as Shelley followed Peacock's mythological scheme, he was *ipso facto* committed to a kind of fatalism. According to that scheme Necessity rules the world, the spirit of evil has been placed in temporary ascendancy, and ultimately the restoring spirit will usher in an earthly millennium. Necessity has established an incontrovertible cyclic plan, whose opponents have virtually no chance at all. Cythna lists Necessity among the "moving things that are," includes "worse Necessity of hate and ill" among the natural and social phenomena which trouble mankind, and asserts that both good and evil perpetuate themselves under the dominion of Necessity.[42] To this extent, at least, Shelley seems to be following, though not wholeheartedly, the scheme of Peacock.

But the whole tenor of Cythna's counsel to the mariners and to Laon is that moral quietism (unquestioning belief in the doctrine of Necessity) is undesirable. The mariners had better not waste time dreaming of a power which "builds for man in solitude." They have only to observe natural and social evils to see that destructive forces are everywhere at work. Men ought to look into their hearts, the real "book of fate," casting out hate and introducing love and joy, which can make "the foulest breast a paradise of flowers." In fact, Love, Justice, Truth, and Joy are the only powers which can guide man out of the present labyrinth of falsehood. Cythna disagrees with the teacher who asserted that men by nature are "weak and sinful, frail and blind," and that man need expect "nought on earth but toil and misery." Virtue and Hope and Love surround the world, and man must be their instrument.[43]

Thus the fundamental teaching of *The Revolt* is ethical. The furtherance of good cannot be entrusted to supernal powers, but is man's own task, and his first step must be self-reform. He must cast hate from his heart and admit love, for according to man's

[41] *Ibid.*, 186-187.   [42] *Revolt*, VII, xxxi; VIII, v; IX, xxv.
[43] *Revolt*, VIII, v; VIII, xx-xxii; VIII, xi; IX, xv; IX, xxiii.

decision, the mind can be a Hell or a Heaven. "Love," as Shelley says in his preface to the poem, "is celebrated everywhere as the sole law which should govern the moral world." Wherever Necessity is alluded to in *The Revolt*, it is evidently regarded as an amoral force; it cannot be trusted, as it was in *Queen Mab*, to produce the millennium. Shelley has not surrendered his hopes for the future. But centuries will pass before the goal is attained, and that attainment is possible only through the efforts of wise, virtuous, and heroic human beings. Though Laon and Cythna will not live to see the earthly paradise, they will join that company of immortals whom Cythna eloquently describes: the moral leaders or philosopher-kings of the past.

> The good and mighty of departed ages
> Are in their graves, the innocent and free,
> Heroes, and Poets, and prevailing Sages,
> Who leave the vesture of their majesty
> To adorn and clothe this naked world;—and we
> Are like to them—such perish, but they leave
> All hope, or love, or truth, or liberty,
> Whose forms their mighty spirits could conceive,
> To be a rule and law to ages that survive.[44]

Shelley's next major poem, the psychological verse-drama *Prometheus Unbound*, is far more successful than *The Revolt* as a consideration of the problem of evil. For Shelley's drama abandons the social-group symbols employed in *The Revolt* and enters directly into the psychological predicament of modern man by the use of symbols of states of mind. Except for the change in poetic strategy, however, *Prometheus Unbound* represents a logical development and re-application of the idea Shelley sets forth through Cythna's statements: that is, self-reform is the only trustworthy means of extirpating evil. Man ought, as *The Revolt* makes clear, to dethrone hate and enthrone love. If man were able to achieve this act of purgation within his own mind, his whole vision would be clarified, the great part of evil (though not all of it) would be eliminated, and except for chance, change, illness, and death, there would be no clogs upon the human spirit and virtually no

---

[44] This is the conviction which Shelley eloquently defends in *A Defence of Poetry* and *Adonais*, and (by implication) in *Epipsychidion* and *The Triumph of Life*.

limits to what the human mind could accomplish. Although Shelley entertained no deep-seated illusions that such an act of spiritual catharsis as he outlines in the *Prometheus* could actually occur on a universal scale, he conceived it to be his duty as poet to present this "idealism of moral excellence" for the edification of his readers.

PART TWO:

THE PROBLEM OF EVIL

4

THE HEART OF THE COSMOS:

PROMETHEUS UNBOUND

Man, one harmonious soul of many a soul,
Whose nature is its own divine control,
Where all things flow, as rivers to the sea.
—SHELLEY IN THE *Prometheus*

Let us believe in a kind of optimism in
which we are our own gods.
—SHELLEY TO MARIA GISBORNE

· I ·

BETWEEN the autumn of 1818 and the winter of 1819-1820, Shelley devoted infinite labors to the composition of the ethical and psychological drama which has ever since been regarded, except by a few unreconstructed dissenters, as his masterpiece. Shelley himself said that it was the best thing he ever wrote, and there is no reason to doubt the statement. He managed to combine in it, for the first though not for the last time, his two most persistent themes, the necessity of social reform and the necessity of societal love, in such a way that they supplement and complement one another. The vehicle for these themes is a poem of the greatest subtlety, ambitious in conception, simple in its larger outlines, imbued with moral grandeur, alive with splendid lyrics, and virtually unmarred by those weaknesses of conception or execution which so often weakened the fabric of his visions. The critical history of *Prometheus Unbound* is replete with minor squabbles as to whether or not it has a meaning and, if it has, what that meaning is. Yet the critical history shows, above all, that the poem partakes of the nature of mythology in being (the phrase is from I. A. Richards) relatively inexhaustible to meditation. Of no other poem by Shelley can this be so truly said; of few other poems by Shelley can it be said at all.

There was a time, in his vegetarian or salad days, when Shelley thought of Prometheus as a villain. The myth, as he assured readers of *Queen Mab*, was everywhere accepted as allegorical: Prometheus represents the human race. Having effected a tragic change in his natural habits, man used fire for culinary purposes, in order to forget, as he gorged on roasted flesh, the antecedent horrors of the slaughter-house. Henceforward "his vitals were devoured by the vulture of disease," and all vice arose. Jupiter and the rest of the gods, foreseeing the unhappy consequences of Prometheus' action, were "amused or irritated" by the Titan's shortsightedness, yet allowed him to continue his vicious practice though they presumably knew that it would act to the ultimate detriment of all men. This, at least, was the gospel according to John Frank Newton.

The passage of five years produced a complete reversal in Shelley's sympathies. When he wrote the preface for *Prometheus Unbound*, though he still attached a moral meaning to the myth, the protagonist had become a suffering and enduring hero and Jupiter a "perfidious adversary."[1] Shelley may, indeed, have begun to turn away from Newton's interpretation almost as soon as it was incorporated into the notes to *Queen Mab*. Some months before *Queen Mab* was ready for the printer, he ordered a copy of the plays of Aeschylus, with translation subjoined.[2] If he read *Prometheus Bound* at this time, however, it had no discernible effect, and though he soon began to show signs of knowing Aeschylus, it was not until roughly 1817 that the plays of the Greek tragedian began to be felt as a major stimulant to Shelley's literary imagination.[3] As at Chamounix in the summer of 1816 he had thought of Peacock's Ahrimanes, enthroned among perpetual snows and pre-

---

[1] *Prometheus Unbound*, preface, paragraph 2.   [2] *Letters*, IX, 36. Dec. 24, 1812.
[3] Shelley quoted *Prometheus Bound* with humorous intent in a letter to Mary, Oct. 25, 1814. *Letters*, IX, 100. Mary's list of his reading for 1816, in White, *Shelley*, II, 542, shows that he read the play in that year. An extensive reading of Aeschylus occurred in 1817. See Mary's journal and the 1817 reading-list in White, I, 524 and II, 544.

paring to loose avalanches with his right hand, so the ascent of Les Echelles in the early spring of 1818 reminded him of the Golgotha of the Aeschylean Prometheus: "vast rifts and caverns . . . wintry mountains . . . and walls of toppling rocks, only to be scaled as [Aeschylus] described, by the winged chariot of the ocean nymphs."[4] Six months later, after four or five weeks of intermittent labor, Shelley completed the crucial first act of his *Prometheus Unbound*. Far from being the carnivorous villain of Newton's argument, the reformed Prometheus at least remotely approached, in majesty and moral excellence, the stature of Jesus Christ, or so Shelley appears to have thought.

It is not difficult to account for Shelley's reversed interpretation of the character of Prometheus. Few students of Shelley's earlier poetry could fail to see that the Aeschylean Titan is a natural prototype for the Shelleyan hero, ready to be adopted whenever Shelley, in the fullness of his literary wisdom, can apprehend him.[5] Once so apprehended, he rapidly displaces Milton's Satan in the forefront of Shelley's affection. "In addition to courage, and majesty, and firm and patient opposition to omnipotent force," wrote Shelley, Prometheus is "exempt from the stains of ambition, envy, revenge, and a desire for personal aggrandizement, which, in the hero of *Paradise Lost*, interfere with the interest." Laon is more Promethean than Satanic, a lonely benefactor of mankind who has endured torture for what may be described as a social principle, and defied established power out of a hope (for Prometheus it is a conviction) that at some future date this power will be overthrown. At the same time, Shelley's Titan is an almost awesome improvement over Laon, being conceived in what Keats might have called "a more naked and Grecian manner," and possessed of a grandeur (partly the result of his Aeschylean heritage) to which the hero of *The Revolt*, sired by the Oriental heroes of Southey and Peacock, could hardly aspire. The measure of the advance may be suggested by saying that Laon is a Gothic man and Prometheus a Greek myth—or, better, that Laon suffers from Shelley's determination to make him a creature of flesh and blood, where Prome-

---

[4] *Letters*, IX, 186 and IX, 293.

[5] Shelley of course makes the Aeschylean Prometheus over in terms of the Shelleyan hero. For a careful contrasting of Aeschylus and Shelley, see O. W. Campbell, *Shelley and the Unromantics* (London, 1924), pp. 197-202.

theus is at all times a typical rather than a realistic figure, a pure mythological character uninhibited by history or by the need of being human. By Shelley's estimate, Prometheus is "the type of the highest perfection of moral and intellectual nature impelled by the purest and truest motives to the best and noblest ends."[6]

Shelley's mature dramatic and philosophical purpose is nowhere better shown than in his conception of Prometheus' character. As in Newton's version of the fable, Prometheus represents mankind, or more specifically, as we shall see, the mind of mankind. But instead of introducing fire, and hence cookery, and hence the reprehensible practice of meat-eating, and hence disease and corruption into the world, the Prometheus of 1818-1819 has at last succeeded in casting corruption forth. The process no longer has anything to do with what man puts, or does not put, into his stomach, but it has everything to do with what man allows, or does not allow, to exist in his mind. It has already been noticed that *The Revolt of Islam* enunciates a relatively simple moral and metaphysical conviction: the furtherance of good cannot be entrusted to superior powers, but is primarily the obligation of man, who can fulfill this obligation only by expunging hatred from his mental processes and admitting love or sympathy in its place. The same principle governs the decisions of the protagonist in the first act of *Prometheus Unbound*, upon which all subsequent developments depend. But instead of showing the world at an exemplary way-station in its slow progress towards perfection, as he had done in *The Revolt*, Shelley chose now to show man at a single symbolic hour—the hour of the world's redemption through man's act of self-reform.

The advance shown in the respective treatments of Laon and Prometheus is paralleled by the marked superiority of Asia over Cythna. Here, however, the advancement has less to do with Cythna's being a woman and Asia a goddess than with the fact that Asia is the realization of the conception towards which Shelley was still groping when he wrote *The Revolt of Islam*. In Chapter Two the development of the Shelleyan heroine was noticed. But it is a far cry from a figure like Mab, a Titania in two-penny muslin who talks like an eighteenth-century bluestocking, or even the vi-

[6] See the preface to *Prometheus Unbound*.

sionary maiden of *Alastor*, who springs full-armed from the pages
of Lady Morgan's latest sensational novel, to Asia, "shadow of
beauty unbeheld," who gathers to herself, with ease and grace, the
whole tradition of Venus Genetrix and Venus Urania. It should be
recalled, nevertheless, that the Asia-concept had been taking gradual shape in Shelley's mind at least from 1815 onwards. Towards
the end of *Alastor* the visionary maiden had been purged of those
fleshly attributes which Mrs. Campbell deplores as more nearly
relevant to "some scantily dressed beauty at a costume ball,"[7] and
had taken on a symbolic condition. In the following year, 1816,
Shelley had projected a completely depersonalized ideal of spiritual power in the *Hymn to Intellectual Beauty*. The dedicatory
poem to *The Revolt of Islam*, composed in the fall of 1817, contains Shelley's attempt to elevate Mary to the Asia-status. Her
presence is said to have fallen on Shelley's "wintry heart" like
"bright Spring upon some herbless plain," an image that is developed with great subtlety in *Prometheus Unbound*. But the attempted apotheosis of Mary, while no doubt sincere, is largely
abortive, and the full realization of the significance of the Asia-
symbol probably did not come until 1818, when, among other
tasks, Shelley prepared his translation of Plato's *Symposium*.

Somewhere between the completion of *The Revolt* in September, 1817, and his beginning the first act of *Prometheus Unbound*
in September, 1818, Shelley seems also to have passed the equa-
torial belt between the immature turbulence of a long poem in
the tradition of Southey's *Thalaba* and the comparatively simple classical lines of his Promethean story. *The Revolt* is cluttered,
while *Prometheus Unbound* displays a clean symmetry, as if in
abandoning forever the extended metrical narrative, Shelley had
discovered in the lyrical drama his true medium. An accession of
subtlety is likewise evident. The violent melodrama of *The Revolt*,
arising at least in part from Shelley's conviction that he must di-
versify his plot with "moving and romantic adventure," made way
for the drama of mind as one finds it in *Prometheus*, a drama deep
and intense, like the deliberate struggle of serpents at the bottom
of the sea, leaving hardly a ruffle of overt action upon the surface
of the play.

[7] O. W. Campbell, *Shelley and the Unromantics* (London, 1924), p. 190.

Shelley's powers of conception and expression were never at a higher point than they were in 1818-1819 while he was at work on what is certainly his greatest poem. Perhaps there is greater ease and fluency in such later works as *The Witch of Atlas*, but there is also a kind of autumnal languor. In *The Masque of Anarchy* and *Oedipus Tyrannus*, born of the weekly political press, he designedly did not attempt the high style or the cosmic conception. Finally, there are signs of mounting fatigue and either self-doubt or *ennui* in his failure to bring to completion such potentially magnificent poems as *Charles I* and *The Triumph of Life*, or to develop fully the fragmentary prologue to *Hellas*. But at this earlier date Shelley stood, fresh and active, in the dawn of his maturing powers.

· II ·

THE dramatic tensions of *Prometheus Unbound* originate in two related situations: the separation and reunion of Prometheus and Asia, and the ancient enmity between Prometheus and Jupiter. The first of these is a version of the Psyche-Epipsyche theme, developed for the first time on what may be called a cosmic scale. The second, though couched in terms of Greek rather than Zoroastrian mythology, is clearly another and greatly superior treatment of the good-evil antithesis as employed in the first and final cantos of *The Revolt of Islam*. The fourth of the major figures, Demogorgon, has occasioned much dispute, largely because, like such earlier characters as Queen Mab and Ahasuerus, he has a particularized name which calls up many associations besides the primary one intended by Shelley. Yet in view of what has been shown in the preceding chapter about the origin and development of the mythological pattern of *The Revolt*, it is evident that he represents Necessity—an enigmatic amoral law in terms of which the struggle between the powers of good and those of evil has been carried on since the beginning.

One way of expressing the fundamental aim of the drama is to say that it is directed towards a situation in which it will be ethically possible for the reunion of Prometheus and Asia to occur. But all spirits are secretly affected by "Demogorgon's mighty law,"[8]

[8] II, ii, 43.

and in Shelley's conception the fate of Jupiter is closely linked with that of Prometheus and Asia. That is to say, as soon as Prometheus and Asia are genuinely ready to be reunited, the reign of Jupiter must end. This consummation is the more fitting in that Asia's second-act exposition of the background of the present action strongly suggests that she was separated from Prometheus at, or soon after, the time of Jupiter's accession to the throne.

Three thousand years before the opening of the drama, Prometheus

> Gave wisdom, which is strength, to Jupiter,
> And with this law alone, "Let man be free,"
> Clothed him with the dominion of wide heaven.[9]

But Jupiter kept "faithless faith."[10] In putting on omnipotence, as is usual with the Shelleyan tyrant, he abandoned love and law.[11] Under his sovereignty, famine, toil, disease, and strife appeared upon the earth. Although Prometheus granted man hope and love, and equipped him with knowledge of the sciences and the arts in order partially to alleviate his multiple woes, Jupiter's reign continued and was destined to continue so long as man's will gave sanction to it by continuing in hatred.[12] Prometheus, the altruistic though as yet imperfect champion of man, was chained in a ravine of icy rocks among the mountains of the Indian Caucasus, while Asia, until then his inseparable companion, went into exile in a far-distant Indian vale, a place as "desolate and frozen" as the scene of her erstwhile consort's agony.[13] The torture and the exile, the immortal hatred of Prometheus for Jupiter, and the mournful longing of Asia for reunion with Prometheus have endured, as the action opens, for thirty centuries.

In *The Revolt* Shelley anticipated more closely than in any preceding poem the careful allegorical scheme which he worked out in *Prometheus Unbound*. Close companions in childhood and lovers in their youth, Laon and Cythna are separated through the machinations of Othman—a kind of parallel to the Prometheus-Asia-Jupiter situation,[14] though the former is much more crude.

[9] II, iv, 44-46. [10] III, iii, 130. [11] II, iv, 47-48.
[12] II, iv, 50-100. [13] I, 826-828.
[14] On the former closeness of Prometheus and Asia, see Prometheus' statement (I, 122-123):
> I wandered once
> With Asia, drinking life from her loved eyes.

Later on Shelley grants Laon and Cythna a brief night of reunion, replete with passionate embraces which have, however, no place in *Prometheus Unbound*; and, following their death at the stake, he gives them an eternity of shared joy in the Temple of the Spirit, along with their "winged child"—again a pattern which is carried out, even to the inclusion of the child, in *Prometheus Unbound*. But in 1817 Shelley was so involved with his intention to write a "mere human story" that he fought as shy as possible of allegory. Therefore the separation and reunion of Laon and Cythna, having little determinable significance in a symbolic sense, seems in the main to be adventitious, the result of chance and accident, of forces applied from without instead of deriving from the mental attributes of the hero, upon whose growth and eventual ripeness the denouement of *Prometheus Unbound* depends.

The relatively compact structure of *Prometheus Unbound* may be ascribed in part to the fact that the whole of the poem is the biography of an Hour (the "all-nameless hour," as has been pointed out, of man's redemption through Prometheus' act of self-reform) together with the events immediately preceding it, and those which directly ensue upon its arrival. At the proper time, emphasis is placed upon the Hour itself; yet the primary stress, because this is a drama of mind rather than of outward action, is on the preparatory circumstances. Everything is made to hinge upon the readiness of Prometheus. The Hour is even said to be "of many, one"—which suggests that it is not a particular predestined time, but any hour at which Prometheus reaches the point of growth which he has now reached.

Shelley's main task in Act I was to make Prometheus' ripeness dramatically convincing, somewhat as Shakespeare had first to render almost, if not quite, palpable the deep electric unrest which is present under the quiet demeanor of Denmark in order to raise the responses of Hamlet to the point at which he is ready for action. In *Hamlet*, the ghost is of course the immediate agent of shock; in *Prometheus Unbound* it is something even less tangible than a ghost: the consciousness that the Hour is imminent, that things are about to happen.

It is perfectly plain that the protagonist has not always been what Shelley calls him in the preface, "the type of the highest perfection of moral and intellectual nature." He has always, of course, had saving graces. Unlike Milton's Satan, with whom Shelley contrasts him, he has been free of envy, malice, and self-aggrandizing ambition. Yet he has shared at least two traits of mind with that otherwise inferior fellow-rebel: an immortal hatred of Omnipotence which has given him the necessary courage never to submit or yield; and a kind of unregenerate pride[15] which can make him exultantly say, even after three thousand years of torture, that when the great Hour arrives, it will drag Jupiter from his throne, "as some dark Priest hales the reluctant victim," to kiss the blood

> From these pale feet, which then might trample thee
> If they disdained not such a prostrate slave.[16]

It is true that Prometheus immediately denies that he has spoken in exultation or in proud disdain:

> Disdain! Ah, no! I pity thee. What ruin
> Will hunt thee undefended through the wide Heaven!
> How will thy soul, cloven to its depth with terror,
> Gape like a hell within! I speak in grief,
> Not exultation, for I hate no more,
> As then ere misery made me wise. The curse
> Once breathed on thee I would recall.[17]

Yet the very suddenness of this recantation, as if he had momentarily forgotten himself into the past and given way once more to a pride intellectually but not emotionally abjured, serves to emphasize the comparative recency of his conversion.

When Prometheus fulfills his promise to recall his curse upon Jupiter, Shelley is able to use the occasion even more effectively than in the opening apostrophe to emphasize the hero's conversion from pride to pity. Summoned from the vale of shadows beneath the grave, the Phantasm of Jupiter is made to repeat the curse; torn by some inner compulsion which it is unable to resist, and even imitating Prometheus' original gestures, the ghost echoes the dire and ancient words:

---

[15] Panthea later remarks (I, 336) that "The Titan looks as ever, firm, not proud." Yet the Phantasm of Jupiter has not long since addressed Prometheus as "proud sufferer." (I, 245.) Cf. also Mercury's reference to Prometheus' "haughty heart." (I, 378.) In the unreformed Prometheus, there is a clear indication of the sin of pride.

[16] I, 51-52.   [17] I, 53-59.

Heap on thy soul, by virtue of this Curse,
Ill deeds; then be thou damned, beholding good;
Both infinite as is the universe,
And thou, and thy self-torturing solitude.
An awful image of calm power
Though now thou sittest, let the hour
Come, when thou must appear to be
That which thou art internally;
And after many a false and fruitless crime,
Scorn track thy lagging fall through boundless space
                    and time![18]

"Were these my words?" says Prometheus to the Earth-mother,
and her affirmative response leads directly to the second recantation:

It doth repent me; words are quick and vain;
Grief for awhile is blind, and so was mine.
I wish no living thing to suffer pain.[19]

The moral reformation of Prometheus is now complete, and the
way for his reunion with Asia has been prepared, so that he is able
to endure with equanimity almost all the remaining tortures, the
most cruel and subtle excoriations of mind, which Jupiter, out of a
vengeful determination to requite him for having had the curse
repeated, now heaps upon him. Even if Shelley had not contrasted
Prometheus and Satan in his prefatory remarks, readers could
hardly miss the ironic suggestion of *Paradise Lost* in the words of
Prometheus' original curse. Like Milton's Satan, Jupiter will heap
ill deeds upon his own soul; like him also he will be damned in the
most excruciating fashion—"beholding good," knowing the bliss of
heaven but being unable to share in it; like Satan, too, though
majestic in his power, he will be shown to be outwardly what he is
internally, an image of all evil; and like Satan, he will fall through
boundless space and time down to "the wide waves of ruin . . .
into a shoreless sea."[20]

Somewhat more obvious, because it is instrumental in the temptation scene which immediately follows the second recantation, is
Shelley's attempt to develop the resemblance between Jesus Christ

[18] I, 292-301.   [19] I, 304-306.   [20] III, i, 71-74.

and Prometheus in both being impervious to temptation, and serene in self-mastery. When Mercury appears as an emissary from Jupiter, with the legioned furies snarling at his heels, he comes ostensibly from Heaven rather than from Hell. But he shortly asserts that whenever in the past he has left the side of Prometheus and returned to Jupiter's domain, Heaven, by comparison, "seems Hell."[21] Even now, he says, the Torturer Jove (Shelley uses the names interchangeably) is arming the "subtle, foul, or savage fiends," who people the abyss, with more slow agonies for Prometheus.[22] Unlike Satan on the Mount of Temptation, Mercury pities his prospective victim; yet, being under the compulsion of a higher power, he executes Jupiter's commands, offering "benefits" if Prometheus will submit, and even suggesting the possibility that instead of enduring the tortures now in prospect, Prometheus might

> dwell among the Gods the while,
> Lapped in voluptuous joy.[23]

Like Jesus Christ, however, Prometheus refuses to quit his Golgotha in the bleak ravine, and the agonies which yet must come, because he knows that the reign of evil will end, after the agony.

With the messenger's departure, the unleashed furies are enabled to begin their subtle tortures, all of them designed to scarify the mind of Prometheus rather than his body. It is noteworthy that he succeeds in withstanding them through serene self-dominance.[24] And it is especially remarkable, in view of Shelley's youthful recriminations against Jesus and in view of the parallelism between the Christ and Prometheus which he has been developing, that the really climactic and almost unendurable torture is a vision of Jesus Christ's agony upon the Cross. When all the other furies have done their worst and returned to the depths, one remains to display this most heart-rending of all emblems. The worst of it is that the faith Jesus kindled has been abused, and his words have acted like "swift poison, withering up truth, peace, and pity," so that crimes have been ever afterwards perpetrated under the protection of his name.[25] When Prometheus' eyes have been directed to the emblem of the crucifixion, which the Fury

[21] I, 358. [22] I, 367-370. [23] I, 424-426.
[24] I, 430, 492. [25] I, 549.

evidently displays like a tableau, the Fury explains its significance in words whose bearing cannot be lost upon the Titan:

> Those who do endure
> Deep wrongs for man, and scorn, and chains, but heap
> Thousand-fold torment on themselves and him.[26]

Quite as bad as this fact, says the Fury, is the deep ignorance of human society:

> [Men] dare not devise good for man's estate,
> And yet they know not that they do not dare.
> The good want power, but to weep barren tears.
> The powerful goodness want; worse need for them.
> The wise want love; and those who love want wisdom;
> And all best things are thus confused to ill.[27]

The Fury ceases with an ironic echo of the words of Jesus: "They know not what they do." But, as the Saviour's words were spoken out of an infinite pity, so Prometheus reacts with pity for man's ignorance. "Thou pitiest them?" says the last of the Furies. "I speak no more!"—and he disappears.[28]

The first act of *Prometheus Unbound* ought thus to be seen as preparatory in purpose, designed to show that the Titan, having cast out pride and hatred while remaining firm and calm in his opposition to the evil principle, is now ready for the arrival of the great hour of man's redemption. A commentator bent on showing the classical symmetry of the act might point out that Shelley has balanced the visitation of the Furies, at the close of this section, with a chorus of fair spirits, who prophesy that love and unselfishness will in the end prevail. It may be assumed that this prophecy provides a salve for the still aching mental wounds of Prometheus.

---

[26] I, 594-596.   [27] I, 623-628.

[28] An observation which one is glad to see has gained no acceptors is that of C. E. Jones, "Christ a Fury?" *MLN* 50 (January, 1935), 41. The notion is that the last remaining Fury is Christ, but it should be plain from the discussion above that the Fury only displays the Crucifix as a device to deepen the suffering of Prometheus. "Behold an emblem," says the Fury. (I, 594.) Prometheus then addresses the vision. He is not, as Mr. Jones alleges, speaking to the Fury, but rather to the silent figure which the Fury is exhibiting. If Shelley thought of *Prometheus Unbound* as in any sense a stage play, he would no doubt have wished to have the emblem placed in a curtained recess, backstage center, where the Fury could have pulled the curtain aside, and revealed, within, the Christian image.

The act closes with a speech of Panthea's which, as it refers to the place of Asia's exile, may be regarded as transitional, since Act ii is to deal with Asia's visit to Demogorgon. But these are formal matters. The most striking aspect of the first act is that Shelley, like the author of the *Beowulf* and many another envisioner of gods and heroes in the great tradition of English literature since the Middle Ages, has suffused a myth of pagan origin with deeply felt Christian symbolism. He has begun with Aeschylus and ended by the representation of an ethic which is close to that of the New Testament.

· III ·

When Peacock made the second prose outline for his *Ahrimanes*, he supposed that the universe was governed by Necessity. Under its rule two antagonistic spirits, Oromaze and Ahrimanes, did unending battle. Shelley, as we know, adopted this mythological pattern for his *Revolt of Islam*. As in Peacock's poem, Necessity dwells apart, taking no discernible hand in the action, yet ready, if the world were ready, to usher in a new order. In Shelley's *Revolt* as in Peacock's poem the world is still dominated by the evil spirit, yet not utterly so, since it is possible for Laon and Cythna to produce a revolution which proves, albeit temporarily, what the world might be like under the rule of the good spirit. Further, as both Peacock and Shelley no doubt told each other in their conversations on mythology, the laws of Necessity required that the spirit of evil would one day be cast down, and that a new age would come, in which the spirit of good would endure through a historical cycle. Laon and Cythna, in their immortal transfigurations, awaited the advent of the new age, the roll of the cycle, in their south polar retreat.

With certain differences, partly the result of his merger of the Greek and the Zoroastrian schemes, Shelley follows a similar plan in *Prometheus Unbound*. In *Ahrimanes* and *The Revolt* the spirits of good and evil join battle under the eye of Necessity. But where the earlier poems of Peacock and Shelley showed a world not yet ready for the return of the Good, the world in *Prometheus Unbound* has at last reached that status, and Prometheus' unbinding can occur. Where the revolution failed in Islam, having been superinduced by outward action, that in *Prometheus Unbound*, having involved and taken place in man's whole mental constitution, must succeed.

Prometheus' opening apostrophe to Jupiter proves that Shelley had something like the foregoing mythological pattern in mind. Jupiter is

> Monarch of Gods and Daemons, and all Spirits
> But One, who throng those bright and rolling worlds.

The "One" is probably Prometheus, who has placed Jupiter in the seat of power.[29] Prometheus' controlling secret is that Necessity must eventually institute what are in effect proceedings of impeachment against Jupiter, for this monarch has been guilty of high crimes, misdemeanors, and malfeasance in office from the moment he assumed the throne. Precisely when this impeachment will occur, Prometheus does not appear to know, but he does know that "it must come." As we have seen, the determining factor is Prometheus' capacity for self-reform, a capacity potentially present, but not successfully invoked, among the human beings who participated in *The Revolt of Islam*.

The second and third acts of *Prometheus Unbound* are the inevitable consequence of the first. As the preparatory act closes, Panthea has alluded to Asia, waiting in "that far Indian vale/ The scene of her sad exile"—a place once cold and desolate but now, because of Prometheus' accession of pity, "invested with fair flowers and herbs/ And haunted by sweet airs and sounds," for the winter of Prometheus' suffering has ended, and Asia's transforming powers are accordingly released.

During the first act, which opens in the dark night of Prometheus' soul, morning has broken. Now dawn and the spring have come to Asia's vale, and as she awaits the arrival of her sister-nymph, Panthea, she knows that the long-looked-for Hour is at hand.

> This is the season, this the day, the hour;
> At sunrise thou shouldst come, sweet sister mine,
> Too long desired, too long delaying, come![30]

---

[29] According to Grabo, the One is "The hypostasis which is truth, beauty, perfection" (*Prometheus Unbound: An Interpretation*, Chapel Hill, 1935, p. 13).
[30] II, i, 13-15.

The significance of Asia's "sisters," Ione and Panthea, like the meaning of Demogorgon, has been variously debated, but it seems plain that Shelley intended them to represent, in mounting order, degrees of love and perceptiveness within the human mind.[31] The lesser of the two is clearly Ione, who is subconsciously aware of the approaching change in the heart of the cosmos without being able to define what it is that vaguely disturbs her usual calm.[32] The unfocused awareness which wakes and inwardly stirs Ione is both focused and much more fully developed in Panthea, to whom, in the course of a dream, comes a clear vision of Prometheus, transfigured with the love he has learned through long suffering.[33] Panthea's perceptions are thus far clearer than those of her sister and it is this quality which enables her to act as the intermediary between Prometheus (representing the mind of man) and Asia (representing the idea of divine love). Panthea is "more fair" than any other except Asia, being the lesser "shadow" or imperfect representation of the ineffable radiance of her elder sister.[34]

[31] Grabo, *op. cit.*, p. 52, calls the sisters "aspects of love," defining Asia as "passionate creative love," Panthea as "sympathetic love," and Ione as "the spirit of Love in Beauty." Douglas Bush, *Mythology and the Romantic Tradition in English Poetry* (Cambridge, Mass., 1937) echoes Grabo in saying that "in some vague way" the sisters represent "aspects of love," while observing that the family in the play—a man, his wife and two sisters-in-law—is a "typical Shelleyan household." Vida Scudder implies that the three sisters may be Faith (Panthea), Hope (Ione), and Charity (Asia), of whom the greatest, as in Paul, would be the last. Kenneth N. Cameron, "The Political Symbolism of *Prometheus Unbound*," *PMLA* 58 (1943), 740, believes that Ione is Memory, Panthea Hope, and Asia, of course, Love.

[32] See Panthea's account II, i, 56-106, but esp. lines 93-99:

> Ione wakened then, and said to me:
> "Canst thou divine what troubles me tonight?
> I always knew what I desired before,
> Nor ever found delight to wish in vain.
> But now I cannot tell thee what I seek;
> I know not; something sweet, since it is sweet
> Even to desire . . ."

[33] Shelley's description of Correggio's "Christ Beatified," which he saw in a gallery in the fall of 1818 while he was at work on Act I, has a number of points in common with this vision of Prometheus transfigured. See *Letters*, IX, 342. Nov. 9, 1818.

[34] Whether or not he owed the conception to Plato, Shelley habitually thought of Divine Love (or as he called it in 1816, Intellectual Beauty) as too bright for the human eye to bear. Only the "shadow" of Intellectual Beauty fell upon him on that memorable occasion in his youth, yet the shadow was enough to produce his ecstatic reaction. In view of the sun and moon imagery used in *Epipsychidion*, one might suggest that Panthea is a kind of moon to Asia's sun, borrowing reflected light. The conception of Asia as sunlike is clearly in Shelley's mind: the vernal

As he develops the dream-sequence which fills the first scene of Act II, Shelley again emphasizes the gradations of the sisters. Panthea's excuse for her tardy arrival in Asia's valley is that her wings were faint with the delight of her "remembered dream," the first of the two which came to her as she and Ione slept at the feet of Prometheus. Her words are inadequate, but by gazing into her eyes Asia herself sees the vision of Prometheus joyously transfigured. It should be noticed that Panthea merely saw and remembered the vision; only Asia can interpret its meaning, and this she immediately does:

> Say not those smiles that we shall meet again
> Within that bright pavilion which their beams
> Shall build on the waste world? The dream is told.[35]

Two other dreams, precisely alike in their significance, have come to Panthea and Asia respectively, and Shelley uses them to start Asia's pilgrimage from her place of exile. In her second dream, Panthea has read the words, "Follow, follow," upon the fallen leaves of an almond tree; in Asia's dream the same enigmatic message seemed to be stamped on every herb and written in shadows on the morning clouds. When Asia repeats the message, echoes take it up, and give the sisters a clue to their destination:

> In the world unknown
> Sleeps a voice unspoken;
> By thy step alone
> Can its rest be broken;
> Child of Ocean![36]

The slumbrous spirit in the world unknown is of course Demogorgon or Necessity. Prometheus' recantation has made it possible for Asia and Panthea to begin their descent to the unknown world of Demogorgon.

Since Asia's interview with Demogorgon in scene iv is the major objective of Act II, the short intervening descriptive and lyrical scenes may be quickly passed over. Scene ii is chiefly memorable

---

phenomena at the beginning of Act II occur when Asia's power is released, and at the end of this act, Asia is compared to the "sun's fire filling the living world." (II, v, 27-30.) In one of the Homeric Hymns, which Shelley translated in 1818, there occurs the name Pandeia, "a bright maid of beauty rare," whose mother is the moon.

[35] II, i, 124-126. [36] II, i, 190-194.

for the colloquy of fauns, who speak somewhat after the manner of Caliban at those times when Shakespeare allows him to describe the enchanted island, and whose dramatic function is to predict. One of them mentions his delight in

> Those wise and lovely songs
> Of Fate, and Chance, and God, and Chaos old,
> And Love, and the chained Titan's woful doom,
> And how he shall be loosed, and make the earth
> One brotherhood.[37]

In scene iii, Asia and Panthea reach a pinnacle of rock above the realm of Demogorgon, and in one of Shelley's most majestic lyrics are beckoned by a song of spirits

> To the deep, to the deep,
>> Down, down!
> Through the shade of sleep,
> Through the cloudy strife
> Of Death and of Life;
> Through the veil and bar
> Of things which seem and are,
> Even to the steps of the remotest throne,
>> Down, down![38]

On the steps of that remote throne, Asia's questioning of Demogorgon elicits answers which are oracular, yet penetrable enough to anyone sufficiently familiar with the combination of Hellenic and Zoroastrian mythology which Shelley uses throughout his poem. Asia begins with a kind of catechism. Who made the living world? Who made all that it contains? Who made the powers of the human mind: thought, passion, reason, will, imagination? Who made that sense of ecstasy so strong that it fills the eyes with tears and leaves the earth a solitude when it departs?[39] Demogorgon's answer is always the same: God. If the sudden interjection of God the Creator into a hierarchy of gods already accepted is at first somewhat puzzling, the puzzle is easily solved when it is re-

[37] II, ii, 91-95. These words anticipate Asia's questions to Demogorgon.
[38] II, iii, 54-62.
[39] Shelley evidently has in mind here some such experience as that described in the *Hymn to Intellectual Beauty*, when, in rapt ecstasy, his eyes streamed with tears. See esp. stanzas V-VI of that poem.

called that in the early version of Peacock's *Ahrimanes* Necessity began by delegating power to El Oran the Creator. But in Peacock, as now in Shelley, God the Creator has done His work long ago and takes no part in the current action.[40]

Asia next inquires into the origin of mental evils, the sundry ways in which the powers of the human mind are perverted and abused. Who made terror, madness, crime, remorse, despair, hatred, self-contempt, pain, and the fear of Hell—in short, all horrors which unsettle the human mind? Once more Demogorgon's answer is always the same: He reigns. Since Jupiter reigns, and since the first act has already shown him to be a past master in the art of mental torture, there can be no doubt of Demogorgon's meaning.

The reader now learns, through Asia, of the events preceding Jupiter's reign and the manacling of Prometheus. Heaven, Earth, Light, and Love were all that existed in the epoch before the birth of time. This age was succeeded by a primitivistic period, under Saturn, in which earth's "primal spirits" merely vegetated, having neither knowledge, power, thought, self-governance, nor love.[41] The Age of Saturn ended when Prometheus taught man science and art, medicine, astronomy, and navigation, but at the same time gave wisdom and power to Jupiter, with what disastrous results we already know.

As she concludes her mythological account, Asia importunately returns to the problem of the origin of evil, urging Demogorgon to name the real culprit. Who rains down evil, "the immedicable plague," which drives man until his will is wrecked, and he becomes a lonely outcast, the scorn of earth? Could it be that Jupiter who trembled like a slave at Prometheus' original curse? Who is Jupiter's master? Is Jupiter also a slave? "All spirits are enslaved,"

[40] This agrees with Grabo, *op. cit.*, p. 74. "It is evident that God the Creator does not reign in man's universe."

[41] Shelley employs a somewhat similar pseudo-historical strategy in his *Ode to Liberty*, published in the volume with *Prometheus Unbound* in 1820. Before the coming of the spirit of Liberty

> This divinest universe
> Was yet a chaos and a curse.

War and despair raged among men and beasts "without truce or terms." Man had not learned the fine arts or even the simpler arts of cultivation, and tyranny hung like a fierce cloud over a waste of waves. This state of things continued until Athens arose.

says Demogorgon, "which serve things evil." If Jupiter does so, then he is a slave. But Asia still seeks the culprit's name. "Whom called'st thou God?" she asks, as if she half-suspected that God the Creator and Jupiter had some alliance.[42] "I spoke but as ye speak," says Demogorgon, "for Jove is the supreme of living things"—a remark which might well imply that God the Creator has had nothing to do with the origin of evil, which arose with the reign of Jupiter, long after the Creator's work was done. Who, then, *is* the master of Jove, if God is not? Demogorgon begs this question: "The deep truth is imageless."[43] But he does assert that all things are subject to Fate, Time, Occasion, Chance, and Change, except eternal Love. The presumption is therefore that Jupiter is somehow subject to Fate (or Necessity), and that the occasion has now arrived when through the happy chance of Prometheus' self-mastery the great change can take place, and eternal Love can be reunited with mankind.

This occasion is now at hand, for to Asia's final question—"When shall the destined hour arrive?"—Demogorgon responds by pointing to a throng of charioteers. These are the immortal Hours, one of whom awaits Asia. Actually there are two especially nominated charioteers, one dark and of a dreadful aspect, the other bright and with dove-like eyes which may predict the coming peace. The dark hour represents, of course, the fall of Jupiter, and the bright hour the simultaneous "rise" of Asia and Prometheus, for what to the protagonists is an hour of joy is to their antagonist one of gloom. The first, who describes himself as "the Shadow of a destiny" even more dreadful than his own aspect, has come to bear Demogorgon to Olympus. The task of the second is to carry Asia to Prometheus. The two charioteers will arrive at their respective destinations at the same time, or, to put it another way, the reunion of the mind of man and eternal Love will coincide with the casting-down of Jupiter, the originator of all those evils of the mind which Demogorgon has earlier enumerated.

The second act closes with a scene descriptive of Asia's transfig-

[42] Asia means, in effect, "Who was it that you called God some moments ago?" The rather awkward preterit, "called'st" is required here, since if the form were "call'st," Asia would be asking, "Who is your God?" This last question is neither asked nor answered in the play.

[43] Shelley could easily have caused Demogorgon to answer this question forthrightly. The master of Jupiter is the reformed Prometheus.

uration. The sisters are *en voyage* in the chariot of the Hour. Although the sun has not yet risen, being estopped with the wonder of the approaching miracle, Panthea observes in the clouds around them an awesome spread of light.[44] It emanates from Asia at this hour of her second birth, as aeons ago, among the Aegean islands, when she first uprose, like sea-born Aphrodite, standing within a veinèd shell,

> love, like the atmosphere
> Of the sun's fire filling the living world

burst from her, and permeated all living things. Now the period of her eclipse is over, and the air is filled with the voices of all articulate beings seeking Asia's sympathy. In one of the two final lyrics of the second act, a corporate voice chants a hymn to Asia, addressing her as "Life of Life," "Child of Light," and "Lamp of Earth"; in the second, Asia herself takes up the strain, comparing her soul to an enchanted boat, upborne upon the sound waves of the hymn, and wafted back to the paradise of a diviner day.[45]

Act III begins on the crest of Olympus, in the midst of the *hybris* of Jupiter, who is rejoicing at the approaching hour of his omnipotence. He imagines, having wrongly interpreted Prometheus' secret, that Demogorgon's arrival will be immediately followed by the extinction of man's defiance, which for centuries has threat-

[44] The great hour, according to the time-scheme of the drama, is high noon. "We shall rest from long labors at noon," says the charioteer. (II, iv, 173.) Shelley evidently intends that Acts I and II fill the time from night to noon. The stage directions for the first act state that while the act is in progress "morning slowly breaks," but do not mention sunrise. The time of Act II, scene i, is given as "morning," but the sun is still below the horizon, and it is only "crimson dawn." In II, v, Panthea remarks that the sun "is yet unrisen." Since, however, the noon hour is so close at hand that Asia's transfiguration has already come, it would appear to be Shelley's intention that on this day of days the sun is to be stationary at the dawn position until the great noon hour arrives. In reply to Panthea's remark, the Spirit of the Hour says that "the sun will not rise until noon," for Apollo is "held in heaven by wonder." It would seem, therefore, that Shelley has been consistent in the application of his idea, though perhaps unintentionally deceptive at one or two points. Thus Asia (II, i, 14) says that Panthea is to arrive "at sunrise." When Panthea arrives, Asia gently upbraids her for being late, which would suggest that she has arrived after sunrise. Despite such slips, however, it is impossible to agree with Woodberry (Cambridge edition, p. 623) that the remark of the Spirit of the Hour is "not to be taken literally."

[45] On the probable derivation of the final stanza of Asia's song from the myth in Plato's *Statesman*, see the letter by E. M. W. Tillyard in *TLS* (Sept. 29, 1932), p. 691.

ened the foundations of his fear-buttressed empire.[46] But when Demogorgon alights from the chariot of Jupiter's dark hour, the casting-down of the Torturer is swift and sure. This event, which in dramatic terms ought to be climactic, does not seem to have been so conceived by Shelley. The mental reform achieved when Prometheus casts hate from his heart in Act i is not only a symbolic anticipation of the cosmic reform achieved by Demogorgon in dethroning Jupiter, but also a direct cause of it. To all intents and purposes the expulsion of Jupiter really took place during Prometheus' first-act recantation. For this play, despite its mythological fabric, is a drama of the inner mind, and evil is represented as a deformity of the mind. What is extirpated there can survive nowhere else in the universe. Or, as Demogorgon puts it in his final words to Jupiter:

> The tyranny of heaven none may retain,
> Or reassume, or hold, succeeding thee.[47]

From this point on it remained to Shelley to explore the consequences of Jupiter's fall from dominance.[48] In scene iii Hercules unbinds Prometheus. Thus, says he, does strength minister to "wisdom, courage, and long-suffering love." Now the Titanic psyche is reunited to his epipsyche, and Prometheus assures Asia that from this time forth they will never be separated. Now the Spirit of the Hour, an Ariel with one more task to do before his freedom is earned, is told to circumnavigate the great globe itself, proclaiming everywhere, through the music of a great conch-shell, the glad news of man's redemption. Now Mother Earth, as the warmth circles down through her marble veins, details a spirit in the like-

[46] Shelley has very considerably altered the original myth at this point in order to bring Demogorgon into his theogony. On the extent of these alterations and their bearing on Shelley's meaning, see Appendix III, "The Father-Son Succession in Aeschylus' *Prometheia* and Shelley's *Prometheus Unbound*." One of the frequent passages of sexual imagery in Shelley is that in which Jupiter boastfully recalls Thetis' passionate words at the moment of their union (iii, i, 37-42). Shelley perhaps has in mind some sort of balance between the Prometheus-Asia relationship and that of Jupiter and Thetis, but he does not develop it. It is in any case an element of Jupiter's *hybris* that he imagines that he has begotten Demogorgon upon Thetis. Actually, of course, Jupiter's whole character is destructive rather than creative, so that the child he thinks he has begotten has no existence except in his prideful imagination.

[47] iii, i, 57-58.

[48] I pass over the pleasant idyl of scene ii in which the sun-god describes Jupiter's fall to the god of the ocean, and both rejoice in the event.

ness of a winged child to conduct Asia and Prometheus, as Laon
and Cythna were in the end conducted, to a far-off temple beside
a windless pool, past Nysa, birthplace of Bacchus, and beyond
Indus. There the Spirit of the Earth tells the assembled company
of the miraculous effects of the sky-borne shell-music, and how
"with little change of shape or hue" all things had put their evil
natures off. Now the Spirit of the Hour appears to report the success of his last journey, and to describe finally the state of man
under the new dispensation:

> The painted veil, by those who were, called life,
> Which mimicked, as with colors idly spread,
> All men believed and hoped, is torn aside;
> The loathsome mask has fallen, the man remains
> Sceptreless, free, uncircumscribed, but man
> Equal, unclassed, tribeless, and nationless,
> Exempt from awe, worship, degree, the king
> Over himself; just, gentle, wise; but man
> Passionless—no, yet free from guilt or pain,
> Which were, for his will made or suffered them;
> Nor yet exempt, though ruling them like slaves,
> From chance, and death, and mutability,
> The clogs of that which else might oversoar
> The loftiest star of unascended heaven.[49]

For many readers the foregoing summarization is the real *ave
atque vale* of the drama, and there has accordingly been some
division of opinion as to whether the concluding act, long known
as Shelley's "afterthought," has any legitimate excuse for being.
Grabo quite properly describes Act IV as a "philosophical epilogue," and one is inclined to regard it, like many epilogues, as a
kind of addendum rather than as an integral part of the drama.[50]
But those who are less interested in the play as a play than as a
vehicle for Shelley's philosophical ideas would be loath to part
with the fourth act: it presents several ideas not hitherto made

---

[49] III, iv, 190-203.

[50] In one particular, and probably in one only, the writing of the fourth act was
dramatically obligatory, for it satisfies the reader's natural curiosity as to whether
Jupiter's threat to drag Demogorgon down with him to the pit was ever carried out.
That the threat was empty is indicated by Demogorgon's reappearance at the close
of Act IV.

explicit, and it develops and re-emphasizes ideas which receive less extended treatment elsewhere in the drama.

Act IV consists of three successive choric movements, each introduced and interpreted by Panthea and Ione. The first movement represents the confused departure, heard from afar off, of the outworn pre-reformational hours "to the dark, to the past, to the dead," and the arrival of the bright nascent hours of the new order. These last are fittingly accompanied by the powers of might and pleasure "from the mind of humankind." Until Prometheus' reformation, they lay trammeled in the dark, but they are now celebrating a new freedom, which they owe to the rebirth of love and light in the human mind.

The second movement in the act is a fanciful love-dialogue between the feminine Moon and the masculine Earth. The conceit, which Shelley carefully develops in sexual imagery, is that the rebirth of love in the Earth has kindled a response in the cold bosom of the Moon, his "crystal paramour," the effect of which is that she is warmed and rendered fruitful. The development of the conceit is the more remarkable in that Shelley equates gravitational attraction with the sympathetic powers of love, and compares the moon's movement around the earth to that of an aroused and "insatiate bride," half-dementedly circling her lover in order to gaze on his form from every side. Since the praise of love is intended here, the equation may be symbolically justified, although the idea that the moon is warmed and fertilized by the proximity of the earth would scarcely gain the assent of astronomers.

In the third movement, which is first antiphonal then hortatory in character, Demogorgon invokes the spirits of men both living and dead, of the earth, moon, and stars, of all fauna and flora, and of all the elements, to hear a final proclamation upon the significance of this great day in the evolution of the universe.

· V ·

THE difficulty in the interpretation of *Prometheus Unbound* arises chiefly from the fact that the leading characters are both characters in a drama and symbolic universals. In reading or describing the play, as in earlier sections of this chapter, one must adopt Shelley's dramatic terminology and follow his conduct of the action as if these personified universals were living people. Yet if one thinks in terms of the philosophical meaning of the play rather than in terms of objective, dramatic representation (Shelley's phrase would be the "impersonation" of "visions"), Prometheus is not a "character" at all but rather an image of the mind of man.[51] By the same token, Jupiter and Asia are ideas in the mind of Prometheus, although one should not speak of the "mind of Prometheus" without remembering that in philosophical terms the designation is inexact, since Prometheus himself is *mind*, that is, the human mind seen in its universal aspect. Two other "characters," God the Creator (who is merely alluded to and remains passive in the play) and Demogorgon (who is Necessity conceived as amoral law) stand somewhat apart from, though they are closely linked to, the mind of man. The first has endowed that mind with invaluable faculties; the second is linked closely enough to the mind to respond to any major changes which occur there. In other words, Prometheus would be perfectly justified in saying, by Act III, that once his self-reform was complete, the rest happened "by Necessity." So long as this fundamental dualism between dramatic representation and symbolic function has been recognized, it can be held in critical abeyance. The foregoing sections of this chapter have followed through in detail the development of the action conceived as dramatic action. The symbolic values which Shelley attached to Prometheus, Jupiter, Asia, Demogorgon, and the unseen and essentially inactive God of creation have just been indicated in general terms. It remains to show what the development of the action signifies in more or less philosophical terms.

The essential meaning is fairly simple: the removal of that repressive force which now manacles and tortures the human mind would not only provide an opportunity for the rebirth of the power of love in that mind, but would also enable man to realize his tremendous potential of intellectual might and spiritual pleasure (or blessedness, as Carlyle would translate it) which has for so long been stifled by fear, hate, selfishness, and despair. The conditional mood of this statement is quite intentional: Shelley is not suggesting that these things have happened, but only that they

---

[51] See Melvin T. Solve, *Shelley: His Theory of Poetry* (Chicago, 1927), p. 91. Among earlier commentators, W. M. Rossetti, J. A. Symonds, and H. S. Salt are in substantial agreement that Prometheus represents the human mind.

ought to happen. The *Prometheus* is one of those "dreams of what ought to be or may be" in the distant future.[52]

Shelley works out his vision of man's achievement of ethical perfection in a broad, pseudo-historical perspective, the groundwork for which is provided by Asia's second-act exposition. As in *The Revolt of Islam*, he pays no attention to specific historical details, but moves upon a highly imaginative mythological plane. The mind of man in the Saturnian Age was undeveloped, and man simply vegetated. At a subsequent period, The Age of Prometheus, he acquired knowledge and power. But at the same time "fierce wants," "mad disquietudes and shadows idle of unreal good" began to appear, levying mutual war and "ruining the lair [the human mind] wherein they raged." As partly compensatory "alleviations of his state" man's mind evolved the creative arts and the useful sciences. Prometheus' granting Jupiter dominance upon only one condition, namely, that man is to be free, means in effect that the mind of man suffered its fierce wants and mad disquietudes to assume command, while at the same time retaining the power of freedom of choice. Mind may at any time shake off these agonies if the inward conditions of that mind can be made right. Yet the paradox has been that the mind's capacity for self-deception is so strong that the almost limitless possibilities inherent in an act of self-reform have long been lost to sight. Hence the mind of man has been subjected to the severest tortures. Eventually, however, the great hour arrives. The mind resolves to rid itself of the attitudes which, as in Plato's myth of the cave, have kept it chained in the darkness.[53] With this resolution the way for the expulsion of the mind's daemon is prepared. This resolution and this preparation provide Shelley with the ethical scheme of Act I.

Precisely at the moment of the expulsion (represented in a preliminary way by the departure of the last of the Furies, and

[52] On the political and scientific interpretations of the poem, see Appendix III.
[53] This, I take it, is the meaning of the song of the spirits at II, iii, 90-98:

> Resist not the weakness,
> Such strength is in meekness
> That the Eternal, the Immortal,
> Must unloose through life's portal
> The snake-like Doom coiled underneath
>   his throne
> By that alone.

finally by the fall of Jupiter), the way is made ready for the entry into the human mind of a harmonizing power long since lost (dramatically represented by Prometheus' reunion with Asia). Until the great hour of its enlightenment, the human mind in its self-induced blindness and self-torture has not been able to comprehend this higher love except as a "shadow of beauty unbeheld."[54] It has had to remain content with imperfect degrees of love (Ione and Panthea). Mind is ultimately released by its own strength (Hercules). We are given to understand that the mad disquietudes may return, although such a contingency is for the time being unlikely. (Prometheus is resolved never again to part with Asia, while Jupiter is safely caged under the bars which cover the abyss.)[55]

The obvious question raised by the play is one of the oldest in philosophic literature: How far is man able to control his own destiny? Since *Prometheus Unbound* was conceived and developed as an ethical and psychological drama, Shelley answers the question in these terms: if the mind of man can rid itself of hatred and vengeance, that mind will be cleansed of "fear and pain," and consequently receptive to the harmonizing power of love. Supreme mental well-being will then ensue; order will succeed disorder; harmony will inform chaos. As one of Shelley's images indicates, man will resemble the leprous child who, having drunk of the healing waters of a secret spring, returns home so completely transformed that its mother does not recognize it.[56]

In describing Shelley's view of the problem of evil, Mary asserted that he thought it necessary only for mankind to will "that there should be no evil, and there would be none."[57] With certain qualifications this is true, although the qualifications must be explicitly stated. For Shelley, in his increasingly strong conviction

[54] It is, of course, the beauty itself which is "unbeheld." Prometheus was able to see the shadow of that beauty in Panthea's eyes. The phrase should be understood as if written, "shadow of beauty-unbeheld."

[55] Lesser characters: Mercury, Jupiter's unwilling emissary, may represent half-enslaved and indecisive intellect disconsolately unleashing further tortures within the mind. Thetis, consort of Jupiter, is some sort of whoredom, probably a personification of lust. Jupiter, being destructive and hence uncreative evil, could beget nothing upon her, as O. W. Campbell points out, *op. cit.*, p. 219.

[56] IV, 388-393.

[57] Cf. Mary's note to *Prometheus Unbound*. Medwin borrowed Mary's phraseology in his *Life of Shelley*. See the new edition, ed. H. Buxton Forman (London, 1913), p. 213.

that matter is a function of mind, evil is largely, though by no means entirely, a remediable defect of spiritual vision, an inability to break through the clouds into the sunlight of moral truth. As such, evil is a daemon which can be exorcised, or a gloomy veil which can be dispelled, by a vigorous act of the virtuous will. Man can then realize his full potentialities or, in Shelley's phrase, he can become "king over himself" because his mind is freed from the tyranny of guilt and pain which his uneducated will formerly suffered to exist there.

But Shelley's Magna Carta contains two restraining clauses or qualifications which make it plain that his beatific vision did not blind him to certain exigencies of life on earth. One of these is that, even under the new dispensation (assuming, as he does, that it were achieved on a world-wide scale), man will still have to contend with "chance and death and mutability." Being king over himself, he can rule these incontrovertible facts as if they were his slaves. Yet change, and chance, and death, if not the poor, we shall have always with us. To this extent, at least Shelley's earlier belief in a mechanical necessitarianism had survived into the 1818-1819 period. The survival was fortunate. It acted, as Solve rightly says, "as a sort of balance wheel upon his too enthusiastic faith in the regenerative power of mind."[58]

The second restrictive clause in Shelley's scheme of the new moral order may be inferred from Demogorgon's final exhortation to the assembled cosmic hosts, namely, that there is no absolute guarantee of a permanent expulsion of moral evil.

> Gentleness, Virtue, Wisdom, and Endurance—
> These are the seals of that most firm assurance
> Which bars the pit over Destruction's strength;
> And if, with infirm hand, Eternity,
> Mother of many acts and hours, should free
> The serpent that would clasp her with his length,
> These are the spells by which to reassume
> An empire o'er the disentangled doom.

Jupiter, the spiritually destructive force, has been cast down into the pit. The named powers of the human mind seal up the "firm

[58] *Shelley: His Theory of Poetry*, p. 87.

assurance" that he will remain there. But the chthonic force is strong, and though the assurance is now firm enough, there is always the possibility that in the long stretch of future "acts and hours," some infirmity will develop which will set this force free once more. The serpent would clasp Eternity with his length: moral evil would perpetuate itself through all eternity.[59] If the torturing force should gain its freedom, the same powers of the human mind that now seal it in the abyss are the "spells" by which man may reassume

> An empire o'er the disentangled doom

which now lies coiled and tangled, in durance vile, under the throne of Eternity.

The place of Demogorgon in Shelley's philosophic scheme should now be evident. Demogorgon is the eternal law of amoral necessity which requires an act of mind in order to be set in motion. In *The Revolt of Islam* Shelley had concluded that the furtherance of good in the cosmos is ultimately man's problem, and that the only way in which the forces of moral good can be activated is through a regeneration in the mind of man. This is "Demogorgon's mighty law."[60] Until the great hour of Prometheus' change of heart, Demogorgon is only a potential or holding force, shapeless and inert. Under his throne the happier destiny of man, a "snake-like Doom," has been coiled since Prometheus first gave power to Jupiter. The spirits who guide Asia down to the steps of that remote throne assert that "such strength" is in "meekness" (or in other words, love is so strong a force) that under its compulsion the Eternal (Demo-

---

[59] The source both of this figure and of Shelley's conception of Demogorgon was observed some years ago by H. G. Lotspeich, "Shelley's 'Eternity' and Demogorgon," *PQ* 13 (1934), 309-311. The pertinent passage is Book I, Chapter I of Boccaccio's *Genealogia Deorum Gentilium*. Shelley's Demogorgon says that his name is Eternity. In Boccaccio Eternity is the *socia* or companion of Demogorgon. The cave of Demogorgon in Shelley has its prototype in Boccaccio. There, too, Eternity is represented as an aged goddess encircled by a snake. Those who are troubled by Shelley's apparent inconsistency in speaking of Demogorgon in the masculine gender, of Demogorgon as Eternity, and of Eternity in the feminine gender, will doubtless find an explanation in the fact that Shelley was combining the "companions" of Boccaccio into a single concept. He may have done so in the interests of dramatic unity. He may have wished to suggest that Demogorgon partook of both the male and the female, thus standing as a kind of ancestor to the Hermaphrodite in *The Witch of Atlas*. Finally, he may have intended to imply that the law of amoral necessity was eternal, an idea which could be figured forth with dramatic economy by making Demogorgon and Eternity one.

[60] II, ii, 43.

gorgon) must unloose man's happier destiny through "life's portal."[61] Asia does not urge Demogorgon to free Prometheus because there is no need for her to do so. Love has already been reborn in the mind of man, and by "Demogorgon's mighty law" the release of Prometheus must follow. There is, however, another side to this law. At the end of Act IV, we are told that man's darker destiny of suffering is coiled under the throne of Demogorgon where formerly the happier destiny of man lay unfulfilled. If the forces of moral good were capable of being set in motion only through a regeneration in the mind of man, the forces of moral evil can reassume their former dominance only through a degeneration in the strength of that mind. This, one may infer, is the other side of Demogorgon's mighty law. But as long as gentleness, wisdom, virtue, and endurance remain in man, he will always have weapons with which to combat moral evil.

Prometheus Unbound is in most ways a beautifully exact and skilfully devised piece of work. The structure is carefully wrought, though it must be understood that the stress throughout is less on action than on revelation, that one of the problems is to offer a timeless event in dramatic time, and that the ordinary rules of dramatic organization have, on the whole, comparatively little relevance. Particularly in the first act, but often enough elsewhere, Shelley achieves a sonorous and masterful blank verse which shows that, if he had gone to school to Wordsworth at the time of *Alastor*, he had not neglected Milton in the meantime. The interspersed lyrics contain a quality of lightness without sacrifice of dignity, which serves admirably to relieve the austerity of the rolling iambs, of which they frequently seem a distant echo, like wind in trees after thunder. Nor are these lyrics, as is sometimes said, mere musical interludes without significant relation to the progress of the play. Their function is roughly that of a dramatic chorus: to mourn or rejoice as occasions require, to mark transitions, to introduce or close the scenes, or to provide commentary on the course of the action. They are, moreover, carefully related to the deep and detailed complexities of the myth Shelley has evolved.

The pertinence of the drama as a treatment of one aspect—as Shelley saw it, the crucial aspect—of the problem of evil, the great care with which the original myth has been modified to meet the

[61] II, iv, 94-98.

demands Shelley places upon it, the psychological subtleties and distinctions of character, and the clean exactness with which the whole is seen, as soon as its purpose is grasped, to fit together— these qualify the *Prometheus Unbound* as an imaginative achievement of the first order. One may find the Hell of Act I more satisfactory than the Heaven of Act IV, but this means only that more is always known of Hell than can be imagined of Heaven, as even Dante and Milton, out of their respective experiences in the imaginative reaction of both, would have freely admitted.[62]

As a myth of moral regeneration, the *Prometheus* needs rather to be understood than to be justified. One has only to grasp the respective psychological attitudes of the self-enslaved and the self-liberated man in order to understand Shelley's meaning. The opening scene shows man's mind as it now is, with reasons. The rest is an image of the mind of man set free, made perfect, made whole:

> One harmonious soul of many a soul
> Whose nature is its own divine control.[63]

Shelley's drama provides poetic affirmation for his belief in "a kind of optimism in which we are our own gods," although that optimism is tempered by his appreciation of the radical imperfections which now exist in both the physical and the moral world. These imperfections in their moral applications are examined with some thoroughness in the conversation-poems of 1818-1819.

[62] Shelley well knew how much more skill was needed to make poetry of beauty, virtue, and harmony than of injustice, deformity, and discord. "Better verses," said he, "have been written on Hell than [on] Paradise." *Prose*, VII, 101.

[63] Josiah Royce finds an instructive parallel between Shelley's poetic expression of this idea and Hegel's concept of a "concrete universal." See his *The Spirit of Modern Philosophy* (Boston, 1931), pp. 225-226.

5

THE HUMAN HEART: THE
CONVERSATION-POEMS OF 1818-1819

> We are assured
> Much may be conquered, much may be endured,
> Of what degrades and crushes us. We know
> That we have power over ourselves to do
> And suffer—what, we know not till we try.
> —JULIAN, IN *Julian and Maddalo*

Nor are the crimes and malevolence of the single Being, though indeed withering and tremendous, the offspring of any unaccountable propensity to evil, but flow irresistibly from certain causes fully adequate to their production. They are all children, as it were, of Necessity and Human Nature. In this the direct moral of the book consists, and it is perhaps the most important and the most universal application of any moral that can be enforced by example. Treat a person ill, and he will become wicked.
—SHELLEY'S REVIEW OF *Frankenstein, or The Modern Prometheus,* 1818

· I ·

ALTHOUGH *Prometheus Unbound* attacked the inmost citadel of the problem of evil, it neglected some of the surrounding bastions. The human heart might one day be reformed according to the formula revealed in Shelley's psychological drama, but the reform had not taken place in the past, nor was there much reason to suppose, as Shelley looked round him, that it was occurring in the years 1818-1819. Whatever might be imagined as taking place outside history, the inside was a record of crime and misery. The crime was that of conspiracy by the masters of society, sometimes conceived of as the tyrannous minority, and sometimes, Shelley would have said, as the blank-faced majority. In either instance, the victims provided the misery: the heroic who suffered martyrdom, the innocent who were menaced by corruption, the sensitive who were faced by obduracy, or the downtrodden who lacked leadership. Had it been generally understood that the social conspiracy against these individuals and groups was one of the major themes in the poetry of Shelley's last years, he would not so often have been characterized as an unmitigated optimist.

In the space of a year between August, 1818, and August, 1819, Shelley conceived and wrote, or brought to completion, three works to which the term "conversation-poems" may be applied. They are all, in effect, conversations on history past and present, and though Shelley is still an uncompromising meliorist, though he still knows the formula by which evil may be overcome, he now lays considerable stress on the power of the chthonic forces in human society.

The departure for Italy, that paradise of voluntary exiles which Shelley reached with his family on March 30, 1818, stimulated his plans for a number of literary undertakings. As yet only partly done was his "modern eclogue," *Rosalind and Helen*, which he had begun at Marlow, but which was not completed until sometime in August, 1818.[1] Towards the end of the month in which he finished this poem, he paid a visit to Byron at Venice, and at Este soon afterwards he wrote that pleasant account of the visit which forms the introductory portion of *Julian and Maddalo*. September and the ensuing months were largely occupied with the composition of Acts I-III of *Prometheus Unbound*. In the interval between the date

---

[1] *Rosalind and Helen* had been so far finished in one form that Mary's journal for Feb. 18, 1818, contains the entry: "Copy Shelley's Eclogue." Before he left for the continent on March 12, Shelley "began sending" sheets of his poem to the printer in London. (*Letters*, IX, 319-320.) White states unequivocally that "Shelley sent it to the printers before leaving London." From a letter recently discovered by Professor D. L. Clark, it is plain that the printer received only an incomplete version of the poem, and evidently complained to Ollier that the piece lacked a conclusion. This, Shelley supplied in August, 1818. See Clark, *MLN* 60 (May, 1945), 330-333. Cf. Dowden, *Life*, II, 220, on this point. White (*Shelley*, I, 739) appears to question Lady Shelley's statement (*Shelley Memorials*, 87) that a large part of the poem was written at Marlow. But since Shelley did not leave Marlow for London until Feb. 7, and since the eclogue was being copied on Feb. 18, Shelley must have written a fairly long piece of his poem before leaving Marlow, unless we are to suppose that he bent himself to this task during his first ten days in London, when he was extraordinarily busy with other matters.

on which he completed the third act of *Prometheus* and August 8, 1819, he wrote *The Cenci.*

These are all dark stories of human suffering, variations on a theme of spiritual isolation on which Shelley had first touched in *Alastor.* They deal with historical situations in which, morally speaking, men are quite unprepared for the kind of regeneration depicted in *Prometheus Unbound.* In view of the general gloom which pervaded his chosen subject matter, and in view of his various explorations of the problem of spiritual isolation, it is worth recalling that in this year also Shelley seriously considered writing a piece based upon the sufferings of Job.[2] The available evidence is so slender that one can only speculate about the probable shape of this poem. But it may be suggested that the story is in some respects a parallel to that of Prometheus as Shelley envisioned it, so that in choosing to exploit the symbols of the Greek myth Shelley rejected, at least tentatively, the Hebrew narrative.[3] Shelley's deep dislike of the concept of the Old Testament God would perhaps have prompted him to treat the subject somewhat in the manner of his *Prometheus Unbound*, with Job as protagonist and Jahweh as the equivalent of Jupiter. Whatever the reason for his failure to undertake the work, it is worth emphasizing that the extremes of human agony were central to the Job story, as also to those of Rosalind, the Maniac in *Julian and Maddalo*, and Beatrice Cenci.

· II ·

IT would be pleasant to dismiss *Rosalind and Helen* with the remark Laurence Housman made in excluding Wordsworth's "We Are Seven" from his anthology. It annoyed him, he said, from beginning to end. Parts of the Shelley poem are annoying because they are excessively sentimental. While the eclogue formally resembles some of the constituent poems in Spenser's *Shepheard's*

---

[2] Mary's note on *Prometheus Unbound* (1839) says that Shelley meditated a lyrical drama founded on the Book of Job, which he never abandoned in idea, but of which no trace remained among his papers. Shelley's own very interesting remarks on Job as a subject of heroic proportions may be found in his "Essay on Christianity," *Prose*, VI, 229.

[3] Dowden suggests (*Life*, II, 238) that the prologue to *Hellas* is a reversion in thought to the Job project of three years earlier, where "The speakers are the angelic herald of Eternity, the Christ, and Satan standing, as does the Adversary in the Book of Job, among the sons of God."

Calender in being cast in the form of a reminiscential dialogue, it has nothing else to do with the English pastoral tradition. The two women of the title, having met after years of separation, relate what has befallen them in the meantime. The first narrator, Rosalind, has been almost incredibly unlucky. As she was on the point of marrying the great love of her youth, her father returned from "a distant land" to reveal that he was also father to her betrothed. Both the groom and the father died of this revelation. Left without means to support her widowed (and fast-sinking) mother, Rosalind married herself off to a husband who turned out to be such an ogre that the three children of the union "laughed aloud in frantic glee" at the news of his death. Even after his death the villain continued to torture Rosalind. His will contained the accusation that his wife was both an anti-Christian and an adulteress; since nobody appeared to doubt this statement, Rosalind became a social outcast.

Helen was more fortunate in her *grand amour*, since her associate was the wealthy and high-born young poet, Lionel. After a brilliant career as satirist, Lionel sought refuge from some mental disorder by protracted wandering in "distant lands," whence he returned to take up residence in Helen's neighborhood. They soon became lovers, though neither believed in marriage. When the "ministers of misrule" imprisoned Lionel for blasphemous utterances, Helen waited out his term, and upon his release accompanied him to his ancestral home, where he lingeringly died, leaving Helen with a son who resembled him strongly. Helen's story and her sympathetic reception of Rosalind serve to patch up the quarrel which has hitherto kept the ladies apart. Rosalind, as the original instigator of the separation, is pleased before her death to see the reconciliation symbolically completed by the union of her daughter with Helen's son.

This sentimental *tour de force* apparently delighted Mary, who had urged the subject upon her husband, and had spurred him on, when his ambition flagged, to finish a poem which he might, without great loss to posterity, have left in a bandbox. Except that the poem imaged forth some of his moral views, Shelley seems to have cared little for it. "The fabric of the composition," he told Ollier, was "light and unstudied." If it had little merit as a work of art, it had as much as it aspired to. He could not expect a priggish public "to desert its cherished wines" in favor of a "drop of dew so eva-nescent."[4] Mary subsequently explained that "Shelley had no care for any of his poems that did not emanate from the depths of his mind, and develop some high or abstruse truth."[5] Evidently *Rosalind and Helen* did neither.

In spite of its very obvious limitations, several aspects of this poem deserve comment. There seems to be no reason to doubt the belief of Dowden and Forman that the framework of the story is founded on the break in friendship between Mary Godwin and Isabel Baxter, a break which occurred at the time of Mary's elope-ment with Shelley in the summer of 1814.[6] The details, however, are Shelley's invention, while the implied conclusion—love with-out marriage is infinitely preferable to the spiritual isolation con-sequent upon a loveless marriage—is one that Shelley had reached as early as 1810, when he was seeking to unite his sister Elizabeth, without benefit of clergy, to that brilliant young poet, T. J. Hogg. One may also notice in passing the brief reappearance of the incest theme in Rosalind's premarital tragedy.

The focus of Shelley's interest is Lionel, who appears to be a composite character, unrealistic enough, yet based on an idealiza-tion of the real aspirations of Shelley and some of his friends. Like Laon, his contemporary in the Shelley canon, he is a singer with a purpose, a desire to realize in fact the now familiar vision of that happy age

> When truth and love shall dwell below
> Among the works and ways of men.[7]

Sunlike truth "flashed on his visionary youth"; he pleaded the cause of men before the "throne of armed power"; the "subtle witchcraft of his tongue" unlocked the hearts of the world's bonds-men. But Faith (*i.e.* Superstition) too strongly supported en-trenched power, and the human will was yet too feeble to vanquish superstition. Lionel's hope accordingly subsided into a restless-ness which drove him across "the world's vast wilderness." Seek-

---

[4] Quoted from the letter printed by D. L. Clark, *MLN* 60 (May, 1945), 330. Shelley, Bagni di Lucca, to Charles Ollier, London, Aug. 10, 1818.

[5] Mary's note to *Rosalind and Helen*, in *Works* (1839), III, 159.

[6] Dowden, *Life*, II, 130-131. Cf. Forman's introduction to the facsimile edition of *Rosalind and Helen*, Shelley Society Publications, No. 17.

[7] *Rosalind and Helen*, lines 606-607.

ing refuge in love, he was deceived by "some strange show," after the manner of the poet in *Alastor*, and somewhat in the fashion of the good prince Athanase.

One grows a little tired of the reiteration of the same features, as if Shelley's inventive faculties were limited by the singleness of his purpose. In fact, they were. But Lionel differs somewhat from his fellows, having begun as a popular satirist. People used to advise one another to read his enormously clever *Banquet in Hell*. A change in public sentiment lost him his sympathetic audience, and he abandoned satire in favor of mournful love-songs, written in *ottava rima* and blotted with tears. From these aspects of Lionel's career some readers may glean a suggestion of Byron, author of *English Bards and Scotch Reviewers*, self-exiled satirist and far wanderer, victim of a change in public sentiment during the Regency period, and like Childe Harold an "outlaw of his own dark mind." Others may observe, in the talk of the winged bright Persuasions who ministered to Lionel in his frailty and lassitude, a preview of the idealized portrait of Keats in *Adonais*.[8] Finally, the description of Lionel's persecution, imprisonment, and release might have involved a recollection of Leigh Hunt's difficulties with the Crown.

· III ·

THE year of the conversation-poems was also the year in which Shelley became deeply interested in the life of Torquato Tasso. Although *Rosalind and Helen* was the first of Shelley's major poems to be brought to completion after his arrival in Italy, the story of Tasso was the first subject to engage his attention. From Milan on the sixth of April he wrote Peacock that he had been meditating "many literary schemes, and one in particular," and that he wished to settle down somewhere as quickly as possible in order to begin writing. The particular scheme in his mind during April was a verse-tragedy on Tasso's madness and imprisonment, a project never brought to completion.

In a villa at Este some six months later Shelley wrote, either in whole or in part, the second of his conversation-poems, *Julian and Maddalo*, and thereby inaugurated a mystery which has continued

---

[8] Compare *Rosalind and Helen*, 746-750, with *Adonais*, stanza XIII. Cf. also *Rosalind and Helen*, 828-833 with *Adonais*, stanza X.

to puzzle Shelley critics ever since. A connection between the abortive Tasso drama and *Julian and Maddalo* has been twice suspected but unfortunately never proved. The crucial question has to do with the real identity of the maniac whose complaint occupies a central position in the poem. Nobody has doubted that the introductory portion of the poem is in the main an autobiographical account of Shelley's visit to Byron at Venice in August, 1818. The difficulty has been that an overwhelming majority of commentators have also wished to regard the story of the maniac as autobiography, a position which raises the questions: To what extent does autobiography figure in this poem, and how far, for critical or biographical purposes, can allegedly autobiographical passages in Shelley be trusted?

Julian and Maddalo is a useful document for the discussion of the critical significance of autobiographical evidence in Shelley: about one-third of the poem is approximately true to autobiographical fact, another third is true to what Shelley thought to be historical fact, and the final third is demonstrably a piece of fiction.

The shape of the poem may be briefly indicated. Of the 617 lines, the first part, 211 lines, describes Shelley's actual visit to Byron at Venice on August 23-24, 1818. Shelley intended his friends to understand that Count Maddalo stood for Byron, and that Julian, the English gentleman who pays the visit, represented himself. The poem opens with an account of Julian and Maddalo riding horseback along the sands of the Lido on an unseasonably cold day. This much is fact. By his own statement, Shelley called on Byron at three in the afternoon of Sunday, August 23, 1818, a cold day for that time of year. After some talk about Byron's illegitimate daughter, Allegra, the two men crossed to the Lido in Byron's gondola and rode horseback along the shore. Their conversation "consisted in the histories of [Byron's] wounded feelings, and questions [from Byron] as to [Shelley's] affairs."[9] They spoke of the Chancery decision which had deprived Shelley of his children by Harriet, and of "literary matters," specifically the fourth canto of *Childe Harold's Pilgrimage* and Leigh Hunt's *Foliage*. Then they returned to Byron's palace. The poem, of course, idealizes this encounter somewhat. The talk of Julian and Mad-

[9] *Letters,* ix, 328.

dalo was first gay, then serious, Julian arguing against despondency, and Maddalo supporting the darker side.

From this point on the poem begins to diverge from the facts as they appear in Shelley's epistolary account of the visit.[10] One example of possible invention is the business about the island madhouse. On the way home from the Lido, Maddalo pointed out a madhouse on an island and made a passing remark about the inmates' being called to vespers. There is no assurance that this happened, although Byron and Shelley could probably have seen from their gondola either the madhouse on San Servolo or the penitentiary on San Clemente.[11] But Shelley's only demonstrable connection with prisons during his visit to Venice was the exploratory call he paid to the then empty dungeons of the Doges' Palace.[12]

There is a strong likelihood that Shelley invented most of the remainder of part one of *Julian and Maddalo* in order to ease his way into the lament of the maniac. Julian goes the next morning to Maddalo's palace, plays for a little while with his host's small daughter, and, when the count appears, resumes the talk of the preceding afternoon, preaching, as he then did, the necessity of aspiration.[13] Again opposing his friend's idealistic views, Maddalo proposes a visit to the island madhouse to which he had pointed the day before. There, by listening to the wild talk of a particularly engaging maniac, Julian can learn something about the vanity of human wishes.

[10] One minor example of this divergence may be found in the immediate aftermath of the ride. In the poem Julian is conveyed to his lodgings where he takes leave of Maddalo; in fact, Shelley returned to Byron's palace and seems to have spent most of the night talking with his host, since his letter describing the visit is dated five o'clock in the morning of Monday, Aug. 24.

[11] Peck, *Shelley: His Life and Work*, II, 102, identifies the madhouse as that of San Servolo, although he notes Browning's statement that Shelley was probably confusing this madhouse with the penitentiary of San Clemente. See Locock, *Shelley's Poetical Works* (1911), I, 586. Medwin's statement that he had often seen the madhouse referred to in the poem may be of a piece with many of his other claims.

[12] *Letters*, IX, 335. According to Hobhouse, in his *Historical Illustrations of the Fourth Canto of Childe Harold* (1818), he and Byron had visited these dungeons earlier in the same year. Byron may have suggested the visit to Shelley, but there is no evidence that he accompanied his friend to the Doges' Palace in August.

[13] Shelley may or may not have returned to Byron's palace Monday morning. He had been up rather late, and had business to attend to at "the Banker's." The playing at billiards with Count Maddalo's daughter sounds like something that might have taken place between Shelley and Allegra, but Shelley's letter does not mention any such meeting. One difficulty is that a part of the pertinent letter is missing. See *Letters*, IX, 328. Shelley may have derived his fictional name from the Julian Alps, to which he alludes in this letter.

The visit is undertaken, and the two friends ascend to a well-furnished apartment where they have an opportunity to observe the maniac, a gentle and pathetic creature who, in some mysterious fashion, has been crossed in love, and who is engaged, by his own account, in some kind of deception. As the visitors listen, he delivers a lament of some 100 heroic couplets. When he falls asleep, Julian returns to Maddalo's palace, dines there, and discusses the maniac with his host. Next morning he leaves Venice, and many years elapse before his return. When he does return, he asks Maddalo's now grown-up daughter what happened to the maniac. The young lady tells him all the facts of the case, but Julian says that he will never divulge them to the cold world.

The conclusion of the poem is clearly fictional. Not only did Shelley revisit Venice several times after his parting with Byron, but Byron's daughter Allegra never succeeded in growing up. The first third of the poem, then, is based on historical fact, modified wherever it suits Shelley's convenience. The last third is fiction. The remaining question is whether the lament of the maniac is fiction or fact. A majority of Shelley's biographers have wished to look upon the middle section of the poem as a veiled chapter in Shelley's autobiography.[14] A close examination of the maniac's story reveals, however, that it is a semifictionalized treatment of the poet Tasso's imprisonment for real or alleged madness in the year 1579.

The probable date of composition of *Julian and Maddalo* coincides precisely with the period of Shelley's interest in the fortunes of Tasso. Shelley's own statement is that his poem was "written at Este," which establishes the date of composition between the latter part of August, 1818, when he accepted the loan of Byron's villa at Este, and early November, when he left Este for Naples. The description of the visit to Byron at Venice was certainly composed after August 24, since it is based on the events which happened on August 23-24. The maniac's lament may have

---

[14] On this point Professor Newman White has no doubts. In both versions of his life of Shelley (*Shelley*, II, 43; *Portrait of Shelley*, 286), he avows his "practical certainty" that the maniac's story has an autobiographical basis, and that Shelley is there describing a "bitter . . . reality" in which he was the central figure. For a consideration of the grounds on which Professor White establishes his case, see the essay, "Shelley's Ferrarese Maniac," in *English Institute Essays, 1946* (New York, 1947), esp. pp. 63-73. On the date of Mary's despondency, see Appendix IV in the present volume.

been written in the August-November period, or it may have been substantially written at some earlier date in 1818, and then built into the conversation-poem during the Este period. Either possibility fits the Tasso interpretation equally well, for Shelley's interest in Tasso's life as the subject of a poem began in April, 1818, or perhaps earlier, and continued until November, 1818, or perhaps later.

The inception of his interest in Tasso's biography, as opposed to Tasso's poetry, may very probably be dated from September 24, 1817, when he read Byron's *Lament of Tasso*, a complaint of 247 lines, mostly in heroic couplets. Here the imprisoned Tasso looks back over his unfortunate love affair with the Princess Leonora d'Este, sister of his patron, Alfonso of Ferrara, and consoles himself for his imprisonment by thinking on three satisfactions: he has completed his two great poems, *Aminta* and *Jerusalem Delivered*; he has forgiven Alfonso for placing him in a cell even though he must stay where he can hear the "long and maniac cry" of other "minds and bodies in captivity"; and he supposes that he will be buried near his beloved Leonora. Shelley was much impressed by this poem, but the section that particularly pleased him, as he told Byron, was that in which Tasso's "youthful feelings" were described. The lines which imply an "indistinct consciousness of its own greatness, which a heart of genius cherishes in solitude, amid neglect and contempt, have," said Shelley, "a profound and thrilling pathos which I will confess to you, whenever I turn to them, make my head wild with tears."[15] The lines which so affected Shelley could only be 149-173, where Tasso is made to say that from birth his soul was "drunk with love," which mingled with all he saw and made him especially fond of natural objects and scenes. When his elders called him idler or punished him, he cursed them in his heart and retired to his bower to weep alone and dream again those "visions which arise without a sleep." He learned early the sorrows of spiritual isolation. Throughout his adolescence, his soul panted with indefinable longings, until at last he found what

[15] *Letters*, IX, 245. Shelley knew Tasso as poet before he read Byron's *Lament*. Mary's reading lists show that he read *Jerusalem Delivered* and *Aminta* in 1815, and that he returned to Tasso in 1816. On April 6, 1818, he began rereading *Aminta* with Mary, and at the same time took up a life of Tasso, probably that of Serassi, partly to practice his Italian.

he had been seeking—the Princess Leonora, in whom he became so completely absorbed that he forgot nature and the world. Readers of Shelley's *Alastor* will not wonder that the poet should have been so much struck by this section of Byron's *Lament of Tasso*. Readers of the lament of the maniac in *Julian and Maddalo* will perhaps recognize an allusion to Byron's poem in the statement that "when a boy," he devoted his nature "to justice and to love," and that he was known as "that love-devoted youth."

Soon after his arrival in Italy on March 30, 1818, and something over six months after his enthusiastic letter about Byron's poem, Shelley probably read Serassi's biography of Tasso, which he finished on April 11.[16] On April 20 he told Peacock that he meant to write a tragedy on Tasso's madness; on April 30 he told Hogg the same thing; and sometime in May he entered in a notebook, now at the Bodleian, brief notations for two scenes of the drama.[17] In one, Tasso was to read a sonnet to Leonora; another was to deal with Tasso's famous visit to his sister Cornelia at Sorrento in July, 1577. Part of the week of May 11 Shelley spent with Count Manso's life of Tasso, and it was probably about this time that he composed the two fragments of the Tasso drama which have survived.[18] One of these is clearly the opening of the play. We are introduced to several characters, one of whom, Maddalo, was probably intended to represent Count Maddalo Fucci, a real historical character with whom Tasso once had a quarrel. The other fragment is a love-song to Leonora. Shelley's interest in Tasso did not, however, cease at this point. In mid-July he spoke admiringly of Tasso's "delicate moral sensibility"; on August 16 he quoted a passage in Italian which he ascribed to Tasso, but which he had probably found in Serassi's life of Tasso.[19] When he visited Byron in Venice a week later he was disappointed that the *gondolieri*, who customarily entertained their passengers with recitations from Tasso, this

[16] For evidence of Shelley's acquaintance with Serassi's biography, see C. B. Beall, *MLQ* 2 (1941), 609-610.

[17] *Letters*, IX, 298-299 and IX, 307. The notebook entry is printed by A. Koszul, *Shelley's Prose in the Bodleian Manuscripts* (London, 1910), p. 148. The entry occurs at folio 41, MS. Shelley e. 4.

[18] Mary's journal entry for May 4 records the reading of Manso's *Vita*.

[19] *Letters*, IX, 312 and IX, 321. Shelley repeated the phrase in altered form to Hunt, November, 1819. See *Letters*, X, 130. He also used it twice in his essays, once in the fragment "On Life" and again in *The Defence of Poetry*.

time failed to do so.[20] In accepting Byron's villa at Este he entered a region filled with reminders of the Estensi, Tasso's patrons, and it was here, by his own statement, that he wrote *Julian and Maddalo*. On November 7, during the journey from Este to Naples, Shelley went sightseeing in Ferrara, inspected the mementos of Tasso, visited Tasso's prison at the Hospital of Santa Anna, and sent Peacock "a piece of wood of the very door which for seven years and three months divided this glorious being from the air and the light." The Hospital was, thought Shelley, "a horrible abode for the . . . meanest thing that ever wore the shape of man, much more for one of delicate susceptibilities, and elevated fancies."[21]

It is therefore evident that Shelley's interest in Tasso's life extended through a period of more than one year, that he seriously intended to write a drama on Tasso's madness, that he sketched out a curtain-raiser and two later scenes, that he composed a love-song to Leonora, that he read at least two biographies of Tasso, that he admired Tasso's delicate moral sensibility, and that even after the Este period, when *Julian and Maddalo* was written, he was sufficiently interested in Tasso so that in leaving Este for Naples he wished to stop at Ferrara to see the Tasso relics.

There is no way of knowing why Shelley abandoned his projected drama on Tasso. Both this play and that on the Biblical character Job were considered and laid aside in 1818, probably about the time that Shelley's interest in the *Prometheus Unbound* began to rise. But from what has been said it seems fairly clear that, as a substitute for the abandoned dramatic project, he embarked upon another mainly modeled on Byron's *Lament of Tasso*, and partly based on the reading in Tasso's biography which he had done in preparation for the tragedy on Tasso's madness. The result was a lament only thirty lines shorter than Byron's poem, to which it bore some resemblance in its opening and closing passages; in the fact that it was presented, like most of Byron's poem, in heroic couplets; in the fact that it showed the protagonist imprisoned within earshot of the howls and blasphemies of other

[20] *Letters*, IX, 335 and note. Shelley's enthusiasm for Tasso as poet had given way by the fall of 1819 to admiration for Dante, Petrarch, and Boccaccio. See *Letters*, X, 86.

[21] *Letters*, IX, 341.

maniacal prisoners, and in the fact that it mentioned the prisoner's youthful devotion to love—a devotion, as we have seen, which Shelley found so moving in Byron's account that a reading of it made his head "wild with tears." Shelley's reason for concealing the maniac's real identity can probably be found somewhere between his personal delight in mystifying even his closest friends, and a possible fear that he might be accused of imitating Byron's *Lament of Tasso.*

Two previous critics have implied or suggested that the maniac was originally intended as a portrait of Tasso in a Ferrarese cell. Although Dowden was unwilling to hazard such a guess, he suggested that some of Shelley's studies for the Tasso drama might have overflowed into the "mournful soliloquies" of *Julian and Maddalo.*[22] In 1930, Professor R. D. Havens published an article in which he agreed with Dowden, pointed out that Shelley got the name Maddalo from his Tasso researches, and observed that while the maniac's story contains no allusions to Tasso or Ferrara, nobody need be surprised, since in transferring the lines to his new piece, Shelley "would naturally drop or change all that were not adapted to it."[23] If either Dowden or Havens had taken note of the resemblance between Byron's *Lament of Tasso* and the maniac's story, or if either of them had looked into Shelley's other sourcebooks, Manso's *Life of Tasso* and the work by Serassi, Professor White would in all conscience have been compelled to accept their conclusions, instead of merely admitting, as he does in a footnote, the possibility "that Tasso was in Shelley's mind as he wrote, but in the background rather than in the foreground."[24]

It will be useful to see, therefore, what data on Tasso Shelley could have assembled from a reading of the biographies by Manso and Serassi. According to the extremely cautious and circumspect life by Count Manso, Tasso pretended that he was in love with one of three ladies of the court of Ferrara, each of whom bore the name Leonora, in order to conceal which of the three was the real object of his passion. However, "alcuni credettero, che la dama di lui, sovra ogni altra amata, ed esaltata, fosse Madama Leonora d'Este,

[22] Dowden, *Life*, II, 238.
[23] R. D. Havens, "Julian and Maddalo," *SP* 27 (1930), 648-653.
[24] White, *Shelley*, II, 558-559.

sorella del Duca Alfonso."[25] Manso adds his own opinion that
Tasso's verses from Sorrento show that the Princess Leonora was
"sua particolar Signora, e favoratrice"—that is, his own lady and
favor-giver. But Tasso was a victim either of gossip or of organized
conspiracy. One of his friends, "with whom he shared everything,
even his thoughts, and from whom he had not completely concealed the secret of his loves . . . repeated one day some details of
the amorous secrets of Tasso." Greatly angered, Tasso struck him
in the face. In the duel which followed, Tasso was getting the best
of it, when his opponents fled, escaping arrest by the Duke Alfonso's men, who were attracted to the spot by the clash of arms.
Tasso was seized and placed in custody, not as a punishment for
fighting but, as the diplomatic Manso points out, in order to pro-
tect him from potential assassins. Tasso failed to understand the
motive behind his arrest, since the duke appeared to be more in-
censed with him than a mere duel would warrant. Putting two and
two together, he concluded that the duke had heard of the gossip
which had caused the fight: that is, the statement that he was in
love with a lady of the ducal court.[26] We are left to infer that the
Ferrarese gentleman babbled about Tasso's secret love for the
Princess Leonora, and that the arrest and imprisonment were, in
Tasso's mind, a penalty for having allowed this affair to reach the
public ear.

Tasso soon broke prison and fled Ferrara. But he chose for his
return the inauspicious moment of the duke's third marriage. The
former favorite of the court was received with such coldness that
he gave vent to his indignation and was again imprisoned, this
time for seven years in the Hospital of Santa Anna. Manso attributes this second imprisonment to the duke's magnanimous desire
to restore Tasso's disturbed imagination to normal. Yet the biographer contrives to be so ambiguous in what he says of Tasso's
madness that he seems to be attempting to leave room for the
widely accepted story (noted by Quadrio and Baruffaldi) that
Tasso was only feigning insanity upon instructions from the duke.
According to the agreement, so long as Tasso pretended to be out
of his mind the duke would keep him in pleasant apartments in the
prison, but would not invoke the death penalty, which would

25 Manso, *Vita*, in Tasso, *Opere*, Firenze, 1724, I, xvii.
26 Manso, *Vita, loc. cit.*, xxiv-xxvi.

otherwise be the inevitable consequence of Tasso's having cast a blot on the escutcheon of the proud House of Este. But while Manso appears to be of two minds on the insanity question, he has much to say about the phantasms which appeared to Tasso, among whom the devil was a prominent visitor.

Serassi, who was very probably the third main source of Shelley's knowledge of Tasso, agrees with Manso at many points, but rejects the implication that there was any real love affair between Tasso and the princess. At the same time, he refuses to believe that Tasso was insane, for he thinks such poetry as Tasso's could hardly have been composed by a diseased mind. Even the level-headed Serassi finds it hard to avoid being touched by the romantic story. He notes the constancy of Tasso's devotion to Leonora, and describes the princess as very beautiful, graceful, modest, and reserved, and given to improving her mind by learned converse with literary men.[27]

All of the necessary hints for the lament of Shelley's maniac can be found either in Byron's *Lament of Tasso*, or in the lives of Tasso by Serassi and Count Manso. The maniac begins, as in Byron, with a remark about the slow passage of time in prison. He mentions the "mask of falsehood" which he must wear, concealing the truth even from his friends. This is a clear allusion to the tradition that Tasso's madness was feigned, a view implied in Manso and Serassi, and stated outright three times in Byron's *Lament of Tasso*.[28] The maniac says that if he made an error, he has had nothing out of it but pain, insult, unrest, and terror. He has not bought repentance with pleasure or "a dark yet sweet offense." He invokes his "spirit's mate" as one who would weep if she knew the true extent of "her lost friend's incommunicable woe." But he will not yield to scorn or hate, which are poor medicines for a mind which scorn and hate have wounded. Here Shelley is closely following Byron. Byron's lamenter admits that he was delirious to aspire to so lofty a love as Leonora, for his life has been blighted, his reputation debased, and his thoughts branded as things to shun and fear. Yet he feels no remorse, having no cause.[29] If it was presumptuous in him to love without design, that sad fatality has cost him dear.[30] But he holds no grudges: he has cast all bitterness from his

[27] Serassi, *Vita* (1790), pp. 149-150.   [28] *Lament of Tasso*, lines 4, 48, 214.
[29] *Ibid.*, 47-100.   [30] *Ibid.*, 140-141.

heart, and even though Leonora will not pity him, he cannot forsake her memory. Despite his sufferings, Shelley's maniac has not changed his basic beliefs or resolutions; he will not sanction tyranny or surrender to avarice, misanthropy, or lust. He longs for the peace of the grave. Byron's Tasso is still too proud to be vindictive; he has pardoned the insults of the prince, and longs only for death.

In the midst of the maniac's soliloquy, his fancy becomes overwrought, and he thinks he sees beside him the phantasm of his beloved. She has taken Death for her paramour, and the maniac says that he will watch from his winding-sheet as she makes the tomb her bridal bed. Manso, as we have seen, describes Tasso's hallucinations at some length. Byron's Tasso complains that his mind plays him tricks. Unwonted lights shine along his prison and a "strange demon" vexes him. Shelley may also have remembered, with some horror, the closing lines of Byron's poem, where Tasso imagines that he and Leonora will be entwined forever—in the grave. When the phantasm disappears, Shelley's maniac says that it has acted like a serpent, poisoning the very breast that warmed it. He recalls the lady's former protest that he did not love her enough; yet he loved her even to his overthrow, while she would like now to forget her former protestation. If they had never met and embraced, he would not have been plagued with present agonies, nor would she have had to endure his love while her own for him was diminishing, nor could she taunt him for imagining that one of his personal appearance should address himself to "love's work." Here Shelley is outreaching Byron. The maniac's lady evidently encouraged his love, but grew cold after the love was consummated. Byron's Leonora was never an active participant, but only a shrine to be worshiped from a distance. Yet Byron's Tasso accuses Leonora of undue pride of station, and of being ashamed that such a one as he could love her.[31] The maniac's statement that he was not personally attractive could have been derived from Manso's very detailed description of Tasso, where the poet is said to have been tall and well-proportioned, but where such other details as his large nose and mouth, thick prominent teeth and thin lips, the depression in his forehead, the peculiar slope of his head, and his sparse black eyebrows, do not add up,

[31] *Ibid.*, 228-230.

whatever the count's intention, to a vision of male beauty.[32] In the remaining lines other Byronic echoes occur. As the maniac writes, his eyes are dazzled with tears. Byron's Tasso blots with tears the final page of his master-work. Shelley's maniac says that he has refrained from suicide in order that his lady will be less desolate. Byron's Tasso will not "sanction with self-slaughter" the lying statement that he is insane. Shelley's maniac says that he has hidden every spark of the love which consumes him beneath the embers of his words. Byron's Tasso says that he has breathed no word of a love which was "sufficient to itself, its own reward." Shelley's maniac ends by calling for death. Byron's Tasso concludes with thoughts of the grave where he and Leonora will be buried under the same laurel-tree. In short, it would appear that the key poem in solving the mystery of the identity of Shelley's maniac is Byron's *Lament of Tasso*, though Shelley's knowledge of Manso and Serassi was doubtless useful to him in completing his conception of the poet's character.

In view of their common interest in the Tasso story, it is not unlikely that Tasso's name should have come up for discussion during Shelley's visit to Byron in the summer of 1818, although it cannot be certainly known that Byron cited the unfortunate career of Tasso as a proof of his belief that men are the playthings of destiny. In any case, the most interesting aspect of the autobiographical portion of the poem is the argument on free will *versus* destiny in which the story of Tasso serves as the *exemplum*.

Shelley's friendship with Byron was based on certain similarities of outlook. He had observed in 1817 that "there must be a resemblance, which does not depend upon their own will, between all the writers of any particular age. They cannot escape from subjection to a common influence which arises out of an infinite combination of circumstances belonging to the times in which they live."[33] But this determinism, though inescapable, allowed for wide divergencies among individuals, and Shelley observed between himself and Byron temperamental differences of the most fundamental kind.

The burden of the conversation between Julian and Maddalo indicates that Shelley wished to present himself as an incorrigible

[32] *Julian and Maddalo*, lines 463-466. Cf. Manso, p. lxxv.
[33] *The Revolt of Islam*, preface.

meliorist and Byron as an equally adamant fatalist. The talk during the ride along the Lido was concerned, according to Shelley,
with "God, freewill, and destiny" and the conversationalists spoke

> Of all that earth has been, or yet may be,
> All that vain men imagine or believe,
> Or hope can paint, or suffering may achieve.

On the grounds that it is wisest "to make the best of ill," Julian
argued for freedom of the will. But Maddalo, prompted by his own
dark pride, chose to support the position that men are victims of
a blind destiny against which it is useless to struggle.[34]

As the gondola passed eastward of the island madhouse during
the return trip, Maddalo ordered the *gondolieri* to cease rowing
so that Julian could hear the bell which summoned the madmen to
vespers. Julian, inveterate foe of religious superstition, remarked
that the madmen had all the skill they needed to pray to their
stern Maker "in thanks and hope for their dark lot." Maddalo, who
had long known his friend as an "infidel," at first accepted the remark as an ironic joke; but then his brow darkened and he cried
that the tolling bell, silhouetted against the setting sun, was a fit
emblem for the human soul, "hung in a heaven-illumined tower"
but summoning thoughts and desires to meet in prayer around the
ravaged heart, like madmen praying for an unknown and unknow-
able good.[35]

When the friends resumed their conversation next morning,
Julian took the offensive. If man were as blind and passive a creature as Maddalo had maintained, if he were the sport of an un-
knowable destiny, there might be little harm in his adherence to
religious superstitions "which break a teachless nature to the
yoke." But the point is that man's nature is not "teachless." Evil is
largely a condition of mind, and man may be capable, through an
act of will, of throwing off the chains and the blindfolds. Evil is
"permitted ill," and it is man who grants the permission. If men
were not so weak, their deeds could match their desires. Maddalo
upbraided Julian for such utopian talk: men are weak, and their
aspirations are therefore vain. Who knows, said Julian, until he
has tried? The chains which bind the human heart may well turn
out to be brittle as straw. The kings of ancient philosophy, those

---

[34] *Julian and Maddalo*, lines 42-52.   [35] *Ibid.*, 106-130.

who reigned before "Religion made men blind," taught that mankind has power to accomplish and endure. Until he has invoked his full potential no man knows how efficacious thought may be. It is not destiny, but man's own "willful ill" which inhibits the march of progress.[36]

Maddalo remains unconvinced. Even if Julian could make his argument impervious to logical refutation "as far as words go," the brute facts of the human predicament would still argue against it. "I knew a man," says Maddalo, "who argued as you do." He then explains that his acquaintance has gone mad and is now incarcerated in the island madhouse. With Julian's permission, they will pay him a visit: the wild talk of the maniac will show "how vain are such aspiring theories" as that of Julian.[37]

Upon Julian the visit made a deep impression. The maniac's words drove the philosophical problem entirely out of the minds of his hearers, and when they returned to Maddalo's house, they talked of nothing but the specific case, trying to guess their way into the mystery of the madman's woe. Despite Maddalo's expectations, however, the island adventure failed to convince Julian of the vanity of human wishes. On the contrary, he imagined that if he were able to study without interruption the ravings of the maniac, just "as men study some stubborn art for their own good," and if he were able to find, by the exercise of infinite patience, an entrance to the caverns of his mind (the expression is Shelley's, but the idea is that of modern psychiatric practice), he might discover the means of reclaiming him "from his dark estate." It was only a hope; the pressure of his own affairs prevented Julian from putting his theory to the test. But he did not, therefore, relinquish his belief that the human mind was reclaimable, or its corollary, that evil is largely a condition of mind which may be vanquished by the exercise of will.[38]

Shelley adopted the same position in *Prometheus Unbound*, which was begun at Este at exactly the period when *Julian and Maddalo* was composed. Although the two poems are as divergent in manner as it is possible for two exactly contemporary works by the same author to be, the fundamental ethic of both is the same, and to one interested in the relationship between Shelley and

[36] *Ibid.*, 160-191 and 202-211.   [37] *Ibid.*, 191-201.
[38] *Ibid.*, 520, 568-583.

Byron, both poems might be construed as the meliorist's answer to the uncompromising environmental fatalist. But Shelley was conscious both of the corrupting effects of social environment and the tragic results of human desperation. *The Cenci*, like the first of his conversation-poems, *Rosalind and Helen*, examined the social aspects of the problem of evil.

· IV ·

To group Shelley's historical tragedy, *The Cenci*, with such conversation-poems as *Rosalind and Helen* and *Julian and Maddalo* may seem at first glance to involve a violation of the somewhat inelastic laws which govern literary *genres*, for *The Cenci* is obviously a stage-drama, composed to be acted. In other respects, however, *The Cenci* resembles the two pieces which preceded it sufficiently to justify its inclusion here. Like them it is made to serve as a vehicle for Shelley's moral ideas. As in the conversation-poems, Shelley projects his ideas through dramatic dialogue, his method being to place two characters vis-à-vis and to develop opposed points of view by means of impassioned conversational interchange. There are accordingly reasonable grounds for considering *The Cenci* in conjunction with the conversation pieces.

Of the three poems to which the present chapter is devoted, *The Cenci* was by all odds Shelley's strongest bid for popular favor. He wrote it with the idea that the well-known Irish actress, Miss O'Neill, could perhaps be induced to play the leading role, and the hope that Kean might be persuaded to act Count Cenci. He toned down the uglier aspects of the original story in order, as he thought, to make it acceptable to a bourgeois theater-going public. He chose a subject which for two centuries had continued to excite wide interest among the Romans. He adopted a plainer style, abjuring high-flown images, and seeking to come as close as his subject allowed to the everyday language of men.

Even more than the first two points, the last two seem to have been part of a definite plan in Shelley's mind, both in the year of the conversation-poems and as late as the year of his death. He now sought story-structures which already existed in popular tradition, and which might therefore be expected to exert a stronger grip on the imaginations of the people. This search for "natural" subjects appears to have had something to do with his choice of the Promethean myth. Like the Greek tragedians, he did not feel "bound to adhere to the common interpretation, or to imitate in story as in title" the great treatments which in the past had been accorded this and other myths. In other words, he found precedent among his peers for allowing himself to invent freely within the general framework of a traditional story. At the same time, he could count on his audience's acquaintance with the general shape of a given myth or legend or historical event, and hence assume from the start a certain sympathy between his auditors and his subject. The Job legend, for example, fitted his plans admirably. In selecting the story of the Cenci, he observed that "*King Lear* and the two plays in which the tale of Oedipus is told were stories which already existed in tradition" before Shakespeare and Sophocles gave them permanent literary form. In Rome, at least, he found that everyone knew as much about the Cenci scandal as if it had occurred two years instead of two centuries before. "This national and universal interest" in the affair first suggested to him, he said, its fitness for dramatic purposes.

He was also coming round, for the time being, to an almost Wordsworthian view of poetic language. "I entirely agree with those modern critics," said he, "who assert that in order to move men to true sympathy we must use the familiar language of men. . . . But it must be the real language of men in general, and not that of any particular class to whose society the writer happens to belong."[39] He was plainly in search of what Coleridge, in the recently published *Biographia Literaria*, had called the *lingua communis*. Equally plain is the reason for his choice: he adopts this language "in order to move men to true sympathy." About the introductory and closing sections of *Julian and Maddalo*, he thought in similar though somewhat more limited terms. Sending this poem to Hunt a week after he had finished *The Cenci*, he observed that Hunt ought to like the manner in which it was written. "I have employed," he said, "a certain familiar style of language to express the actual way in which people talk with each other whom education and a certain refinement of sentiment have placed above the use of vulgar idioms."[40]

[39] Preface to *The Cenci*.   [40] *Letters*, x, 68. Aug. 15, 1819.

In the three years of life which remained, Shelley never wholly abandoned the belief that one way to enlist popular sympathy was to employ a selection of the language really used by men—provided, of course, that the subject sanctioned it. He continued to write certain poems designed only for the eyes of the esoteric few. He felt that the familiar style was hardly feasible "in the treatment of a subject wholly ideal, or in that part of any subject which relates to common life, where the passion, exceeding a certain limit, touches the boundaries of that which is ideal."[41] Otherwise he believed in, and in such poems as *The Masque of Anarchy* carefully experimented with, the *lingua communis* and the familiar style.[42]

Besides a more or less systematic attempt to enlarge his circle of listeners, Shelley obviously gave some thought in the year of the conversation-poems to the nature of tragedy. *Prometheus Unbound*, though roughly modeled after the Aeschylean original, had not turned out to be a tragedy in the Greek tradition, and certainly not a tragedy in the English sense of that word. Shelley had shown Prometheus rejecting hatred, admitting love and pity, and triumphing at last over the sufferings which beset the human mind when it is not its own sovereign. Of such agony as Prometheus endured he had presumably some personal knowledge, as he had had, for example, personal knowledge of the mental state of the *Alastor* poet. But in writing *The Cenci*, as he later remarked to Trelawny, his object was to see how well he could succeed in describing passions he had never personally felt.

He was also, and again for the time being, focusing his attention more on Elizabethan than on classical models. Wishing to show a true picture of human beings in action instead of treating the kind of subject he called "ideal," he turned from mythology to history, and from his "beautiful idealisms of moral excellence" to the dark

[41] *Ibid.*, pp. 68-69.

[42] Had *The Cenci* been phenomenally successful, or had *Julian and Maddalo* been published and popular in his lifetime, Shelley might have done more conversation-poems, or at least poems designed for the people. Work done in the familiar style, besides the *Masque of Anarchy*, would include *Peter Bell the Third, Oedipus Tyrannus*, some of the lesser political lyrics, the poem to Mary introducing *The Witch of Atlas, The Sensitive Plant*, the *Letter to Maria Gisborne*, and some parts of the fragmentary *Charles I*. The other poems of the period 1819-1822 move in the realm of the "ideal," as in *The Witch of Atlas, Adonais, Epipsychidion, Hellas*, the fragmentary *Magic Plant*, and the fragmentary *Triumph of Life*.

realities of moral turpitude and error. Up to this time, as he told Hunt, his writing had consisted of "little else than visions" which "impersonated" (that is, projected by means of intentionally symbolic personages) his own "apprehensions of the beautiful and the just: . . . dreams of what ought to be or may be." The published pieces (*Queen Mab, Alastor,* and *The Revolt of Islam*) showed those "literary defects incidental to youth and impatience." Now he laid aside "the presumptuous attitude of an instructor" and turned to "sad reality." The *Prometheus Unbound* had depicted the results in the human mind of moral reform; *The Cenci* showed the results in human society of moral deformity.

For Shelley, tragedy consisted in moral deformity. At the same time, he believed that no tragedy written for the stage should be "subservient to what is vulgarly termed a moral purpose." He had purposely laid aside the presumptuous attitude of an instructor, which meant that he had abrogated direct moral preachment. "It is nothing," he told Peacock of *The Cenci,* "which by any courtesy of language can be termed either moral or immoral." He felt that had anything like the Promethean kind of moral or poetic justice been employed in telling the story of Beatrice, the effectiveness of the play as tragedy would have been diminished. "Undoubtedly," said he, perhaps with his recent experience of the *Prometheus* in his mind's eye, "the fit return to make to the most enormous injuries is kindness and forbearance and a resolution to convert the injurer from his dark passions by peace and love." Undoubtedly, also, revenge or retaliation or even atonement are "pernicious mistakes." Yet if Beatrice had acted with kindness and forbearance, and if she had used the instruments of peace and love instead of appealing to the hatred which the assassins Marzio and Olimpio bore towards her father, she would not, in Shelley's opinion, have been a tragic character.

In selecting the old Italian story as the subject of a tragedy, the nineteenth-century meliorist became involved with a moral problem for which there was no easy solution. Shelley's dilemma in composing *The Cenci* was that of a writer whose moral disapproval of any act involving bloodshed was close to absolute, yet who was compelled, by the very circumstances of his source-story, to make his heroine resort to bloodshed as the means of extirpating a ruthless and triumphant social and domestic evil which was itself close to absolute. If Shelley were really to write a tragedy, it was unthinkable to invent a denouement in which Beatrice succeeded in converting the injurer "from his dark passions" by the exercise of peace and love. His admiration for Beatrice is evident, and it was necessary to engage the sympathies of the audience by painting Beatrice as a fundamentally admirable character. One might be led to conclude on the basis of Shelley's evident admiration that in his view any act which stamps out evil on earth is not only excusable but also desirable. Such a conclusion would, however, be quite in error. Shelley never sanctioned bloodshed, even when the blood was as black as Count Cenci's. To him Beatrice was admirable in spite of, not because of, her taking arms against a sea of troubles, as Hamlet was admirable in spite of, not because of, his act of vengeance. The words which he applies to Beatrice—"a most gentle and amiable being . . . violently thwarted from her nature by the necessity of circumstance and opinion"—could no doubt with equal justice be applied to Shelley's reading of Hamlet's character.[43]

The contrast between *Prometheus* and *The Cenci* is the contrast between what might be and what is. As in the *Prometheus*, Shelley subjected his central figure to all the diabolical rapier-thrusts and bludgeonings that mind and flesh could bear. But this time the reaction was more complicated, as the individual human being is always more complicated than any symbol which can be devised for him. This time no ethical conversion renovated the world. Instead, under indignities of the most horrible kind, a gentle and innocent girl was turned into an efficient machine of vengeance, coolly planning, imperiously executing, denying her part in, and at last calmly dying for the murder of her father. After it was over, history, that "record of crimes and miseries" in human society, moved on as before.

In the summer of 1819, while he was at work on *The Cenci*, Shelley spoke feelingly of "that ever-present Malthus, Necessity," and the implication is, since Malthus was a thoroughgoing economic determinist, that however much Shelley may have trusted in the regenerative powers of the mind, he still regarded some form of Necessity as a strong and perhaps ineluctable force in human social organization.[44] Under the compulsion of such forces, even nom-

---

[43] *The Cenci*, preface.   [44] *Letters*, x, 57.

inally virtuous human beings might be driven from the paths of righteousness. He had already anticipated this position during the preceding year in his review of his wife's novel, *Frankenstein*, where he observed that the crimes and malevolence of the monster flowed "irresistibly from certain causes fully adequate to their production." All these crimes, he urged, were the offspring "of Necessity and Human Nature," and they served to emphasize, dramatically, the direct preachment of Mrs. Shelley's novel: "Treat a person ill, and he will become wicked."[45] Although Beatrice becomes "wicked" only long enough to murder her father and to perjure herself at the trial, the moral of *The Cenci* (despite Shelley's disavowal of a moral purpose) is essentially that which Shelley found in *Frankenstein*.

The point has often been made that *The Cenci*, like the *Prometheus*, is designed more for reading than for acting, mainly because Shelley's interest in characterization is greater than his determination that the action shall move forward. As the play stands, the point is well taken. Not only did Shelley think himself better qualified for the delineation of minute and subtle distinctions of feeling than for what might be called the kinetographic elements of the drama, but he was also quite ready to admit that in *The Cenci* he had laid considerable emphasis on character-analysis. At one point, Orsino begins a long, self-analytic soliloquy with the following remark:

> 'Tis a trick of this same family
> To analyze their own and other minds.
> Such self-anatomy shall teach the will
> Dangerous secrets; for it tempts our powers,
> Knowing what must be thought, and may be done,
> Into the depth of darkest purposes.

Such pauses for "self-anatomy" as Shelley allows to the count, Beatrice, Giacomo, and Orsino serve to reveal their characters with varying degrees of fullness, but there is no doubt that these pauses act to the detriment of the play as a piece of action.

While it appears to have been generally agreed that if Shelley succeeded as a playwright at all, he succeeded chiefly in the area

---

[45] *Prose*, VI, 264. This is not to be confused with Shelley's preface to the novel, which he wrote at Mary's behest.

of character analysis, there have been few attempts to take Shelley at Orsino's word, and to discover precisely what his conception of the leading characters was, or what constitutes the psychological basis of the central struggle. Shelley's desire to anatomize and lay bare the secrets of other minds led him quite literally "into the depth of darkest purposes." To cast what light one can into these depths is basic to a critical study of the play.[46]

The count is a complex character. The widespread belief that his is a motiveless malignity ignores Shelley's careful exposition throughout the play; the father of the Cenci family has three major reasons for his conduct. One basis of his motivation is explicitly a perverted sexual drive. During his first-act conversation with Cardinal Camillo, allusion is made to the count's fiery youth, remorseless manhood, and unrepentant old age. Camillo wonders that such a man is not miserable. But Cenci is miserable only in that the onset of old age has left him less ready than formerly to translate his every thought into immediate action. He is confessedly a "hardened" man. His youth was notorious for sexual promiscuity. When the diet of what he calls "honey" palled, he required stronger stimulants, which he found in the sight and sound of physical suffering in others. But his sadistic appetites took in the end a deeper turn. Now he is satisfied only when he is able to afflict some new victim with extreme mental agony—and be there to watch its outward manifestations. In this last refinement upon his earlier methods of self-gratification, the count has simply habituated himself to what Hawthorne was to exploit fictionally as the unpardonable sin, that is, the desire to finger the soul of another human being, and it appears that the hardening process in the count is now virtually complete. In starting from a groundwork of sexual perversion, Shelley was closely following, though cleaning up considerably, his manuscript source, "The Relation of the Death of the Family of The Cenci," where it is stated that the historical count was a thrice-convicted sodomist.[47]

The second of the count's motives is avarice, a condition of mind the less fortunate for his family in that it frequently comes into

---

[46] The excellent study of the play by Ernest Sutherland Bates (New York, 1908) seems least satisfactory in the chapter devoted to the characters.

[47] The source-manuscript in Shelley's own translation may be consulted in Woodberry's edition of the play, Belles Lettres Series, Boston, 1909.

conflict with his insatiable appetites. Both in the source and in Shelley's play the count buys immunity for his deeds through the payment of large fines to Pope Clement. The voracity of his desires and the sly vigilance of the Pope's agents are such that his fortune—which he values as a guarantee of future immunity from prosecution—is rapidly diminishing. His wish to conserve it partly explains his maltreatment of his sons, who are a drain upon his resources and have lately received a judgment from the Pope which requires the count to support them. Hence the father's delight when the two boys suffer accidental deaths in Spain, and his reason for stealing, by a legal trick, the dowry-money in the possession of his eldest son, Giacomo.

But Shelley is both refining and enlarging upon his source-manuscript, as his development of a third complicating motive shows. The source explains the count's inhuman treatment of Beatrice as a combination of avarice and sexual perversion. He imprisoned his daughter to prevent her following the example of her sister, who had fled the palace, married, and through the Pope's intercession had extracted from the count a good-sized dowry. According to the source, the count's attempts to debauch Beatrice were far more frequent and ugly than Shelley's play indicates: he sought her naked in bed, compelled her presence during his encounters with sundry courtesans, and tried to persuade her "that children born of the commerce of a father and his daughter were all saints." Shelley either omits or merely hints at such horrors because he wishes to make dramatic capital of a single sexual attack. Moreover his portrait of the count subordinates avarice to a third motive, vengeance.

This is not, as Shelley builds it, a simple block-like vengeance, but a whole nervous complex of deeper drives, where the deepest has no place, except by inference, in the source-account. It appears that the count's desire for vengeance arose from his relations with his first wife, who died, according to the source, "after she had given birth to seven unfortunate children." The count had always been a domestic tyrant *in extremis*, and nothing enraged him so much as defiance of his authority, whether as parent or (observe his treatment of his second wife, Lucretia) as husband. Shelley is following his source in saying that from their earliest days he abused his children.[48] When they were too weak to help themselves, Lucretia served them as protector; in recent years the maturing Beatrice has assumed this office. As a result the daughter has been brought into sporadic conflict with a domestic tyrant content only with absolute power over the minds and bodies of his family.

Although the sourcebook is so vague about the vengeance motive that it must be regarded as Shelley's own refinement, the play leaves the impression that the count's hatred of his children and his desire to dominate them stems ultimately from his hatred of their mother. The first wife was "an exceedingly rich lady" who married a complete profligate. If the count in those days was running true to form, he lost no time in establishing his dominance over both her fortune and her person. The fact that she bore him seven children would not in itself suggest a ruthless sexual campaign were it not that the count even now displays his faith that sexual domination is a trustworthy means to the subduing of women. At the close of the banquet scene, the count dismisses his nubile daughter with the boast that he knows a charm to make her meek and mild. The charm he contemplates is sexual intercourse. Why should he imagine that it would render her meek instead of desperately resistant unless his importunate sexuality had produced that very reaction in her mother? It is entirely in character for the count to suppose that through the persecution of his dead wife's offspring he can continue to wreak vengeance upon her memory.

In any event, he is not long in putting his "charm" to work. During his visit to Beatrice's chamber some hours after the banquet he manages, though without overt declaration, to make it clear to Beatrice that he intends to rape her. At that point she is still able to face him down with "a stern and an inquiring brow." But on the following morning, his sudden appearance in a room where she is talking with Lucretia and her younger brother catches her unprepared and opens the first seam in her defiant reserve. Seeing her fear, the count gleefully capitalizes upon it.

> Never again, I think, with fearless eye,
> And brow superior, and unaltered cheek,

[48] The source states that the abuse began while the children "were yet too young to have given him any real cause of displeasure."

And that lip made for tenderness or scorn,
Shalt thou strike dumb the meanest of mankind;
Me least of all. Now get thee to thy chamber!

That his joy comes from the satisfaction of a long-postponed desire to break her spirit is clear enough. That he is even then thinking of her mother becomes evident when he immediately turns to her brother Bernardo with the words of dismissal:

Thou, too, loathed image of thy cursèd mother,
Thy milky, meek face makes me sick with hate!

It is finally worth noting that as soon as Beatrice and Bernardo have gone he immediately consolidates his feeling of complete domestic mastery by cruelly brow-beating his second wife, Lucretia.

A strong desire for vengeance emanating from the conditions of his first marriage would seem therefore to be a third element in the motivation of Count Cenci. The isolation of these motives, which collaborate in many ways to explain the count's actions, indicates that his malignity is by no means motiveless, while if one simply writes him off as a "devilish incarnation of the principle of evil," one ignores Shelley's careful, though not always perfectly explicit, presentation of the true bases of his character.

The usual reading of the character of Beatrice has also been unsatisfactory. A frequent objection to Shelley's conduct of the fifth act is that Beatrice there appears as an ignoble liar. She steadily denies any part in the murder of the count, even though her associates are being tortured for information, and she displays no compunction when she imperiously compels the hired assassin Marzio to withdraw the confession which has implicated her in the crime. Since this behavior appears to contradict the notion that Beatrice embodies the spirit of good, the fifth act is held to be inconsistent with the remainder of the play, and in reading criticisms of the trial scene one sometimes gains the impression that it is not so much Beatrice as the author himself who is up for judgment.

The critical discomfiture over Beatrice's conduct in the fifth act, like the sneaking suspicion that Count Cenci is far too black to be credible, rests upon a failure to appreciate the intricacies of Shelley's intention. In brief that intention is to display the perhaps inevitable corruption of human saintliness by the conspiracy of social circumstances and the continued operation of a vindictive tyranny. At first glance this intention may seem to refute the ethical conclusions of *Prometheus Unbound*. Actually it only brings those conclusions down to earth and works them out in a specific human situation. Where Prometheus, during several millenniums, falls short of ideal standards of conduct, his conversion is at last accomplished through his act of self-reform, and he emerges as "the type of the highest perfection of moral and intellectual nature." In *The Cenci* this order is reversed.[49] Beatrice begins in a state of almost saintly innocence. For long years she lives the Christian life: she is devout, chaste, dutiful, forgiving, and altruistic, and she gains strength and the power to endure through her conviction that she is clothed in the armor of righteousness. Shelley is at some pains to show how, under blows repeated day after day and week after week for years, this armor cracks, until Beatrice is ready to cast it off in favor of the cloak of a murderess. As Prometheus in Act i rejects hatred and vengeance, so Beatrice in Act iii embraces both with a determination born, like that of Prometheus, out of prolonged agony. Shelley still believed in the course followed by Prometheus, and specifically blamed Beatrice for not having done likewise. But he was not now seeking to prove an ethical point—he was writing a tragedy. The tragic flaw in Beatrice, in Shelley's mind, was the crack in the armor of her righteousness.

Something analogous to the hardening of soul which Count Cenci describes as his most conspicuous trait now begins in Beatrice. As in the *Prometheus*, the "conversion" when it comes is both sudden and complete, but Shelley's exposition has carefully prepared the way for it. In the past Beatrice has tried every device of moral persuasion upon her father. At first she endured his malice through an innocent belief in the rightness of paternal judgment; then she sought to bend him with love and tears; next she tried prayer; then she petitioned the Pope; finally, at the banquet, she came desperately into the open with a plea for aid from the assembled guests. All these efforts came to nothing because Beatrice had the misfortune to exist in a social milieu from which scruple was absent.

[49] Compare Shelley's review of *Frankenstein, or the Modern Prometheus*.

But this is not the only restraint upon Shelley's heroine: she is also held back by her own conscience. When she asks herself the crucial question—"Where shall I turn?"—one wonders why she has not turned to flight. She is, of course, a prisoner in the Cenci Palace just as certainly as Tasso was a prisoner in Santa Anna; yet even if this were not so, she would have chosen to remain: her stepmother and her younger brother must have her assistance. This sense of duty, as well as her religious fear of the consequences, have prevented flight by suicide. Yet she is not defeatist, partly because she believes her armor is strong. As late as the banquet scene she retains her self-possession, and even offers to pray with her father for the salvation of his soul.

Her evident fear of the count on the morning after the banquet is the first sign that her will to endure is beginning to give way before her father's relentless pressure. Her appearance that morning is so deeply altered that Lucretia at once observes it: an unseen visitor's lifting of the doorlatch induces a hysterical response. When the visitor turns out to be, not the count, but a messenger bearing the false report that the Pope has rejected her petition, she settles into an utter depression of spirits, a dead center of indifference best summarized in her statement, " 'Twere better not to struggle any more." With the count's arrival, his new found mastery becomes evident. The formerly imperious girl cringes at sight of him, and he is not long in following up his advantage. Sometime in the course of that very night he completes his dominance with an overt sexual attack.

It is the supreme irony of the drama that the means chosen by the count to establish final mastery are the best means he could have fixed on to harden Beatrice's soul to the point where she is ready to do murder. Out of the darkest experience of her life, the temporary derangement caused by her father's attack, Beatrice rises with a resolution:

> Ay, something must be done;
> What, yet I know not.

Suicide is out of the question, and legal action is quickly rejected. Murder, the bold redress of the insufferably wronged, remains.

In making herself the prime agent of her father's destruction, Beatrice explicitly rejects the moral position to which she has hitherto been devoted. There must be no forbearance, no remorse. For the time being she enters that state of implacable hardness which is necessary to the fulfillment of her purpose. She becomes, in her own phrase, "the angel of [God's] wrath," and her only rule of conduct, until just before her execution, is to play a ruthless game to the top of her bent—intriguing, bribing, conniving, and lying, without regret, without remorse, without pity. Only once, as she hears her death-sentence (to which she responds almost in the words of Shakespeare's Claudio in the comparable section of *Measure for Measure*) does her hard demeanor show signs of breaking down under the force of fear. Twice her buried life rises to the surface. Once, with Lucretia's head on her shoulder, she sings the equivalent of Desdemona's "Willow Song"; again, readying their necks for the executioner's axe, she and Lucretia bind up each other's hair, quietly, tenderly, and finally. For the rest, neither the trial judge, nor Marzio, nor any of the other culprits is able to penetrate her self-possession. Lady Macbeth, summoning to her breast the murdering ministers, is not more willfully callous to all accepted moral codes than she. Nor is the comparison a mere literary ornament. Every reader of *The Cenci* and *Macbeth* knows how closely Shelley modeled the count's murder, and its aftermath, upon the murder of Duncan. It is very probable that through most of Acts III, IV, and V, Shelley wrote of Beatrice with one eye on Lady Macbeth.[50]

If Shelley's conception of character is in some respects Shakespearean, his management of the action reveals influence from classical tragedy. Bates believes that the conduct of the scenes, which usually consist "in a dialogue between two persons, or of a

[50] That Beatrice resembles Lady Macbeth in her complete resolution and Desdemona in her few moments of tenderness are points which seem to have escaped Bates, whose treatment of Elizabethan and particularly of Shakespearean parallels is otherwise excellent. In his study of *The Cenci*, Bates lists some 13 other passages where Shelley is following *Hamlet, Othello, Lear, Macbeth, Measure for Measure, King John, Richard III, Twelfth Night,* and *The Merchant of Venice. Op. cit.,* pp. 54-55. He observes also that Orsino's machinations resemble those of De Flores in Middleton's *The Changeling,* although Iago seems as good a parallel. He suggests that the trial scene may owe something to the trial of Vittoria in Webster's *The White Devil.* He compares the prison scenes in Act V to those in Milman's *Fazio,* which Shelley saw performed, with Miss O'Neill as Bianca, in 1818. A more recent consideration of Shakespeare's influence on *The Cenci* is in D. L. Clark, "Shelley and Shakespeare," *PMLA* 54 (1939). *The Cenci* is discussed on pp. 278-286. See also S. R. Watson, "*Othello* and *The Cenci,*" *PMLA* 55 (1940), 611-614.

succession of such dialogues with changed speakers," is more Greek than Elizabethan.[51] Although the idea deserves mention, it should be pointed out that Shelley had handled in this way every major scene in every major poem from *Queen Mab* to *Prometheus Unbound*, so that habit rather than classical influence probably fixed his course in *The Cenci*.

A much clearer instance of classical influence appears in Shelley's handling of the count's fourth-act *hybris*, which so closely resembles that of Jupiter in the third act of *Prometheus Unbound* as to suggest that Shelley was recalling his most recent verse-drama as he led Count Cenci nearer and nearer the brink of disaster. Classical *hybris*, as in the *Hippolytus* of Euripides, is always charged with dramatic irony. Jupiter's fall from the ramparts of Olympus occurs just after he has smugly supposed that Demogorgon's arrival will confirm and perpetuate his nearly absolute dominion over the minds of men. But the audience, which has already overheard Asia's interview with Demogorgon, knows all along that *Ate* is about to descend upon the master of Olympus. When Count Cenci takes his family to Castle Petrella, high on a rock among the loneliest Apennines, he believes himself as secure as Jupiter upon Olympus. There he plans the final stroke in his attack on Beatrice—the establishment of his supremacy not merely over her body (which he accomplished with the assault in Rome) but also over her mind. His single aim at Petrella is to force Beatrice's agreement to his incestuous suit, and thus "to poison and corrupt her soul," to break her stubborn will

> Which, by its own consent, shall stoop as low
> As that which drags it down.

In this intention he is in effect seeking to attain a Jupiter-like power, for it is Jupiter's dominion over the mind of man which has kept Prometheus bound to the rock. The count's anticipation of success is as firm as that of Jupiter. The real peak of his *hybris* is reached in the midst of his curse upon Beatrice. When the awed Lucretia reminds him that God punishes such prayers, the count tempts Necessity with a supreme histrionic boast: "He does his will, I mine!" Two scenes later he is dead.

[51] Bates, *op. cit.*, p. 57.

In spite of its lengthening stage history, *The Cenci* has always been treated more like an heirloom extracted from a glass case for temporary exhibit than like a piece of serious stagecraft.[52] If it were ever to be launched as a popular play, it would undoubtedly require cutting, transposition of scenes, and some other editorial tinkering, particularly among the supporting characters. Shelley's interest is so closely centered in the count and Beatrice that his development of the other *dramatis personae* seems, as the play stands, only slightly better than adequate. The prelate Orsino emerges as a kind of minor Iago, driven by his unrequited love for Beatrice to implement a murder through which he hopes to bring her into his debt and therefore into his power. Yet her dependence upon his machinations is so slight that his role could be eliminated without doing violence to the central story. The misfortunes of Beatrice's surviving brothers, and especially those of Giacomo, are intended to deepen the audience's sense of the count's viciousness as an adversary. Yet, like Lucretia, they are little more than foils for the heroine, while their softness and naïveté are far less engaging than Beatrice's purposefulness, so that one is more likely to scorn than to sympathize with them. If *The Cenci* were to be cut to three-act length, most of its weaknesses could be eliminated, and in view of the economy and force with which Shelley handles the central story when he is giving it his undivided attention, there is no reason why, given effective actors, the play should not succeed. Shelley has fully realized his avowed aim of increasing the ideal and diminishing the actual horror of the events "so that the pleasure which arises from the poetry which exists in these tempestuous sufferings and crimes may mitigate the pain of the contemplation of the moral deformity from which they spring."[53]

By and large, *The Cenci*, like the other dialogue-poems, presented Shelley's view of the human predicament as it could be found in history. In *Rosalind and Helen* and the two stories drawn from the Italian past he chose to work in the area of domestic

[52] For an excellent, and probably exhaustive, account of the stage history of *The Cenci*, see the article of that title by K. N. Cameron and Horst Frenz in *PMLA* 60 (1945), 1080-1105.

[53] The quotation is from Shelley's preface to *The Cenci*. It should be kept in mind in interpreting Shelley's statement that "incest is, like many other incorrect things, a very poetical circumstance." *Letters*, x, 124. This statement was made on Nov. 16, 1819, in the course of some comments on Calderon's *Cabellos de Absolom*.

tragedy, projecting on a lesser scale, and in essentially nonpolitical terms, the same sort of unendurable, unrelenting oppression of the weak by the strong, and of the principled by the unscrupulous, which he had writ large in *The Revolt of Islam* and *Prometheus Unbound*. The impression to be gained from these poems is not that of an untroubled world. Malicious intrigue, abuse of power, cruelty, betrayal, false witness, corruption, madness, lust, avarice, and murder: these were the red letters upon the calendar of history as Shelley viewed it, and he was to discover further corroboration for his views in the state of England during the years 1819-1820, even to the extent of implying an ominous parallel between nineteenth-century England and sixteenth-century Italy.

6

THE MYTHOLOGY OF POLITICS

These . . . are awful times. The tremendous question is now agitating, whether a military and judicial despotism is to be established by our present rulers, or some form of government less unfavourable to the real and permanent interests of all men is to arise from the conflict of passions now gathering to overturn them. We cannot hesitate which party to embrace; and whatever revolutions are to occur, though oppression should change names and names cease to be oppressions, our party will be that of liberty and the oppressed. —SHELLEY TO HUNT, NOVEMBER, 1819

· I ·

ALTHOUGH Shelley assured the Gisbornes in November, 1819, that he was "full of all kinds of literary plans," there is no indication that he had in mind any works of such magnitude as the two dramas, *Prometheus Unbound* and *The Cenci*, which he had sent off to London, one in manuscript and one in print, a few weeks earlier.[1] His apparent readiness to be blown in whatever direction the winds of chance or doctrine might dictate could probably be traced partly to his simple relief at having completed two major works, and partly to the fact that, for the time being, he had said effectively the more difficult things which he had to say. The looseness of his ends and the paucity of his means are indicated by his momentary determination to compose other poems after the manner of *Julian and Maddalo*: that is, to multiply into a tetralogy a kind of poem of which even then he entertained no very high opinion.[2] As the scene of his conversation-poem had been Venice

---

[1] *Letters*, x, 121.

[2] He thought of it as a "little Poem" (*Letters*, x, 68) and later spoke of it as a "*sermo pedestris* way of treating human nature." (*Ibid.*, 168.)

(and Tasso's cell at Ferrara), so he thought of doing three companion pieces, using Rome, Florence, and Naples as his locales, and as his subject matter such "dreadful or beautiful realities" as he had developed in *Julian and Maddalo*.[3] Nothing came of this project. But the reformer's instinct was still in him, and while the wheel on which he had fashioned the *Prometheus* and *The Cenci* still turned with the dying force of its own momentum, he was able to strike off with careless ease two poems which the state of England in the fall of 1819 seemed to justify. In the summer of 1820 he did another which was marked by a similar mood and arose from a similar impulse; and in the fall of 1821, activated this time less by critical fervor than by a determination to glorify the cause of liberty wherever it might show signs of renascence, he wrote the last of his major political poems.

The comparative ease with which *The Masque of Anarchy, Peter Bell the Third, Oedipus Tyrannus,* and *Hellas* were turned out is indicated by the fact that although together they are considerably longer than the first three acts of *Prometheus Unbound,* over which Shelley had intermittently labored for the greater part of eight months, they required, among them, probably no more than eight weeks of his time. On September 5, 1819, Shelley read a newspaper account of the "execrable enormities" which in mid-August had taken place at Manchester; by the 23rd he had completed and sent to Ollier the ninety-two stirring stanzas of his response, *The Masque of Anarchy*.[4] Towards the end of October he began a satire on Wordsworth's *Peter Bell* which, like Rip Van Winkle, had suddenly started up in the preceding spring after a twenty-year sleep in manuscript. In "a few days" Shelley set down and Mary was set to copying the 765 lines of his extravaganza, *Peter Bell the Third*.[5] Precisely ten months later, having followed with amused irritation the story of the Prince Regent's attempt to keep his errant queen from sharing in the coronation ceremonies, Shelley devoted a week to the business of dragging through a literary pigsty the royal family's already well-smudged reputation, and emerged with a two-act mock tragedy, *Oedipus Tyrannus*.

[3] *Letters*, x, 135.
[4] For an exhaustive account of the massacre and Shelley's reaction to it, see A. S. Walker, "Peterloo, Shelley, and Reform," *PMLA* 40 (1925), 128-164.
[5] *Ca.* Oct. 24-28. See *Shelley and Mary*, I, 421. It was sent to Hunt, Nov. 2.

The time spent upon the composition of *Hellas*, his only other lyrical drama, is uncertain, but could hardly have been great. It was virtually finished by October 22, 1821, roughly fourteen months after the mock tragedy. On the 25th, Edward Williams baptized it. It was copied out between November 6 and 10, and then sent directly off to Charles Ollier, since Shelley believed, not without reason, that whatever interest the poem might excite depended upon its immediate publication, while the revolution in Greece was still current.

These were all occasional items, post-box poems, or (in the phrase from Horace which Shelley used to describe the first decade of Byron's work) "disjecti membra poetae." The first three were elicited by Shelley's indignation, variously grave or gay, over the cumulative stupidities of the monarch, his queen, and his petty officials, and at what Shelley regarded as the almost equally reprehensible failure of Wordsworth to maintain his political and artistic integrity. The fourth, though marked off from the others by a return to the grand manner of the earlier Shelley, and from all but *The Masque of Anarchy* by its high seriousness, is of a piece with the other political poems of this two-year period. Each of these poems contains passages of considerable power, chiefly in the lyrical mode; all are marked by a looseness of structure and an openness of texture which betray the relative slightness of Shelley's care.

Yet Shelley had a more serious design in writing these and other shorter poems on political subjects than his apparent carelessness would suggest. In the *Prometheus* he had been able to imagine in titanic terms what might happen if all men were to succeed in the great task of self-reform. But he had been obliged to go outside history in order to fabricate this vision. With *The Cenci* he had reentered history, in the middle of an extremely dark chapter, and had imagined his way into a situation where even a person of such fine sensibilities as Beatrice was hardened, by the conspiracy of social circumstances and her father's moral deformity, into an efficient murderess. What engaged Shelley's attention in the two years following the *Prometheus* and *The Cenci* was contemporary history: the utter moral deformity of England's rulers and the widespread (though perhaps corrigible) ignorance of the oppressed majority. In the condition of England during the autumn of 1819, and in the condition of Europe for two years thereafter, Shelley needed no more than his liberal's nose to detect a malodorous conspiracy of social circumstances which seemed in England to forebode armed insurrection and civil war, and which elsewhere saw these forebodings become bloody actualities. Shelley's serious purpose in writing the political poems on England was to head off civil war by unifying liberal thought among all classes; his purpose in writing the *Hellas* was to predict and glorify the coming liberty and the coming peace in a country where, as it seemed to him, the spirit of freedom was far stronger than in his native land.

Even if Shelley had not shown, by the composition of such prose tracts as *A Philosophical View of Reform* and the open letter on Richard Carlile's alleged blasphemies, that he had a completely rational basis for his views on the cause and cure of England's ills, and if his only remedy had been the poems here under consideration, it would still be unwise to accuse him of political naïveté. The effectiveness of inspirational or satiric poetry, even the merest doggerel, during a time of social storm and stress, is well enough known, and if Shelley's youthful experiences in Ireland did not make him a seasoned campaigner, they had not left him completely unaware of the variety of organizational techniques open to the serious participant in political action. Nothing written only to be read could be expected to have the value of such forthright political action as was represented by "Orator" Henry Hunt's assemblage of workers on the field of Peterloo, particularly since the arrant stupidity of the militarists, in hacking their way through a dense crowd well strewn with women and children, provided the working classes with a large group of political martyrs. But Shelley was in Italy, attempting to operate on a sick country by proxy only, and was obliged to employ those techniques which were readiest to his hand. It is a sign of his deliberate intent that his operative techniques showed so wide a range as is represented by *The Masque, Peter Bell, Oedipus,* and *Hellas.*

· II ·

THE MASQUE OF ANARCHY is the longest of a group of six poems which were the immediate result of Shelley's attempt to promote "a frank and spirited union of the advocates for liberty."[6] He knew very well that liberal elements were not confined to any one financial or educational bracket: English gentlemen like Lord Byron and himself, English bourgeois like Leigh Hunt, and English proletarians like Henry Hunt bore sufficient witness to the spread of liberal ideas. But Shelley wished his words of exhortation to penetrate as deep as possible into the body politic, and he gave particular attention to the problem of communication. As recently as the preceding summer he had agreed with the proposition that "in order to move men to true sympathy," one must use "the familiar language of men," although he had immediately specified that "it must be the real language of men in general, and not that of any particular class."[7] In such a nominally Christian country as England, the vocabulary and syntax of the English Bible, suitably purged of the less familiar archaisms, will come very close to representing the *lingua communis* which Shelley sought to use as an instrument of communication. This may account for the semi-Biblical tone of these half-dozen political poems. By the same token Shelley sought to call into service the familiar songs of the people. The "Song to the Men of England," had it ever been hawked among the British working-classes, could have been chanted to almost any simple, stanzaic hymn-tune.

> Men of England, wherefore plough
> For the lords who lay ye low?
> Wherefore weave with toil and care
> The rich robes your tyrants wear?
>
> . . . .
>
> Wherefore, Bees of England, forge
> Many a weapon, chain, and scourge,
> That these stingless drones may spoil
> The forced produce of your toil?

If ploughs and forges are rare in the average beehive, the fact is of little consequence to a successful political song. Shelley's version of the national anthem is somewhat more careful of its images. Based on the notion that Liberty, England's erstwhile queen, had been done to death in the course of recent months, and could be

---

[6] *Letters*, x, 118.   [7] Preface to *The Cenci*.

revived only through the concerted efforts of her bereaved subjects, it was made to be sung to the tune of "God Save the King."

> God prosper, speed, and save,
> God raise from England's grave
> Her murdered Queen!
> Pave with swift victory
> The steps of Liberty,
> Whom Britons own to be
> Immortal Queen.
>
> . . . .
>
> Be her eternal throne
> Built in our hearts alone—
> God save the Queen!
> Let the oppressor hold
> Canopied seats of gold;
> She sits enthroned of old
> O'er our hearts Queen.

Although the "Lines Written During the Castlereagh Admin-
istration" and the angry invocation "To Sidmouth and Castlereagh" are less successful than the preceding pair as incendiary
chants, they employ the black-and-white name-calling strategy
familiar to many veteran orators. The first poses as an epithalamium for the wedding day of the Tyrant and his paramour, Ruin.
In the second, the ministers addressed are compared to carrion
crows, vultures, scorpions, wolves, and vipers, as well as to a shark
and a dog-fish wrinkling their gills in happy anticipation of a feast
as they follow in the wake of a trans-Atlantic slave ship. Having
begun his career as viewer-with-alarm in the public interest some
seven years earlier, Shelley was by this date well acquainted with
the less subtle techniques of the political pamphleteer.

He made a sharp mental distinction between poems like *The
Masque*, which he classified with the "exoteric species," and such
works as *Prometheus Unbound* or *The Witch of Atlas* which,
though broadly political in purpose since both were concerned
with moral reformation, were presented in a manner designed to
appeal only to the "esoteric few." In sending off his poem for what
he hoped would be quick publication he asked Hunt to print it,
not in the elegant *Indicator*, which was generally dedicated to the

fine arts, but in the more down-to-earth and "practical" *Examiner*, where it would presumptively attract the attention of the liberal-minded.[8]

Had Leigh Hunt printed the fifth of Shelley's poems he might well have spent another term in jail. The sonnet indicts the dragoons for perpetrating, the Prince Regent for countenancing, the Law for allowing, and the Church for ignoring the Manchester massacre, and does so in terms so severe, so candid, and so seditious that in mailing the piece to Hunt on December 23, Shelley remarked, "I don't expect you to publish it, but you may show it to whom you please."[9] As a measure of Shelley's nausea at the thought of the blood-soaked mud in Peterloo Field, it was worth showing and is worth reprinting, though it is a poor sonnet.

> An old, mad, blind, despised and dying king;
> Princes, the dregs of their dull race, who flow
> Through public scorn—mud from a muddy spring;
> Rulers, who neither see, nor feel, nor know,
> But leechlike to their fainting country cling,
> Till they drop, blind in blood, without a blow;
> A people starved and stabbed in the untilled field;
> An army which liberticide and prey
> Makes as a two-edged sword to all who wield;
> Golden and sanguine laws which tempt and slay;
> Religion Christless, Godless—a book sealed;
> A Senate—Time's worst statute unrepealed,
> Are graves from which a glorious Phantom may
> Burst to illumine our tempestuous day.

The devices employed in *The Masque of Anarchy* run parallel, on a scale only slightly more elevated, to those of the lesser poems of the same period: simple allegorical structure, plain moral exhortation, analysis blocked out in terms too large to miss, a powerful organizational anthem, and, clad in armor bright

[8] *Letters*, x, 129. Mary's note to the poems of 1819 expressly states that Shelley had an idea of publishing a series of poems addressed directly to the people and commemorating their wrongs. "He wrote a few, but in those days of prosecution for libel they could not be printed. They are not among the best of his productions, a writer being always shackled when he endeavors to write down to the comprehension of those who could not understand or feel a highly imaginative style."

[9] *Letters*, x, 138. Dec. 23, 1819. The Cambridge edition of Shelley's poems, ed. G. E. Woodberry, p. 365, errs in giving the date as *November* 23.

enough to illuminate the scene, the glorious Phantom of Liberty.

Shelley might have learned from Wordsworth or Coleridge the trick of the simple beginning. He opens *The Masque* with a stanza close to the level of doggerel, yet bare and monosyllabic enough to arrest the eye and beat a tattoo upon the ear-drum.

> As I lay asleep in Italy,
> There came a voice from over the sea,
> And with great power it forth led me
> To walk in the visions of Poesy.

Although he does not subsequently commit another such inversion as that of line three, the quoted stanza typifies the studied simplicity of his narrative manner throughout the poem. But after the first quatrain, with a speed which recalls Coleridge's famous dream, he quickly enters the realm of apocalyptic vision.

The vision for which he provides a mythological fabric in the first thirty-six stanzas of *The Masque* is a development in miniature of the image of the four horsemen in the *Book of Revelation*, with such Petrarchan or Spenserian modifications as suit his purpose.[10] In triumphal procession at the height of their power, the four horsemen go a progress across the fields of England. Although their names are Murder, Fraud, Hypocrisy, and Anarchy, the first three riders in this "ghastly masquerade" are said to resemble Castlereagh, Eldon, and Sidmouth. The resemblance is obviously not coincidental. Yet Shelley does not similarly identify Anarchy with a specific historical personage, and unless we are to suppose that this skeletal figure, who wears a "kingly crown," represents the prince regent denuded of his upholstery, it seems wisest to assume what the whole conduct of the poem seems to bear out, that Shelley intended his four horsemen, like those of St. John, to be concepts rather than people. Anarchy, astride a blood-smeared white horse (the pale horse of *Revelation*) is Dictatorship posing as Divine Law, or cynical political Force wearing the mask of Necessity.

---

[10] The procession recalls several of those which Spenser scattered through *The Faerie Queene*, but especially that of the Seven Deadly Sins. (*F.Q.*, i, iv, 21-43.) White, *Shelley*, ii, 105, 576, compares "the triumphs or masques of Petrarch," noting Mary's journal-entry for Sept. 17, 1819: Shelley "reads the 'Trionfe della Morte' aloud in the evening."

The real clue to Shelley's simple meaning, however, is that each of these evil concepts is wearing a disguise. For *The Masque of Anarchy* is actually a masquerade, in which all the more vicious (because inwardly destructive) evils which beset human society have managed to assume the garb of ordinarily respectable individuals: Murder looks smooth in his wide cloak; Fraud wears an ermine gown like a Lord Chancellor; Hypocrisy clothes himself "with the Bible as with Light"; Anarchy, though his pallor suggests "Death in the Apocalypse," could otherwise pass for a scion of the House of Hanover, and a befuddled and bedazzled people loudly acclaim him both as God and as Law.

As in other masquerades, however, the moment of unmasking arrives, revealing that the people have been only ironically right, for Anarchy is a God of Misrule operating under the Law of Force. Just as the Leader of the cavalcade directs his henchmen to seize the Bank of England and the Tower of London, and begins to move in upon his "pensioned parliament," a maniac maiden named Hope, the last descendant of many hungry generations, hurls herself in the path of the procession. She misses being trampled into oblivion only through the intercession of the magnificent winged figure of resurgent Liberty, arrayed in shining mail, who rises momentarily between the maiden and her foes. Thereupon the processional quickly becomes a recessional, Anarchy lies vanquished upon the field, and the pale horse of Death, "tameless as wind," takes his departure.

The remaining fifty-six stanzas of the poem add up to a plea for another Peterloo, with the difference that this one will be decisive. Shelley writes an educational and inspiration anthem, comparable in some respects to the *Marseillaise*, in which slavery and liberty are successively defined in homely terms which Shelley intended all workers to understand. These definitions are followed by a concrete remedial proposal: an assembly shall take place "on some spot of English ground," with all "the fearless and the free" in attendance—that same "spirited union of the advocates of liberty" which Shelley promised to promote. There, on the field of a new Peterloo, the people are to solemnize their declaration of independence. There, too, although waves of horsemen with gleaming scimitars are unleashed against them, they are to stand side by side with folded arms, defenseless except for their mutual resolution and the probability that their assailants will retire in shame in the end. The slaughter of the advocates of liberty will unify the nation against the tyrants.

> And these words shall then become
> Like oppression's thundered doom,
> Ringing through each heart and brain,
> Heard again—again—again!
> Rise like lions after slumber
> In unvanquishable number!
> Shake your chains to earth, like dew
> Which in sleep had fallen on you—
> Ye are many, they are few!

In short, *The Masque of Anarchy* is a proposal for passive resistance by a united popular front.

It has sometimes been suggested that Shelley contradicted himself in urging the oppressed majority to rise up against the few "like lions after slumber," only to instruct them in the next breath not to fight. There is a certain fault in the image, assuredly, yet Shelley was trying to walk the ethical knife-edge which was sharpened by his hatred of violence. To him the united popular front seemed to make any other big stick unnecessary, and he was simply putting into verse the conception of strength in union. The clue to his position may be found in his remark to Hunt: "The great thing to do is . . . to inculcate with fervour both the right of resistance and the duty of forbearance," a remark which provides an extremely interesting commentary upon his most recent tragedy.[11] When he read with mounting indignation the packet from Peacock in which the Manchester affair was described, and while he awaited news of the British people's reaction to such "bloody murderous oppression," he felt so much like Beatrice Cenci after her father's gross assault that he quoted in a letter the very words he had put into her mouth as she reeled with horror: "Something must be done. What, yet I know not."[12] If the news from England made him feel like a woman raped under the foulest circumstances, however, he conspicuously refused to sanction the error he had condemned in the parricidal Beatrice. The doctrine preached in *The Masque of Anarchy* is not only the right of resistance to unen-

[11] *Letters*, x, 130-131. [12] *The Cenci*, iii, i, 86-87.

durable oppression, a course which Beatrice had bravely followed up to the moment of her father's assault, but also the duty of forbearance, which she had finally, and as Shelley saw it tragically, rejected.

Not one of the six poems here considered was published in Shelley's lifetime. Medwin first printed the epithalamium for Tyranny and Ruin and the poem on the bestial aspects of Sidmouth and Castlereagh in 1832. *The Song to the Men of England*, the sonnet, and the national anthem appeared under Mary Shelley's editorship in 1839. Hunt did not print *The Masque of Anarchy* in his *Examiner* either in 1819 or later. Instead he edited the poem with a historical introduction and brought it out as a pamphlet ten years after Shelley's death, explaining his failure to publish the poem in the *Examiner* by saying that in his opinion at that time "the public at large had not become sufficiently discerning to do justice to the sincerity and kindheartedness of the spirit that walked in this flaming robe of verse." Perhaps not, since Hunt, the journalist in England, could assess public opinion somewhat better than Shelley, the poet in Italy. But another reason, which is no slur upon Hunt's integrity but rather a compliment to his hardearned caution, could probably be found in the British proverb, "Once bitten, twice shy."

· III ·

THE irony which hid Shelley's political thoughts was continued in the instance of *Peter Bell the Third*. As *The Masque of Anarchy* had originated through the effect of a newspaper story upon Shelley, so he first heard of Wordsworth's *Peter Bell* in the columns of Leigh Hunt's *Examiner*. The publication of this poem in late April, 1819, created a minor stir in London, where Wordsworth's pontifical manner and his habit of hurling conversational aspersions at his contemporaries had for some years both amused and irritated men like Hunt, Keats, and John Hamilton Reynolds. When Reynolds heard that Wordsworth's *Peter Bell* had been scheduled for April publication, he hastily wrote a skit, *Peter Bell: A Lyrical Ballad*, which he brought out under a Taylor and Hessey imprint on or about April 15, some days before the appearance of Wordsworth's poem.[13] In order to ensure the success of his venture, Reyn-

---

[13] Keats, *Letters*, ed. M. Buxton Forman (London, 1931), II, 345.

olds asked Keats to bring the lampoon to Editor Hunt's attention, a request with which Keats complied by writing a short notice for the *Examiner* of April 25.[14] The Reynolds pamphlet opens with a boastful preface, signed "W.W." where the bogus Wordsworth is represented as saying that it has been his aim and his achievement to "deduce moral thunder from buttercups." The remainder of the preface follows the same general line. The poem itself shows an aged Peter Bell, poking about in Cumberland churchyard, laboriously spelling out, with appropriate comments, the epitaphs of Simon Lee, Betty Foy, Alice Fell, Goody Blake, Harry Gill, and other Wordsworthian characters, until he is brought up short by a stone inscribed:

Here lieth W. W.
Who never more will trouble you, trouble you.

Keats' reaction to Reynolds' joke was one part amusement to three parts of regret that it had been perpetrated, so that the tone of his review, as he tries to speak a good word for Reynolds without unduly disparaging Wordsworth, is equivocal. But when Leigh Hunt reviewed the real *Peter Bell* in the following issue, he was much more forthright, mercilessly ridiculing the conclusion, wherein the rough and cruel Peter has turned soft and pious, as a reformation induced about equally by "harebells and hell-fire."[15] Hunt's determination to find something sinister in Wordsworth's innocuous work was such that his commentary spilled over into the May 9 issue of the *Examiner*. There he praised Shelley's *Rosalind and Helen* much more highly than it deserved by contrasting it with *Peter Bell*, which he damned rather more severely than he need have done. "The object of Mr. Wordsworth's administrations of melancholy," said he, "is to make men timid, servile, and . . . selfish; that of Mr. Shelley's, to render them fearless, independent, affectionate, infinitely social. You might be made to worship a devil by the process of Mr. Wordsworth's philosophy; by that of Mr. Shelley you might reseat a dethroned goodness. The Poet of

---

[14] *Ibid.*, 354. The early draft of the *Examiner* notice may be read here, and the final version in the *Examiner*, No. 591 (April 25, 1819), 270. Reynolds wrote another parody of Wordsworth, called *The Dead Asses: A Lyrical Ballad*. See W. S. Ward, "Wordsworth, The 'Lake' Poets, and their Contemporary Magazine Critics, 1798-1820," *SP* 42 (1945), 951.

[15] *Examiner*, No. 592 (May 2, 1819), 282-283.

the Lakes always carries his egotism and 'saving knowledge' about with him, and . . . will go in a pet and plant himself by the side of the oldest tyrannies and slaveries; our Cosmopolite-Poet would evidently die with pleasure to all personal identity, could he but see his fellow-creatures reasonable and happy." The contrast emphasized throughout is between Wordsworthian egotism as sanctioning tyranny and slavery, and Shelleyan altruism as dedicated to freedom and the full-sided development of the individual.

The "Cosmopolite-Poet," situated on the peripheries of the Cockney group, belatedly rang his own changes on the Bells of Reynolds and Wordsworth. The subject fitted his own political interests in the fall of 1819 because, by Leigh Hunt's account, Wordsworth was a turncoat who had allied himself with tyrants. The pertinent copies of the *Examiner* seem to have reached Shelley at Leghorn in June. He was amused, but evidently not immediately inspired, for it was not until October that he added his own castigations to those of Reynolds and Hunt, taking from the latter's *Examiner* articles of May 2 and May 9 a number of cues for his own poem.[16]

Shelley plays with his subject partly like a child with a new game and partly like a philosopher with a syllogism. He parodies as precisely as possible Wordsworth's scheme of presentation, with a prefatory motto, a prologue, and a division of the poem into several parts. Wordsworth dedicated his poem to "Robert Southey, Esq., P.L." (for Poet Laureate); Shelley addressed his to "Thomas

[16] The date when Shelley received and read the *Examiners* for April 25, May 2, and May 9, is my surmise. According to Mary, a critique on Wordsworth's *Peter Bell* (she does not mention the critique on Reynolds' *Peter Bell*) "reached us at Leghorn." See her note, *Collected Poems*, 2nd ed., 1839. The Shelleys were at Leghorn proper in mid-June, though they continued to live nearby until Sept. 30. It is possible, if Mary meant by Leghorn the city *and* its environs, that Shelley did not see Hunt's critique until later in the summer. Yet it normally required only two weeks for London mail to reach Leghorn (see *Letters*, x, 60, 77-78), and Shelley evidently received several numbers of the *Examiner* together from time to time. (See *Letters*, x, 74.) Shelley's dedicatory epistle states, "Mr. Examiner Hunt presented me to two of the Mr. Bells." This might be interpreted to mean that Hunt also forwarded copies of the two poems. Shelley had evidently seen a copy of Wordsworth's poem before he wrote his own. The stanza about the people in the parlor, "all silent and all damned," which he used as a motto to his *Peter Bell the Third*, appeared in the first two editions of Wordsworth's poem (both 1819) but was subsequently deleted in order not to offend "the pious." I suspect from his characterization of the manner of the poem in his prologue that Shelley had also seen a copy of the Reynolds parody. The only other internal evidence is the fact that both Reynolds and Shelley rib Wordsworth as the creator of Betty Foy.

Brown, Esq. H.F." (for Historian of the Fudges).[17] The letter to Southey descants upon modern criticism; Shelley's letter to Brown playfully supposes that "when London shall be a habitation of bitterns, when St. Paul's and Westminster Abbey shall stand, shapeless and nameless ruins, in the midst of an unpeopled marsh, . . . some transatlantic commentator will be weighing in the scales of some new . . . system of criticism the respective merits of the Bells and the Fudges and their historians." In the prologue Shelley plays with the idea of the three ages of man. Reynolds' *Peter Bell*, having beaten Wordsworth's to publication, is labeled the "antenatal Peter"; Wordsworth's shows the "polygamic potter" in his earthly guise; and Shelley's poem represents Peter as having descended into Hell after death.

In general outline the poem looks like as severe an attack upon Wordsworth as Hunt had made in the columns of the *Examiner*. Taking up where Wordsworth left off, Shelley pretends that Peter's self-reform was both short-lived and superficial; when the hero dies, therefore, the devil has no difficulty in buying Peter's soul and in persuading the ex-potter to become his footman. Hell is a populous city not unlike London, full of lawyers, confidence men, and flirts, and the devil occupies a mansion in Pandemonium's Grosvenor Square. Among the guests who attend the *petits-soupers* of Peter's new master and are served by Peter the footman is a "subtle-souled psychologist" (Coleridge), whose table-talk renders the poetic calling so attractive to Peter that he gives the devil notice in order to devote himself to writing. But the devil, with a craftiness worthy of a Tory angel to the *Quarterly*, persuades the reviewers so to lambaste Peter's first book that the novice turns sour. He is soon writing hortatory odes to the devil himself:

> Slash them at Manchester,
> Glasgow, Leeds, and Chester;
> Drench all with blood from Avon to Trent.
> Let thy body-guard yeomen
> Hew down babes and women
> And laugh with bold triumph till heaven be rent.

---

[17] Early in July, 1818, Peacock sent Shelley a box of books and magazines, including "The Fudge Family in Paris." See his letter of July 5, 1818, in *Shelley and Mary*, I, 293.

Upon the devil's demise, therefore, Peter is promoted to his place, becoming a thoroughgoing, knee-bending, bourgeois Tory. But he pays for his new glory by contracting dullness, a writer's disease so infectious to readers that it has presently set to yawning all the inhabitants within some 2,000 cubic miles of Peter Bell.

Shelley did not choose to attach his own name to the piece, and implied that he wished to remain anonymous because he did not consider the poem worthy of him. But if the poem had been published at this time, and if Wordsworth had chosen to institute a libel suit, the implications of the poem with respect to Wordsworth (particularly the broad hint that he approved the Manchester massacre) might have brought Shelley once again into the toils of Chancery. It is just possible that a realization of this possibility confirmed Shelley in his decision to remain anonymous.

From his choice of the *nom de plume* Miching Mallecho it is clear that Shelley meant mischief. One of the most mischievous aspects of the completed poem is that Peter Bell III can be equated with Peter Bell II only part of the time; the rest of the time, despite Shelley's private disavowal of the fact, Peter Bell is William Wordsworth. When she published the poem later on, Mary tactfully (and perhaps self-protectingly) asserted that "nothing personal to the Author of *Peter Bell*" was intended, and that Shelley's poem moved upon an "ideal" plane. But she had to add that Shelley's poem constituted a warning to men of genius who abandon their "glorious calling of discovering and announcing the beautiful and good," and who impart to the unenlightened, not "that ardor for truth and spirit of toleration" which Shelley believed necessary, but "false and injurious opinions, that evil was good and that ignorance and force were the best allies of purity and virtue."

It was Leigh Hunt's notion that Wordsworth's *Peter Bell* had propagated such false and injurious opinions, and he made no bones of saying so in the *Examiner*. Shelley makes Peter Bell III go morally to seed, decide that "happiness is wrong," and become so habitually the *advocatus diaboli* that the hard old potter he once was is "born anew within his mind." He looks pitilessly upon his dying country's face, turning away with "hardened sneer" and planning only to impale her with an elegy after her death. This is the point which Hunt so forthrightly makes about Wordsworth in the *Rosalind and Helen* review. The conclusion is inescapable that the serious undertone in Shelley's mischief is mainly derived from Hunt, and that Shelley was very exactly describing one aspect of his poem when he called it a "party squib."[18]

But such is the ambiguity of Shelley's purpose that his poem sometimes rises above the squib into the realm of serious literary criticism. The best parts of the poem come when Shelley is thinking of two Wordsworths—first, the writer he had for many years admired, quoted, and imitated; and second, that aging moralist who had exhumed a rather silly poem and dedicated it to a liberal-turned-reactionary, the new Poet Laureate, Robert Southey. Praise of Wordsworth as a literary pioneer is unmistakable in the following passage:

> Peter's verse was clear, and came
> Announcing from the frozen hearth
> Of a cold age, that none might tame
> The soul of that diviner flame
> It augured to the Earth;
>
> Like gentle rains on the dry plains,
> Making that green which late was gray,
> Or like the sudden moon, that stains
> Some gloomy chamber's window panes
> With a broad light like day.[19]

This impressionistic characterization of Wordsworth's place as pioneer is hardly a match for another more closely analytical passage which will strike many readers as excellent criticism, whatever they may think of it as poetry:

> He had a mind which was somehow
> At once circumference and centre
> Of all he might or feel or know;
> Nothing went ever out, although
> Something did ever enter.

[18] Peacock had added some grains of powder to the squib with his description of the poet's activities during the elections in July, 1818. Brougham was a candidate from Westmoreland and by Peacock's account (July 5), "Wordsworth has published an Address to the Freeholders, in which he says they ought not to choose so poor a man as Brougham, riches being the only guarantees of political integrity. He goes further than this, and actually asserts that the Commons ought to be chosen by the Peers. Now this is a pretty rascal for you. . . . Of course, during the election, Wordsworth dines every day at Lord Lonsdale's."

[19] v, xiii-xiv.

He had as much imagination
As a pint-pot; he never could
Fancy another situation,
From which to dart his contemplation,
Than that wherein he stood.

Yet his was individual mind,
And new-created all he saw
In a new manner, and refined
Those new creations, and combined
Them, by a master-spirit's law.

Thus—though unimaginative—
An apprehension clear, intense,
Of his mind's work, had made alive
The things it wrought on; I believe
Wakening a sort of thought in sense.[20]

One may wish to revise the statement that Wordsworth was lack-
ing in imaginative power by pointing out that if he had not (except within rather narrow limits) that capacity for self-projection
which was so important an aspect of Shelley's concept of imagination, yet he had in superlative degree another kind of imagination:
the ability to re-create freshly all he saw, to combine or fuse these
new creations under the law of a sovereign spirit, and thus to vital-
ize and objectify the inner workings of his mind. In what Shelley
says of the earlier Wordsworth, therefore, it is easy to discover the
bases of his continuing admiration.

This perfectly sincere praise had now been conditioned by Shelley's disappointment in the anticlimactic Wordsworth. For Shelley, the publication of *Peter Bell* in April, 1819, showed that the
Wordsworth of that date stood at a "low-tide in soul." Not only
had the poetic stature of the pioneer been substantially reduced
by a ridiculous production, but also, and more important, the cold
touch of a limited and exclusive moral philosophy had evidently
extinguished the last spark of political fervor in Wordsworth.
Shelley could only remark bitterly (what it is hard to suppose he
really believed even then) that

[20] IV, vii-x.

From the first 'twas Peter's drift
To be a kind of moral eunuch;
He touched the hem of Nature's shift,
Felt faint—and never dared uplift
The closest, all-concealing tunic.[21]

Shelley's motives with respect to Wordsworth are therefore fairly complicated. He is disappointed, amused, and angry with the author of *Peter Bell*, for literary, political, and moral reasons. Yet he is unable to forget, and is careful to record, the very real virtues of Wordsworth, whether as the gardener who helped to develop the finest flower of the romantic movement, or as biographer of the deeper recesses of the individual mind. Hunt—a lesser poet, even a poetaster—had reacted violently to the unwelcome stimulus of *Peter Bell*. Keats and Shelley, whose personal experience of some of Wordsworth's more felicitous poems had been too intense to be so easily disregarded, softened their blows. Shelley's wish to be gentle with Wordsworth is suggested by his instructions to Ollier to change a name in the text of *Peter Bell the Third* from *Emma* to *Betty* because, after he had sent the MS to England, he recalled that Emma was the name "of the sister of a great poet who might be mistaken for Peter."[22] The only other possible construction that can be put upon this request is that Shelley feared prosecution for libel, since Peter Bell III and the "great poet" are so unmistakably one in many passages of the poem that Shelley's request would otherwise make little sense.

That Shelley was both punishing and praising Wordsworth in *Peter Bell the Third* is further corroborated by the fact that on May 8, 1820, he sent Mrs. Gisborne a little lyric called "An Exhortation," where he developed a comparison between poets and

[21] Shelley, of course, fancied himself as a remover of Nature's veils. Had he been able to read the Mount Snowdon episode at the close of *The Prelude*, where Wordsworth's imagination moves out from an epicenter to grasp in a magnificent figure the concept of the One which remains, Shelley would have been obliged to see Wordsworth as an Actaeon rather than as a moral eunuch. His admiration for Wordsworth as a poet of nature, as well as his disappointment in Wordsworth's conservatism, is indicated in the sonnet, "To Wordsworth," published with *Alastor* (1816).

[22] *Letters*, x, 168. This request was made soon after he sent "An Exhortation" to Mrs. Gisborne.

chameleons which he characterized as "a kind of excuse for Wordsworth."[23]

> Chameleons feed on light and air;
> Poets' food is love and fame;
> If in this wide world of care
> Poets could but find the same
> With as little toil as they,
> Would they ever change their hue
> As the light chameleons do,
> Suiting it to every ray
> Twenty times a day?
>
> Poets are on this cold earth,
> As chameleons might be,
> Hidden from their early birth
> In a cave beneath the sea.
> Where light is, chameleons change;
> Where love is not, poets do;
> Fame is love disguised; if few
> Find either, never think it strange
> That poets range.
>
> Yet dare not stain with wealth or power
> A poet's free and heavenly mind.
> If bright chameleons should devour
> Any food but beams and wind,
> They would grow as earthly soon
> As their brother lizards are.
> Children of a sunnier star,
> Spirits from beyond the moon,
> Oh, refuse the boon!

The lyric may well be thought of as Shelley's ironic commentary
on a text from Wordsworth, the famous sonnet beginning

> The world is too much with us; late and soon,
> Getting and spending, we lay waste our powers:
> Little we see in Nature that is ours;
> We have given our hearts away, a sordid boon.

[23] *Letters*, x, 167. Cf. the reference to the chameleon growing "like what it looks
upon" in *Prometheus Unbound*, iv, 483-484.

The boon which Shelley would deny to poets is the "sordid boon" which Wordsworth had once deplored. Shelley was sadly certain that his "great poet" had laid waste his powers. Yet, as he well knew from his friends and the newspapers, there was too little love and too little light in the England of 1819-1820. Perhaps Wordsworth should not be condemned too harshly, in the dearth of his proper food, for having turned his coat to display drab colors, and for having become, to all outward appearances, a brother to the lizards.

In the story of Peter Bell and his historians, the president of the literary immortals had one more chapter to write. Although Shelley did not choose to make anything of it in *Peter Bell the Third*, the fact that Wordsworth's poem should have been thought worthy of publication after having lain in manuscript for twenty years was one of the causes of his amusement.[24] If Shelley had been able, like Troilus, to look back from some "sunnier star" upon the ultimate disposition of *Peter Bell the Third*, his ironic laughter might have matched that of Chaucer's hero. The poem was not published until Mary included it in her second edition of the collected poems in 1839. It had lain in manuscript for exactly twenty years.[25]

· IV ·

"I WONDER," wrote Shelley to Medwin on July 20, 1820, "what in the world the Queen has done. I should not wonder, after the whispers I have heard, to find that the Green Bag contained evidence that she had imitated Pasiphäe, and that the Committee should recommend to Parliament a bill to exclude all Minotaurs from the succession. What silly stuff is this to employ a great na-

[24] See the lyric, *To Mary*, introductory to *The Witch of Atlas*, where Shelley refers to "the overbusy gardener's blundering toil" which kept Wordsworth laboring over *Peter Bell* intermittently for nineteen (actually twenty) years. It is interesting to recall that in 1820, Wordsworth wrote and published a sonnet "On the Detraction Which Followed the Publication of a Certain Poem"—the reference is to *Peter Bell*—in which he scornfully shrugs off the "harpy brood" which "with foul claws" had clamorously fallen "on Bard and Hero." He presumably did not know that Shelley was among the harpies. In the following year Shelley himself was vigorously attacking those harpies whom he charged with having driven Keats into an early grave.

[25] Mary finished copying *Peter Bell the Third* on Nov. 2, 1819, and sent it off the same day. *Shelley and Mary*, I, 426.

tion about. I wish the King and the Queen, like Punch and his wife, would fight out their disputes in person."[26]

A month later Shelley began his *Oedipus Tyrannus,* a kind of Punch-and-Judy show with classical trappings, where the queen not only engaged her estranged husband in person but also, in full hunting regalia, booted and spurred and mounted on a Minotaur, gave him aggressive chase, as if he had been a Tory fox and she the Mistress of Hounds at the Boeotian Hunt.

During the summer of 1820, the "conflict of passions" between George IV and Queen Caroline had reached a crisis which was a persistent topic of conversation among the British expatriates in Italy.[27] But the whispers Shelley heard in Pisa were roars of admiration, laughter, or disgust in London. The queen's precipitate return to England and the uncrowned king's abortive efforts to divorce her on grounds of adultery were a comic substitute for the tragedy of Peterloo Fields. The opposition sprang to the queen's support with scurrilous cartoons and pamphlets, which were answered in kind by the less dignified elements of the Tory press until a paper war was in full swing.[28]

Although the crisis in George's household had only recently come to a major political issue, the scandal had been in preparation for a quarter of a century. In April, 1796, when Shelley was a child of four, George and Caroline had separated with mutual recriminations. Shelley had just turned twenty-two when Caroline went over to the Continent in 1814. Her conduct during a distinctly unregal progress around the Mediterranean Basin was perhaps sufficiently unlovely, but it might have passed for what it was—the last fling of an embittered and disappointed woman—had not George III, *pater-familias,* brought matters to a head by dying on January 29, 1820. The new king, long anxious to divorce a wife he had not even seen for thirteen years, had deputized a formal commission, with headquarters in Milan, instructed to document the queen's misdemeanors. Having heard that the coronation was scheduled for August 1, and that plans were afoot for excluding her person from the ceremonies and her name from the liturgy,

[26] *Letters,* x, 192. July 20, 1820. [27] See Mary's note to *Oedipus Tyrannus.*
[28] See Newman I. White, "Shelley's Swell-foot the Tyrant in Relation to Contemporary Political Satire," *PMLA* 36 (1921), 334. For examples of the shilling-pamphlets on the scandal, see the Cruikshank collection at the Princeton University Library.

the queen recrossed the Channel on June 6. George hastily postponed the coronation, and with the help of his Milan Commission set about preparing a bill of divorcement (which was in effect also a bill of impeachment) against his queen-consort. The evidence, including the testimony of a number of paid domestics, was assembled in the famous Green Bag for presentation to the House of Lords.[29] The Tory prosecution summed up on September 7. Brougham opened for the defense on October 3. He was so successful in his refutation of the Green Bag witnesses that the Bill of Pains and Penalties was abandoned on November 10, and on the 29th of that month the absolved and impenitent queen, accompanied by a sorry little group of retainers, gave thanks for her acquittal at St. Paul's.

One might have concluded that there was some chivalry left. But the account of the queen's continental meanderings had not made pretty reading, and the cynicism of a majority of the pamphleteers, Shelley included, is well summarized in a contemporary quatrain:

> Gracious Queen, we thee implore,
> Go away and sin no more;
> But if that effort be too great,
> Go away at any rate.[30]

Cynically or otherwise, however, the Opposition had made capital of George's persecution of his queen. Lord Liverpool ruefully told his monarch that the Whigs and their associates were apparently "determined to make a party question of the whole business,"[31] and although it is decidedly inaccurate to say, as one commentator has said, that "the Queen's domestic agitation was to engender and hasten the coming of the Reform Bill,"[32] it is clear that the queen's stand against her persecutors provided Opposition groups with a standard around which they enthusiastically, though no doubt quite cynically, rallied.[33]

[29] On the radicals' use of the Green Bag as a symbol of the Tories' desire to ruin the queen, see White, *PMLA* 36 (1921), 335.

[30] Shane Leslie, *George the Fourth* (Boston, 1926), p. 109.

[31] A. Aspinwall, ed., *The Letters of George IV* (Cambridge, 1938), II, 361.

[32] Shane Leslie, *op. cit.*, p. 105.

[33] Shelley's own position is clear: "Nothing . . . shows the generous gullibility of the English nation more than their having adopted her Sacred Majesty as the heroine of the day. I . . . wish no harm to happen to her, even if she has, as I firmly be-

Shelley, operating from Italy, was not in touch with the radicals chiefly responsible for fomenting the campaign, though he had had at least a nodding acquaintance with one or two of them before he left England. His sources of information were Hunt and Peacock, his regular correspondents and moderate liberals both, and somewhat belated copies of the *Examiner* and Cobbett's *Political Register* which were sent to him from London. Galignani's *Paris Messenger* also reached him from time to time. The probability is that he knew little of the actual trial, for *Oedipus Tyrannus* was completed long before the Tory ministers' case against the queen had been fully broached. In sum, therefore, since he held no particular brief for the queen except as a rather tawdry symbol of "the oppressed," it seems likely that Shelley was simply holding up his end of the Whig party line, and adding one more pamphlet to the dozens of far less worthy literary efforts which were being dangled under the noses of George IV, Liverpool, Castlereagh, Wellington, Eldon, and Sidmouth.[34]

Like Shelley's other party squibs, *Oedipus Tyrannus* claimed little of his time. At the Baths of San Giuliano on August 24, 1820, he was reading his *Ode to Naples* aloud to his wife and a sympathetic visitor, Mrs. Mason.[35] His declamation was drowned out by the "grunting of a quantity of pigs," which had been assembled for sale at a village fair then in progress in the square outside their

---

lieve, amused herself in a manner rather indecorous with any courier or baron. But [it is] one of the absurdities of royalty, that a vulgar woman . . . and a person whose habits and manners everyone would shun in private life . . . should be turned into a heroine, because she is a queen, or . . . because her husband is a king; and he, no less than his ministers, are so odious that everything, however disgusting, which is opposed to them, is admirable." *Letters*, **x**, 186.

[34] Professor K. N. Cameron, in a careful comparison of Shelley's prose pamphlet, *A Philosophical View of Reform*, with other reform proposals of the period, believes that Shelley was moving further to the left in the emphasis he now wished to place on popular action. It is suggested also that the tone of Chapters II and III of this pamphlet is closer to that of Cobbett's *Political Register*, a radical reform weekly, than to that of the more moderate *Examiner*. Cameron finds, however, that Shelley "was not known even as a figure of minor consequence in the reform movement," so that in spite of his "real capacity for political analysis," he should be regarded only as "an eagerly sympathetic observer." See K. N. Cameron, "Shelley and the Reformers," *ELH* 12 (1945), pp. 62-85, and esp. pp. 84-85. It should be pointed out, however, that the *Examiner* was anything but moderate in its editorial attitude toward the king in the Caroline affair, as a perusal of the *Examiner* volume for 1820 will prove to any interested reader.

[35] Mary's note says Shelley read aloud his *Ode to Liberty*. This is possible, since the poem was published with *Prometheus Unbound* in the summer of 1820. But the *Ode to Naples*, composed Aug. 17-25, 1820, was probably what she meant.

windows. The cacophony, which intruded impolitely upon the music of his *Ode*, reminded Shelley of the frogs in Aristophanes, and with that enthusiastic levity which sometimes activated his imagination, he began to extemporize a political satire on the Caroline affair, with the San Giuliano pigs as chorus. The plan of the drama was perhaps not quite so spontaneously evolved as Mary supposed in giving the foregoing account of its inception, for a kind of classical beast-fable is implicit in the letter to Medwin written in late July.[36] Six days after the Italian pigs had entered their new sties, the pigs of *Oedipus Tyrannus* had been eternized on paper. Mary wrote in her journal for August 30 the cryptic statement, "Read Swell-foot."

Oedipus Tyrannus or Swell-foot the Tyrant achieves, within the limits imposed by the short time which Shelley devoted to its composition, an amusing merger of Pasiphäe and Punch, of classical learning and newspaper erudition. The substitution of the San Giuliano pigs for the frogs of Aristophanes is only one of many such blending tricks. He playfully surrounds his cow-queen, in this Battle of the Barnyards, with memories of Europa, Pasiphäe, and Io. "We long," says one of the gullible boars, "to hear what she can possibly have done." Says Purganax, sly master of the art of innuendo:

> Why, it is hinted, that a certain Bull—
> This much is *known*:—the milk-white Bulls that feed
> Beside Clitumnus and the crystal lakes
> Of the Cisalpine mountains, in fresh dews
> Of lotus-grass and blossoming asphodel
> Sleeking their silken hair, and with sweet breath
> Loading the morning winds until they faint
> With living fragrance, are so beautiful!
> Well, *I* say nothing; but Europa rode
> On such a one from Asia into Crete,
> And the enamoured sea grew calm beneath
> His gliding beauty. And Pasiphäe,

[36] Peck suggests (*Shelley: His Life and Work*, II, 174) that Shelley derived the idea for the chorus of hogs from Professor Porson's "A New Catechism," which appeared in the *Examiner* for Aug. 30, 1818. But the date makes the possibility rather remote.

Iona's grandmother—but *she* is innocent!
And that both you and I, and all assert.[37]

Aside from the allusion to the Europa story, Shelley is recalling (as he had done in his letter to Medwin in July) the eclogue in which Vergil describes Pasiphäe's passion for the snowy bull, and exclaims, "Ah! unlucky girl, now wandering across the hills, while he, resting his snowy flanks among soft hyacinths, chews his cud of pale grass beneath a dark ilex-tree and pays court to some heifer of the great herd."[38] Shelley's making Pasiphäe the grandmother of his Iona Taurina carries the further implication that Caroline's love for the British people (the Ionian Minotaur or John Bull) is comparable to Pasiphäe's love for the snowy bull in Vergil.

But Iona Taurina is chiefly modeled on the figure of Io, whose career, as Shelley perceived with delight, showed remarkable parallels to that of Caroline. Beloved of Zeus, and thereby incurring the jealous wrath of Hera, Io was transformed, for her own protection, into a handsome white cow. She thereafter wandered widely (as Caroline had done since 1814) around the continent of Europe and the fringes of Asia, being tortured en route by a gadfly, sent for that purpose by Hera. With that neatness and high-handedness which usually characterized his reworking of ancient mythology for modern ends, Shelley saw that the malicious gadfly of the myth of Io was a natural prototype for some one of the members of the Milan Commission. So he named the queen *Io*-na Taurina, and set a gadfly upon her.[39]

Another notable instance of Shelley's clever use of old materials is his redaction of the initial situation in Sophocles' *Oedipus the King*, where a plague has developed (in Shelley a famine) and where a chorus of suppliants (the lean swine of Shelley) are seeking relief. The suggestion, as in Sophocles, is that a purgation of the land is in order, and in Shelley as in Sophocles, some business is devoted to the interpretation of an oracular prophecy. With

[37] II, i, 59-72. The passage is no doubt typical of the kind of gossip purveyed among the English expatriates in Cisalpine Italy and beside the crystal lakes of Switzerland.

[38] Eclogue, VI, 45-60.

[39] The story of Io appears, among other places, in Aeschylus, *Prometheus Bound* (786 *et seq.*); in Ovid, *Metamorphoses* (I, 724 *et seq.*), and in Apollodorus, *Library*, II, i, 3.

Sophocles, the prophecy is all important. Shelley follows him by expressing in another prophecy the semiserious preachment of his play:

> Boeotia, choose reform or civil war,
> When through thy streets instead of hare with dogs,
> A Consort-Queen shall hunt a King with hogs,
> Riding on the Ionian Minotaur.[40]

This prophecy, like that of Sophocles, indicates the general direction of the dramatic action. Shelley wishes to show how a conspiracy of Oedipus and his Theban ministers against Queen Iona Taurina was defeated by the queen's sharp thinking and aggressive action in turning the enemies' chief weapon (the Green Bag) back upon themselves.

Another sign of Shelley's blend of classical learning with the latest advices from England is that, like Spenser and Milton before him, he amuses himself with playfully learned etymologizing. He knows that Oedipus (Swell-foot) was so named because of a permanent deformity in his ankles, the result of their having been too tightly bound during his exposure as an infant. But the name fits George IV both because of the king's renowned obesity and because George's gluttony might well have afflicted him with the gout. Purganax, minister to Oedipus, is a Greek transliteration of Castle-reagh (*Purg*: tower or castle and *Anax*: king). Dakry (Greek *Dakru*: a tear) is Shelley's name for Lord Eldon, who seems to have had a reputation for lachrymosity on the bench, and whose crocodile tears had already been alluded to in *The Masque of Anarchy*. Laoktonos, which appears to be derived from Greek *Laos*, or people, and *Ktonos*, or slayer, was in Shelley's view a fitting designation for Wellington, whose military exploits would have earned him the title. The crowning example of Shelley's etymological experimentation is his handling of the Minotaur, who explains:

---

[40] The hunting figure was used in a shilling pamphlet called *The Radical Ladder or Hone's Political Ladder* (London, 1820), p. 16:

> A Royal Stag hunted by bloodhounds is seen,
> But not chaste Diana, the bold huntress Queen,
> They would hunt him, till thirsty and panting for breath,
> And then slake his thirst with the chalice of death.

I am the Ionian Minotaur, the mightiest
Of all Europa's taurine progeny. . . .
I am called Ion, which, by interpretation,
Is John; in plain Theban, that is to say,
My name's John Bull.

Shelley's calling Caroline Iona Taurina implies that she has the support of John Bull, the spirit of the British people, in defending her right to remain their queen.[41]

Aside from the subtler touches of caricature and certain more or less tangential political allusions, the "tragedy" is simple and effective. Oedipus opens with an apostrophe to his obesity and to that of his Tory supporters, refusing the Whiggish pleas of the hog-populace for food, and using methods to cut down their numbers which would have made Malthus shudder. To Purganax and Mammon (Castlereagh and Liverpool) the future looks dark, particularly in view of the prophecy that Queen Iona Taurina will hunt down Oedipus with the aid of her lean hogs. In an effort to stave off the inevitable, the ministers call in the Leech, the Rat, and the Gadfly (the Milan Commission), whose testimony about the queen's conduct has been condensed into a poisonous dew in the Green Bag.[42] With characteristic guile Purganax then persuades the lean hogs that their queen will easily survive the ordeal by poison, and will emerge as an angelic figure, too bright for a hog's eye to endure without the aid of smoked glass, who will float gloriously above their heads and rain down comfits. Everything proceeds as planned until the moment of the test when, as in *The Masque of Anarchy*, the transforming Spirit of Liberty gets to work. Just as

[41] I am indebted for assistance in these derivations to my friend and colleague, Professor George Duckworth of the Classics Department, Princeton University. Some of the other figures in Shelley's drama were stock characters in contemporary political satires. Dowden (*Life*, II, 346) so describes the Rat and the Leech. White, *PMLA* 36 (1921), corroborates Todhunter's suggestion (*A Study of Shelley's Poetry*, p. 207) that Mammon is intended for Lord Liverpool. He also identifies the Leech with Vice-Chancellor Sir John Leach, the Rat with Lt. Col. Browne, and the Gadfly with William Cooke. These last three were members of the Milan Commission, charged with investigating the queen's conduct, and are probably the "Committee" to which Shelley alludes in his letter to Medwin on July 20. See *Letters*, x, 192.

[42] White, *PMLA* 36 (1921), 336, points out that this idea was possibly derived from a remark in the *Examiner* for June 9, 1820, where Hunt alludes to the Crown's tampering with witnesses, in order to gather "poison for one of those venomous Green Bags, now to infect the Queen."

the Green Bag is about to disgorge its liquor upon the queen's head, she suddenly snatches it from Purganax, and empties it over Oedipus and his court. They are transformed into badgers, otters, hares, wolves, and stinking foxes, and vanish into the fens and forests. As the lean hogs scramble for loaves from the altar of Famine, the Minotaur, who can "leap any gate in all Boeotia," invites the queen to pursue her obscene quarry, and the drama closes to the hunting-cry of tally-ho.

Since Mary Shelley reprinted the poem in her collected edition with the apologetic remark that the world had a right to everything her husband wrote whether or not a particular item did him honor, it has been the critical fashion to deplore *Oedipus Tyrannus* as a plain failure. Measured by the yardstick of *Prometheus Unbound* and *The Cenci*, the little mock-tragedy looks dwarfish; but when it is placed over against the work of other contemporary pamphleteers who dealt with the same subject, its distinctive qualities are at once apparent. Anyone who has taken the trouble to examine the circumstances surrounding the trial of Queen Caroline will be struck both by the ludicrous precision with which Shelley has made his beast-fable conform to the political facts as he knew them, and by the cleverness with which he has hit off the meretriciousness and pusillanimity of the Tory Party in the late Regency period. The poem is not great, but it is clever and it is mildly funny. Had it escaped the notice of the so-called Society for the Suppression of Vice, and had it been set off with George Cruikshank's inimitable cartoons, *Oedipus Tyrannus* might conceivably have become a very palpable hit, even though the trial it celebrated had ended before the poem appeared (probably in December, 1820), and the attendant furor was rapidly subsiding.

Only seven copies of the pamphlet had been sold when the Vice Society threatened the publisher with a libel suit, and the remaining copies were withdrawn from circulation. Like *The Masque of Anarchy*, "The Song to the Men of England," the new National Anthem, and *Peter Bell the Third*, Shelley's satire entered the limbo of lost causes. There it remained until it was festooned with the cobwebs of history, and when it emerged at last, another queen than the luckless Caroline was the cynosure of English eyes, as she methodically fumigated the royal household and rendered it holy.

HELLAS, the last of Shelley's major political poems, was written in the fall of 1821 and published in the spring of 1822. Its aims are three. The first is fundamentally political: to celebrate the Greek War against the Turks "as a portion of the cause of civilization and moral improvement." The second is ethical: to hold up as an *exemplum* for the modern world the wonderful achievement of Athens in the fifth century, B.C., and to envision, as a lofty ideal towards which the world ought to move, a new Athens, conceived in liberty and dedicated to the spread of brotherly love. The third is metaphysical: to assert that thought is the sole reality and that all else in the world is a shadow and a dream. *Hellas* so well summarizes the end-result of Shelley's career as a political poet that it must be considered, out of its chronological order, in the present chapter.

Politically speaking, *Hellas* is an ode to liberty in a semidramatic setting, and may be regarded as the culminating poem in the long series which began in the days of *Queen Mab*. Shelley had made a lifelong habit of commemorating in verse all signs of democratic movements which came to his attention. Having heard in 1812 that a new republic was imminent in Mexico, he composed a lyrical tribute to its success, addressed "To the Republicans of North America." His "Feelings of a Republican on the Fall of Bonaparte," published with *Alastor* in 1816, exulted over the defeat of one who had, according to the author, danced for a number of years upon the grave of liberty.

During the fall of 1819 there occurred a brief interlude, already described, in which Shelley composed a number of experimental poems, written in language carefully simplified, and addressed directly to the British lower classes in the hope that they might thereby form a united front against their oppressors. The failure of this attempt did not, however, discourage him from saluting in a series of heroic odes the resurgent spirit of liberty in Spain, Italy, and Greece, though in so doing he abandoned his plan to activate the lower classes, and returned to what Mary called "the loftier poetry of glory and triumph."

The Spanish revolution elicited two such "lofty" poems, which appeared with *Prometheus Unbound* in 1820, while the constitutional "revolution" at Naples produced a third. The first of these, "An Ode, written October, 1819, before the Spaniards had recovered their liberty," is of little account as poetry, and its simple message is perhaps best summarized in the initial lines of its stanzas: "Arise, arise, arise! . . . Awaken, awaken, awaken! . . . Wave high the banner! . . . Glory, glory, glory!" But the second, called simply an "Ode to Liberty," is among the best of Shelley's political poems in the grand style. The voice of liberty, coming out of the deeps of thought, charges with might the wings of his song, says Shelley, and he provides an idealized history, first of the rise of Athenian liberty out of chaos, and then of liberty's long decline under the Roman Empire and the oppressive forces of institutional Christianity. "A thousand years the Earth cried: Where art thou?" to the slumbrous spirit of liberty, but its shadow was only fleetingly seen—by Saxon Alfred, by Martin Luther, by the "spirit-sighted" eyes of John Milton. The light it had to shed was darkened by the "blood and tears" of the French Revolution, and even further obscured by the mingled armies of Napoleon. Until the present generation, that light had not shone, except as a fitful gleam, anywhere in Europe. But now the Spaniards, by their magnificent example, exhorted a sleeping England, a desolate Italy, and a king-deluded Germany to rekindle the lamps of liberty "within the dome of this dim world." Shelley chose to greet the proclamation of a constitutional government at Naples in 1820 as a response to "Spain's thrilling paean," and in the "Ode to Naples" paid the Neapolitans the tribute of his solemn music as the latest intercessors against the league of tyrants. The theme of *Hellas* was therefore nothing new in Shelley's poetic experience, and the lyrical utterances of this last political poem are part and parcel of his protracted effort to glorify the spread of liberty across the continent from Spain towards the East, and to salute what he hoped was a new race of liberty-conscious men, "nursed in the abhorrence of the opinions which are its chains."[43]

Shelley's own characterization of *Hellas* is fairly exact: "a sort of imitation of the *Persae* of Aeschylus, full of lyrical poetry."[44]

[43] Even as he voiced such hopes, Shelley felt the weight of the actual. "I hear no political news," he told Byron in October, 1821, "but such as announces the slow victory of the spirit of the past over that of the present." *Letters*, x, 331.
[44] *Letters*, x, 333.

The imitation, as in the instance of *Oedipus Tyrannus*, consists chiefly in borrowing a pattern which Shelley then embroiders. The "action" of *Hellas* takes place in Constantinople, capital of the Turkish Empire, as that of Aeschylus' drama occurs in Susa, the ancient Persian capital of Darius and Xerxes. In each of the plays messengers are employed to bring home reports of Grecian victories—with consequent lamentation in the camp of the enemy. Where the messengers in Aeschylus describe the slaughter of Persian heroes on the Island of Psyttalea and at sea off Salamis, the messengers in Shelley confound the Turkish Pacha, Mahmud, with news of the moral victory of a group of beleaguered Greeks at the "Battle of Bucharest," and an account of the limited triumph of the Greek fleet at Nauplia. Like the Dowager Queen Atossa in Aeschylus, Shelley's Mahmud has dreams of dreadful omen before the battle-news arrives. In *The Persians*, Darius' ghost is conjured up to share in Persia's mourning, while in Shelley the "imperial shade" of Mohamet II is made to rise from his throne "in the abyss" and to remind Mahmud that all tyrannies are subject to the laws of mutability.[45]

With these parallels, however, the resemblances between *Hellas* and *The Persians* end. Unlike Aeschylus, Shelley is speaking as a prophet rather than as a poetic historian of old victories. When *Hellas* was composed, the issue of the Greek war still hung in the balance, where it remained three years later when Byron personally entered the struggle. Shelley had misunderstood and therefore rejected the catastrophe used by Aeschylus in the *Prometheus Unbound*. Now, although he could have wished it otherwise, the actual historical situation compelled him to reject the catastrophe used by Aeschylus in *The Persians*. "The decision of the glorious

[45] Woodberry has observed these parallels, and others (including two alleged minor echoes of the *Agamemnon*) which seem on examination to be remote. Since the *Hellas*, like *The Revolt of Islam*, is a *beau idéal* of revolution, it is hardly surprising that Shelley's battle descriptions, despite his prefatory apology for a display of "newspaper erudition," have little to do with the actual historic events of 1821. As White concludes [*SAQ* 20 (1921), pp. 53-54, 60] after painstaking comparison of Shelley's battles with the reputable histories, "The naval victory which Shelley . . . describes was apparently based entirely on rumor—and Aeschylus." That is, Shelley was "merely retelling the story of Salamis in terms of modern warfare." White might, however, have saved himself this trouble. "Until the conclusion of the war," said Shelley, "it will be impossible to obtain an account of it sufficiently authentic for historical materials. But poets have their privilege." Shelley's privilege was to rewrite Aeschylus.

contest now waging in Greece being yet suspended," said Shelley, "forbids a catastrophe parallel to the return of Xerxes and the desolation of the Persians." He had therefore to content himself with a "series of lyrical pictures" by which he sought to paint "upon the curtain of futurity" such "indistinct and visionary figures" as would suggest the ultimate triumph of the Greek cause. Unlike Aeschylus he was looking forward to, rather than back upon, a glorious victory. The poet of *Hellas* was trying to fulfill one of the functions of the poet as defined in his own *Defence of Poetry* of the preceding March: to be, in effect, one of "the hierophants of an unapprehended inspiration," one of the "mirrors of the gigantic shadows which futurity casts upon the present," one of the "unacknowledged legislators of the world."

The ethical parts of *Hellas* ought to have arrested Matthew Arnold's attention since they embody, though imperfectly and often only implicitly, a version of his own Hellenic idealism. For Shelley, the poem's title signified not so much a modern nation as a body of eternal ideas, the best of what had been thought and said in the ancient world. Only secondarily did the term *Hellas* mean the embattled Greece of 1821, where an abortive insurrection pitifully struggled to be born amid the mud and blood of a run-down peninsula. The vision of ancient Athens, purged of those limitations to which Shelley alluded in his essay on the literature, arts, and manners of the Athenians, burned through the tale of strife and murder which he had to tell. The poem is in a sense apocalyptic. The four horsemen gallop through its pages; ignorant armies clash in a world which is moribund through sheer ignorance; Greek *Niké* is counterblasted with *Allah-illah-Allah.* Yet behind the sunset of hope, the wrecks of old dreams, and the melancholy roar of a receding ocean of utopian faith, the unrealized possibility of a brighter Hellas rears up in visionary splendor: a world unborn, a paradise to be regained.

Ancient Greece had evolved and promulgated what seemed to Shelley the basic controlling *ethos* of the western tradition. The "imperial spirits" of the Athenian city-state in the age of Pericles are said to "rule the present from the past." It is not the rule of a dead hand, but the survival of a vital magnanimity which persists in the realm of thought far below the present strife:

Greece and her foundations are
Built below the tide of war,
Based on the crystalline sea
Of thought and its eternity.

Since the Athenian supremacy, nothing quite like it had arisen. Shelley even describes the spirit of Jesus Christ as a "burning morrow" to "Plato's sacred light." In short, *Hellas* represents a romantic apotheosis of the Hellenic ideal as Shelley saw it. He had already summed up in prose his views on the difference between the Periclean and succeeding ages. "The study of modern history," he wrote, "is the study of kings, financiers, statesmen, and priests. The history of ancient Greece is the study of legislators, philosophers, and poets: it is the history of men, compared with the history of titles. What the Greeks were, was a reality, not a promise. And what we are and hope to be, is derived, as it were, from the influence and inspiration of these glorious generations."[46] The most striking passages in *Hellas* are those inspired by Shelley's vision of ancient Greece.

If, as Shelley believed, the influence and inspiration of the Greeks had determined, and would continue to determine, the direction of the world's development, that fact helped to establish the metaphysical position which he had reached by 1821, and which he had strongly implied in his *Defence of Poetry*: namely, that amid the flux of things only thought is eternal. Although he lauded the military victories of the modern Greeks as evidence of the rebirth of an ancient spirit of liberty, the victories were only events which belonged to the dark flux of things. Whether she won or lost, Constantinople, like all the proud cities of the past, would bow her towered crest to mutability. If, in the meantime, it should turn out that modern Greece should be devastated in the struggle, there was consolation in the thought that its fragments would inevitably reassemble

And build themselves again impregnably
In a diviner clime,

[46] *Prose*, VII, 226. Shelley's chief objections to what he otherwise regarded as the most memorable period in the history of the world were three: Greek "regulations and sentiments respecting sexual intercourse"; the existence of slavery; and the inferior status given to Athenian women.

> To Amphionic music, on some Cape sublime
> Which frowns above the idle foam of time.

This cape, this clime, and this music belong to the realm of thought, and it is to this realm, in his later days, that Shelley increasingly turns as to the sole reality. The wise old Jew, Ahasuerus, one raised above his fellow men by thought, is resurrected in the midst of *Hellas* to serve as the mouthpiece for Shelley's metaphysic. Much of what he says has the tone of *Ecclesiastes*. But he goes further than to aver that all things pass:

> This firmament pavilioned upon chaos,
> With all its cressets of immortal fire. . . .
> Is but a vision; all that it inherits
> Are motes of a sick eye, bubbles, and dreams;
> Thought is its cradle and its grave, nor less
> The future and the past are idle shadows
> Of thought's eternal flight—they have no being;
> Nought is but that which feels itself to be.[47]

Like Hamlet, Ahasuerus surveys the overhanging star-fretted firmament as something ineffably magnificent but is most struck by the "foul and pestilent congregation of vapours" which lies beneath it. Like Prospero, he asserts that the great globe, and all that it contains, are only the baseless fabric of a vision. Bush calls Ahasuerus "a mystic who re-utters Prospero's speech in the spirit of Berkeley."[48] He might have added that it is the spirit of Calderon, as well. Thus augmented, the phrase aptly characterizes Shelley's state of mind when he wrote *Hellas*.

Shelley's attempt to be a legislator for the world, and to make his poetry into what he called an "ardent intercessor" in the promotion of a new order, was not conspicuously successful. One of the numerous ironies in the reception of his political poetry was that *Queen Mab*, which he rejected in 1821 as more likely "to injure than to serve the cause of freedom," was to become in the early Victorian period an instrument to the radical reformers, and was to earn the praise, in the 1880's, of such Fabian socialists as George Bernard Shaw. Shelley's political ineffectiveness with his

---

[47] *Hellas*, 772-785.
[48] Bush, *Mythology and the Romantic Tradition in English Poetry*, p. 164.

contemporaries is easily explained. In his Italian exile he was out of touch with the springs of political action, and was therefore denied any means of reaching the popular ear except through the written word. The words he wrote, moreover, were so candid in their criticism of English domestic rule, and rulers, that they either went unprinted because of the publishers' understandable fear of prosecution and imprisonment; or, if printed, were immediately suppressed by the Vice Society; or, if not suppressed, were too little read or too little understood to be of any practical political consequence at that time.

His failure to acquire even a limited group of readers, let alone sympathetic popular support, was borne in upon Shelley in his last years. "The reception the public have given me might [go] far enough to damp any man's enthusiasm," he moodily wrote in 1820. "I can compare my experience in this respect to nothing but a series of wet blankets."[49] Even as he wrote the *Hellas*, he felt that stifling of his ardor. "I try to be what I might have been," he said of the poem, "but am not successful."[50] Slowly the mood froze to the conviction that he was irrevocably committed to a lost cause. "I wish," said he, "I had something better to do than to furnish this jingling food for the hunger of oblivion, called verse: but I have not, and . . . cannot hope to have."[51] When at last he received the printed *Hellas*, and noticed that the book, seen through the press by another, contained fewer *errata* than usual, he gratefully wondered who had acted as midwife to this last of his orphans, "introducing it to oblivion" and himself to his "accustomed failure."[52] It was remarkable that he continued to write at all. "One would think I were the spaniel of Destiny," he wrote in another connection, "for the more she knocks me about, the more I fawn on her."[53]

Spaniel of destiny or watchdog of liberty, Shelley stuck to his mastering ideals. Perhaps his experiences with the mythology of politics had taught him that to overthrow the world's oppressors might well require more force than poetry could muster unassisted. He had tried all the devices at his disposal: hortatory pamphlets

[49] *Letters*, x, 222-223. November, probably 15, 1820.
[50] *Letters*, x, 333. Oct. 22, 1821.
[51] *Letters*, x, 342-343. January, probably 11, 1822.
[52] *Ibid.*, x, 370. April 10, 1822.   [53] *Ibid.*, x, 295.

like *The Masque of Anarchy,* closely reasoned analyses like *A Philosophical View of Reform,* satires like *Peter Bell the Third* and *Oedipus Tyrannus,* popular songs like his new version of *God Save the King,* and letters to the editors of liberal periodicals. When these failed, only direct personal participation, such as he had once tried as a boy in Dublin, remained to him. Although he dreamed of going to Spain in 1820, and although, after the manner of Aeschylus, he celebrated the military prowess of the Greeks, he was too much a believer in gradualism and too deeply the proponent of brotherly love to place any strong faith in bloodshed as a means to human progress. Thought, rather than direct political action, was becoming for him the sole reality, and in the realm of thought he lived and worked.

PART THREE:

THE SPIRIT'S SPLENDOR

7

THE VISIONARY RHYMES OF 1820

Blest too is he who knows the gods of the woodlands, Pan, and old Silvanus, and the sister Nymphs. He will not be moved by honors that the people can give, by kings' purple, or by any discord which separates brother from brother. —Vergil in the *Georgics*

Courage! when we meet we will sit upon our melancholy and disorders, bind them like an evil genius and bury them in the Tyrrhene sea, nine fathoms deep. —Shelley to Medwin, 1820

It is . . . quite possible to conceive an imaginary society in which there should be no aggressiveness, but only sympathy and fairness—any small community of true friends now realizes such a society. Abstractly considered, such a society on a large scale would be the millennium, for every good thing might be realized there with no expense of friction.
—William James, *The Varieties of Religious Experience*

· I ·

His preoccupation with the state-of-England question in the autumn of 1819 seemed to Shelley like a temporary departure from the happy oases of literature in favor of a journey across the "great sandy desert of politics." Yet even in the arid wilderness, as he was quick to add, he was not "without the hope of finding some enchanted paradise."[1] He never entered the paradise of public popularity, however, and he must have been disappointed by Leigh Hunt's failure to print either his closely reasoned letter on the trial of Richard Carlile or his impassioned plea to the victims of Peterloo, as well as by Hunt's tacit refusal to complete negotiations with

[1] *Letters*, x, 121.

Ollier looking to the publication of *Peter Bell the Third*. But Shelley had recourses of which political crises formed no part. Within the six-month period from March to August, 1820, he thrice re-entered the "odorous gardens" of poetry, producing three "visionary rhymes," half parables, half intellectual playthings, as if to console himself for his failure to discover, except perhaps as a constantly retreating mirage, the enchanted paradise he had sought in the dry desert of politics. Perhaps the importance of these rhymes consists chiefly in what they reveal of Shelley's state of mind and his habits of composition after eight years of poetic effort.

Something of the stylistic differentiation and variety previously noticed in the political poems can be observed in these poems: a similar admixture of gravity and gaiety, of fact and fable, of morality and irresponsibility. Like *The Masque of Anarchy*, *The Sensitive Plant* is markedly plain in style and sober in manner, though it lacks the moral determination with which *The Masque* is infused. *The Letter to Maria Gisborne* displays a relaxed and melancholy gaiety. The language, as in *Peter Bell the Third*, is ready to his pen, and the poet sits at ease, entertaining himself and one of his close associates with a philosopher's dream: the physical, mental, social, and cultural well-being consequent upon the simple life with a few friends in an Italian haven. In *The Witch of Atlas*, as in *Oedipus Tyrannus*, Shelley swoops like a leisurely comet among the staid old mythological stars and the wide literary domains opened to him by long association with the classics of the western world, masking a sober purpose behind an effortless rush of images, never at a loss for motive power, undeterred by considerations of form, attracting all rich metals into his orbit, and breaking off without further ado when he has run his course.

Although these poems are various in style and eclectic in imagery, they share, with varying emphasis, in two themes: the immortality of love and beauty, and the desirability of human brotherhood. In *The Sensitive Plant*, though Shelley indicates that gentle creatures like the plant itself may suffer extinction in a neglectful world, he is equally certain that the fair Lady (Love) and her garden of beautiful forms will endure since thought endures and they exist in thought. The compensatory value of friendship in a world of darkness is the essential theme of *The Letter to Maria Gisborne*, while the Witch of Atlas, who stands for immortal love in somewhat the same way as does the Lady of the garden in *The Sensitive Plant*, is dedicated to the development and spread of human sympathy. Shelley had read Keats' *Endymion* at least once and perhaps twice by the spring of 1820,[2] and although he found it prolix, he could hardly have failed to recognize that the two themes which he engages in the visionary rhymes figured prominently in Keats' poem. He is ready to assert with Keats that a thing of beauty can never pass into nothingness, despite the dearth of noble natures and the dark, unhealthy ways which the human spirit must traverse. A shape of beauty can help to delete the darkness of the soul. The theme of the proem to *Endymion* has thus an important attraction for Shelley. His realization of this fact may have had something to do with his invitation to Keats to come to Italy during that glorious summer when he wrote the poems here considered, while his growing sense of intellectual companionship with Keats was evidently one of his reasons for writing *Adonais* after Keats' death in 1821.

· II ·

THE SENSITIVE PLANT, composed at Pisa in the spring of 1820, is a nature-parable in which several related themes are developed: the failure of vision which prevents the human imagination from fulfilling its appointed task of apprehending ideas of love and beauty; the fate of gentle poetic natures in a loveless world (for which the fate of Keats some months later was to show what Shelley must have regarded as corroborative evidence); and the survival powers of tough, insensitive minds, which are able both to exist and to establish precedence over more finely organized intellects because they require nothing more than the material world provides. One might conceivably regard the poem as a very simple allegory, with the Sensitive Plant as a defenseless innocent, with the flowers of the garden as damsels in distress, and with the unlovely forms which usurp the garden as the villains of the piece. But so simple a description does little credit to the complexity of Shelley's inten-

[2] A cancelled passage in Shelley's letter to Ollier (*Letters*, x, 71, probably Aug. 20-24, 1819) indicates that he had received *Endymion* by that date, while his invitation to Keats (*Letters*, x, 193-194, July 27, 1820) contains the statement: "I have lately read your Endymion again."

tion. The author of *Alastor* and *Prometheus Unbound* is still interested in psychological problems. He is using the seasonal phenomena of growth and decay as a complex metaphor of certain tragic limitations in the human mind.

Although Part I of the poem has something of the atmosphere of Erasmus Darwin's *Loves of the Plants* (its denizens are too insistently sweet, their human attributes are overdone, and one cannot forget the similar failings of *The Botanic Garden*), Shelley is trying something much more difficult than Darwin undertook. Where the earlier poet personifies flowers in order to make their respective attributes memorable, and to remind the amateur botanist of their pistil and stamen structures, Shelley is trying to project a vision of abstract and perfectly harmonious love and beauty in terms of flowers, to which he secondarily attaches human qualities in order to elicit the reader's sympathy.

The garden where the Sensitive Plant flourishes is represented as an "undefiled Paradise"—a visionary landscape of absolute perfection. Under the beneficent vernal sun, "like the Spirit of Love felt everywhere," a variety of flowers exists in complete harmony. The emphasis falls less upon their variety than upon what may be called their "mutuality." Each fills the atmosphere with a radiance and fragrance in which all share, as all share in the light of the sun.

> For each one was interpenetrated
> With the light and the odor its neighbor shed,
> Like young lovers whom youth and love make dear,
> Wrapped and filled by their mutual atmosphere.

From the radiant companions in whose presence it exists, however, the Sensitive Plant is in one important way set off: it is able to contribute nothing to the perfect beauty of its environment; it has, of its own, neither blossom, nor radiance, nor fragrance. But if it differs from its associates in that it cannot interpenetrate, it shares their capacity to be interpenetrated. That is, it blissfully feels from root to topmost leaf an infinite receptiveness to love; and it is animated by a single pervasive desire (the all-mastering *eros*-drive of Plato's *Symposium*) to possess what it does not itself have: the beautiful. This, for Shelley, is the indubitable mark of the sensitive mind: its capacity for aspiration towards perfection, its thirst for the unattainable.

This "undefiled Paradise" contains a presiding genius, to whom Part II of the poem is devoted. In the opening line of this section she is called a "Power," and in the second line, "an Eve in this Eden." The power is that of Love, as the Lady's every act proves; but Milton's Eve provides the literary image in terms of which the visionary genius of the garden is rendered visible to the mind's eye. The Lady is therefore closely related, both in idea and in imagery, to the Promethean Asia, to the Witch of Atlas, to the Urania of *Adonais,* and to the Idea which bears the name of Emilia in *Epipsychidion.*

Since Shelley's aim in the first two sections was to portray an unspoiled paradise, his recollection of Eve was natural. He returned, a few months later, to the fourth book of *Paradise Lost* in order to find hints for his portrait of the Witch of Atlas. Shelley's garden, like Milton's Eden, contains "flow'rs of all hue," fresh fountains, vernal airs, and all sweet odors.[3] Shelley's picture of the descent of evening over the garden is a kind of improvisation after Milton's more careful account of evening in Paradise.

> Now came still Ev'ning on, and Twilight gray
> Had in her sober livery all things clad;
> Silence accompanied; for Beast and Bird,
> They to thir grassy couch, these to thir nests,
> Were slunk, all but the wakeful Nightingale;
> She all night long her amorous descant sung;
> Silence was pleased.

> And when evening descended from heaven above,
> And the Earth was all rest, and the air was all love,
> And delight, though less bright, was far more deep,
> And the day's veil fell from the world of sleep,
> And the beasts, and the birds, and the insects were
>   drowned
> In an ocean of dreams without a sound,
> Whose waves never mark, though they ever impress
> The light sand which paves it, consciousness;
> Only overhead the sweet nightingale
> Ever sang more sweet as the day might fail,

[3] *Paradise Lost,* IV, 256. Cf. *ibid.,* IV, 690-702 for Milton's catalogue of Eden's flowers.

And snatches of its Elysian chant
Were mixed with the dreams of the Sensitive Plant.

One may note that Shelley's only (though striking) addition to the Miltonic picture is the sandy-floor figure for consciousness. The rest is stolen from Eden.

Milton's Eve and the Lady are so obviously counterparts that one might say of Shelley what Milton says of Satan:

> Eve separate he spies
> Veil'd in a cloud of fragrance, where she stood
> Half spi'd, so thick the Roses bushing round
> About her glow'd, oft stooping to support
> Each flow'r of slender stalk, whose head, though gay
> Carnation, purple, azure, or speckt with gold
> Hung drooping unsustain'd. Them she upstays
> Gently with myrtle band.[4]

With a similar assiduity and tenderness, Shelley's Eve "tended the garden from morn to even," watered the sun-stricken plants, emptied rain from the cups of the heavier flowers, and

> Lifted their heads with her tender hands,
> And sustained them with rods and osier-bands.

Into the blissful bower of Milton's Eve, "Beast, Bird, Insect, or Worm durst enter none."[5] Shelley's Eve has her own device for ridding her domain of "killing insects and gnawing worms," and "things of obscene and unlovely forms." She bears them in a basket "into the rough woods far aloof." Thus, while the Lady is present, such unlovely forms are unable to attack the Sensitive Plant or to defile the garden.[6]

---

[4] *Paradise Lost*, IX, 424-431.　　　　[5] *Paradise Lost*, IV, 704.

[6] Always on the watch for real-life prototypes of Shelley's heroines, Medwin started the persistent rumor that the former Lady Mountcashel (a good friend of the Shelleys who in 1820 was living in Italy with a Mr. Mason by whose name she was known) was the original of the Lady of the Garden, while according to Hogg the garden itself was doubtless an idealized recollection of one into which he and Shelley had stumbled during their rambles around Oxford. Shelley later compared the Lady of the Garden to Jane Williams, though he playfully added that "this must have been *a pure anticipated cognition*," since he had written the poem a whole year before he knew her. Like many other identifications of Shelley's heroines with real people, these allegations are misleading: the Lady seems to be purely a literary creature, like the Witch of Atlas, and her garden probably never existed except in Shelley's mind.

But the Lady's vigilance in banishing destructive beings from this bower of bliss is brought to an end by her untimely "death," and the monstrous shape of ruin, as in the ninth book of *Paradise Lost*, invades the garden. Since Shelley's parable uses symbols drawn from nature rather than from Milton's version of the Genesis myth, he shows ruin, not as an intrusion and temptation by Satan, but as an autumnal assault by "forms of living death"—rank weeds, pulpous fungi, and venomous blights. One by one the lovely blooms of Part I are destroyed and "massed into common clay." Winter seals all in the rigors of death. When spring returns, the Sensitive Plant is "a leafless wreck," but the crude and indefatigable mandrakes, toadstools, docks, and darnels rise up once more like the loathsome forms of the exhumed dead.

Shelley's attempt to develop his fable in terms of natural phenomena involved him in several logical fallacies. In trying to be true to the requirements of his vision, he is occasionally false to nature. With Shelley, however, the vision is usually more important than the natural fact, and as soon as the transcendental meaning of his parable is stated, it is easy to see how the difficulties arose. The garden of Part I is evidently the realm of beauty and love, at some time when the sensitive mind is fully awake to these ideas, and when the spirit of love and sympathy is felt everywhere. The flowers themselves are the perfect "forms" with which sensitive minds have established contact, and their mutual "interpenetration" signifies the essential unity and interdependence of such ideas, a common neo-Platonic notion. The Sensitive Plant does not itself contribute to these perfections, but its aspiring character makes it deeply receptive to their influences. The death of the Lady signifies the withdrawal of the spirit of love from the apprehensive powers of the sensitive mind, and is the symbolic representation of a failure of vision quite as much as it is a way of suggesting the departure of love from the mind of man—as Asia's withdrawal to her Indian vale signified both a failure of understanding on the part of Prometheus and a departure of those forces which could have helped to maintain the world in pristine harmony. The ensuing autumn and winter represent the long dark period which is the natural consequence of such a failure, and of such a withdrawal. During the second spring, the triumphant reemergence of the unkillable weeds and fungi, the "monstrous undergrowth," suggests the survival power of insensitive minds in a world where the idea of love is no longer either widely understood or cherished. The destruction of the Sensitive Plant appears to mean not only that the apprehensive powers of even the most finely organized human beings may fall short of perfection in a world from which the ideas of love and beauty are absent, but also, and more particularly, that actual destruction of such sensitive beings may occur—an anticipation of the idea Shelley entertained about the causes of the death of Keats.

Shelley's "Conclusion" shows that he has in mind a failure of the human apprehensive powers, but at the same time a Keatsian faith in the immortality of beauty and love. Whether the animating spirit of the Sensitive Plant and the Lady's "gentle mind" were destroyed along with their outward forms (root and leaf, flesh and fell), he does not know. The dream-world which we all inhabit is full of mockeries, and one of them may well be death itself. But what can be unequivocably affirmed is that

> That garden sweet, that lady fair,
> And all sweet shapes and odors there,
> In truth have never passed away:
> 'Tis we, 'tis ours, are changed; not they.
>
> For love, and beauty, and delight,
> There is no death nor change: their might
> Exceeds our organs, which endure
> No light, being themselves obscure.

The beautiful can never fade into nothingness; it is an idea in the mind and, as such, is impervious to the laws of dissolution and decay which govern the material universe. The destruction of love and beauty is therefore always apparent rather than real. What is destroyed, or at any rate limited, is the human capacity for apprehending supernal beauty and love. In the gloom of error, ignorance, and strife which enwraps humankind, the very organs of perception are obscured: they cannot endure the white radiance of that eternity in which the sublime ideas exist.

So far as the poem succeeds in establishing this point, it is sound enough. But it is inferior to the *Prometheus* in its failure (largely, perhaps, a failure of the chosen image) to emphasize the necessity of moral decision and action. The Plant is too weak, too frail, too amenable to destruction; the Promethean spirit of rebellion has been lost, and no discernible stoicism has entered in its place. The melancholy of *The Sensitive Plant* is elegiac; its savor is of acceptance, its manner suffused with that autumnal languor which one sorrowfully observes in the conduct of the chief mourner among the mountain shepherds at the funeral of Adonais. What survives in the poem, however, is Shelley's vision, that vision of harmony and "mutuality" of which he never seems, in his major poems, to have lost sight. If the literalist stands appalled before *The Sensitive Plant*, the transcendentalist can say that, whatever the defects of the "rhyme" in this visionary rhyme, the quality of the vision strengthens and saves it.

A final word should be said on the relation between the substance of *The Sensitive Plant* and the moralistic epilogue which serves as its conclusion. The poem proper might well be seen as an expatiation on a text from *Hamlet*. For it develops a melancholy picture of the world as "an unweeded garden" gone quite to seed and dominated by "things rank and gross in nature." With Hamlet Shelley cries "Fie on't!" With Hamlet he could wish that the sullied flesh would melt. The epilogue, however, indicates where the real goal of his aspiration lies—in a vision of that divine order and harmony which knows neither cessation nor decay.

The use of natural phenomena as emblematic of mental states is a frequent trick of Shelley's. In several of the well-known lyrics of 1819-1820, and most notably, perhaps, in *The West Wind, The Cloud*, and *The Skylark*, one finds him seeking in the natural world for analogies by which to reassure himself that regeneration follows destruction, that change does not mean extinction, and that there is yet hope for the world if it will pay heed to those unacknowledged legislators, the prophetic poets. He invoked these analogies once again in *Adonais* where, as in all of these lyrics, the underlying contrast is between the transitory and the permanent. The underlying hope of the odes is either that the melancholy world can be exchanged for some bright world of the hereafter, or that the world as it is can be converted into the world as it ought to be.

In the *Ode to the West Wind*, Shelley voices the complaint for which he was so severely castigated by Irving Babbitt—"I fall upon the thorns of life! I bleed!"—and records his conviction that "a heavy weight of hours has chained and bowed" one who was formerly, like the wind itself, tameless and swift and proud. Yet the concluding petition of the poem, where the poet wishes that the fierce wind might serve him as a trumpet by which to wake the unawakened earth, and as an instrument by which his inseminating principles might be spread, is hardly defeatist. In *The Cloud*, if one may legitimately assume that some other than a naturalistic meaning is intended, such statements as "I change but I cannot die," and "I silently laugh at my own cenotaph" could be accepted as evidences of Shelley's belief in some kind of immortality, as well as his yearning towards a supernal status. The comparison of *The Skylark* to a poet hidden "in the light of thought," whose singing converts the world to "sympathy with hopes and fears it [formerly] heeded not" might be construed as evidence of Shelley's continued hopefulness about the possibility of the world's redemption through the power of human thought when it is given memorable expression in poetry. If it is true that Shelley was at this period seeking in nature some analogical confirmation of his own highest hopes, these lyrics would suggest, more forthrightly than *The Sensitive Plant*, that he found what he was seeking: an emblem of permanence in a world of change.

· III ·

The spider spreads her webs whether she be
In poet's tower, cellar, or barn, or tree;
The silkworm in the dark green mulberry leaves
His winding sheet and cradle ever weaves;
So I, a thing whom moralists call worm,
Sit spinning still round this decaying form,
From the fine threads of rare and subtle thought—
No net of words in garish colors wrought
To catch the idle buzzers of the day—
But a soft cell, where when that fades away
Memory may clothe in wings my living name
And feed it with the asphodels of fame,
Which in those hearts which must remember me
Grow, making love an immortality.

So, and again with a natural analogy, opens *The Letter to Maria Gisborne*, a poem not intended for publication and for that very reason a useful document of self-revelation. Shelley is proud of having resisted the temptation to spin a web of garish colors by which to catch the plaudits of those idle buzzers, the critics. Moralists call him a worm. Very well, then, he will be that kind of worm which is able to become a butterfly. He will spin round his name a soft chrysalis of words, out of which, in God's good time, his name will emerge like a handsome moth to feed upon the asphodels of fame which grow in the hearts of those who must, and will, remember him. The doctrine of love he has perpetually celebrated will accordingly be strengthened and continued.

Because Shelley had suffered public neglect, he felt driven to insulate his spirit against public contumely. In order partially to compensate for his having been denied access to the paradise of public popularity, he surrounded himself with the fabric of a vision, a chrysalis of words. A second compensation for public neglect, and one on which *The Letter to Maria Gisborne* lays great stress, is the consciousness that one has at least a few tried friends who are sympathetic with his visionary aims.

Like Keats day-dreaming *Sleep and Poetry* in Leigh Hunt's booklined study, Shelley sits now among the mechanical debris of Henry Reveley's study at Leghorn, addressing the boy's mother in London, and spinning couplets out of the heterogeneous array of unpoetical objects with which he is surrounded:

> Whoever should behold me now, I wist,
> Would think I were a mighty mechanist,
> Bent with sublime Archimedean art
> To breathe a soul into the iron heart
> Of some machine portentous . . .

The mood, like that of Keats, is Spenserian. On the table before him rests a walnut bowl filled, not with wine, but with quicksilver, and he develops the suggestion into a humorous picture of gnomes turning from their subterranean toil to toast in brimming bowls of mercury the latest exploit of the earthquake demons. Shelley's skill with the humorous vignette, as also in the picture of Queen Iona Taurina floating above the heads of her subjects, was so real, and yet so seldom invoked, that it is worth noticing here. In the hope that something else will catch his fancy, he delightedly names over the protean disarray of objects: "shapes of unintelligible brass," screws, cones, wheels, books of chemistry and mathematics, a half-burned match, a broken tea-cup, a block of ivory, a heap of rosin, and a mysterious object with a lead center for which he can find no adequate title and which makes him exclaim

> I'll leave, as Spenser says, with many mo,
> This secret in the pregnant womb of time,
> Too vast a matter for so weak a rhyme.

If he fails to breathe a soul into the iron heart of Reveley's machines, the effort has at least served to launch his poetic epistle, and "the self-impelling steam-wheels of the mind" are now spinning fast. Still following Spenser, he compares himself to "some mysterious Archimage,"[7] plotting spells, and preparing "devilish enginery"[8] like Milton's, to use in a holy war against the reviewers.

Outside, the *libeccio* howls; in the pauses of the blast he hears the murmur of the awakening sea; thunder growls among the distant mountains; in the foreground of his vision a hill "looks hoary through the white electric rain." But what fixes his attention is not the gathering storm or his plots against the reviewers. It is rather one patch of blue in the lowering sky, like "the eye of Love" smiling down upon "the unquiet world." To one who witnesses such a picture, says he, the roaring elements, the war of worms, and the shriek of the world's "carrion jays" (the reviewers) seem of little consequence.

In various permutations and combinations this image dominates Shelley's major poetry in 1820-1821: Love is seen as an inextinguishable sun, a perpetual fountain of light set over a darkling world, a bright emanation which sometimes descends through the lowering sky to consume the clouds of mortality. As early as 1816 he had bemoaned the evanescence of the spirit of Intellectual Beauty, which in passing away left the human spirit "vacant and desolate" in a "dim vast vale of tears." Its light alone, he asserted, gave "grace and truth to life's unquiet dream"; it nourished human thought, and its influence could redeem the world from its "dark slavery." In *Mont Blanc*, that same year, he had described another

---

[7] *Faerie Queene*, Bks. I and II, *passim*.　[8] *Paradise Lost*, VI, 553.

trance-like state during which his mind seemed to hold "an unremitting interchange" with "the clear universe of things around." In the *Lines Written Among the Euganean Hills* (1818) he had recorded how, while he stood at noontide looking down upon the surrounding country, his spirit was "interpenetrated" (the word should be noticed in connection with *The Sensitive Plant*) by the "glory of the sky"—

> Be it love, light, harmony,
> Odor, or the soul of all
> Which from heaven like dew doth fall.

The ineffable brightness of Asia transfigured in *Prometheus Unbound* partakes of this same image. Like the Witch of Atlas and like Emilia in *Epipsychidion*, Asia veils the splendor of her light in order that the eye can bear to look upon her. Shelley's faith in the immortality and immutability of Love and Beauty led him to say in *The Sensitive Plant* that their mingled might

> Exceeds our organs, which endure
> No light, being themselves obscure.

In a world of "error, ignorance, and strife" we are all but lost. Now in Reveley's study, as the storm clouds whirl in from the mountains behind Leghorn, Shelley's attention is fixed upon that rift in the clouds through which the eye of Love seems to be looking down. It is comparable to the star image with which he closes *Adonais*, and the moth rises from its chrysalis of words towards that light.

The other consolation for having to inhabit the Cimmerian desert is that it contains bright oases of friendship. Shelley's epistle goes on to recall past joys with Mrs. Gisborne: walks by the sea "under the roof of blue Italian weather"; frugal feasts and companionable talks; readings together in the "starry autos" of Calderon; and those occasions when his addressee listened sympathetically to his "visionary rhymes." From the recollection of things past, Shelley turns to the present, and *seriatim* characterizations of Mrs. Gisborne's probable companions in London: Hunt, Hogg, Peacock, Horace Smith, and perhaps Coleridge, his radiant mind muffled in dark despair like a "cloud-encircled meteor." He contrasts the drab loneliness of London with the landscape which meets his eyes in this paradise of exiles, Italy. From this contrast he moves on to the future, a pleasant day-dream of another winter, when with his few good friends, Hunt, Hogg, Peacock, Horace Smith, and Maria Gisborne, and with the help of tea and toast and books and talk, he can hold a friendly, winter-long "philosophic revel" until the time of parting comes again. It is plain that these friends, though few, are invaluable to him in his present state of mind. He might have concluded his epistle with a sentiment he had used in a letter to Hunt a few months earlier: "Affectionate love to and from all. This ought not only to be the *vale* of a letter, but a superscription over the gate of life."[9]

· IV ·

DIDO, Queen of Carthage, abandoned by Aeneas, deeply distraught, and planning her own death, deceived her sister Anna about her real intentions with a manufactured story about a Massylian priestess who could cure the pangs of love, and whose assistance she therefore meant to seek. "Near the boundaries of the ocean and the sinking sun," said she, "lies far Ethiopia, where most mighty Atlas bears upon his shoulders the star-marked turning sphere. There, I have learned, abides a priestess of the Massylian race, guardian of the temple of the Hesperides, she who gave sweets to the dragon and watched over the sacred limbs of that tree, strewing fresh honey and sleep-producing poppies. She says that with her spells she can set free the hearts of whomsoever she wishes, although to others she can bring harsh love-pangs. . . . You and your dear life are my witnesses, sweet sister, that against my will I undertake to arm myself with magical devices."[10]

The story of the Priestess of Atlas, who boasted that by her magic spells she could set free the hearts of human beings or afflict others with the pangs of love, appears in the fourth book of the *Aeneid*, which Shelley finished on April 1, 1820. It is probable that this speech of Dido provided the germ of the idea which developed during the last week of the following August into *The Witch of Atlas*.[11]

[9] *Letters*, x, 138. Dec. 23, 1819.   [10] *Aeneid*, IV, 480-493.
[11] Douglas Bush, whose perceptive essay on *The Witch of Atlas* (*Mythology and the Romantic Tradition in English Poetry*, Cambridge, Mass., 1937, pp. 138-143) observes many of the parallels indicated below, notes the resemblance between Dido's priestess and Shelley's Witch.

Mary had read Vergil. Whether or not she recognized the connection between *The Witch of Atlas* and Dido's priestess, whether she likewise saw in the poem the almost innumerable literary echoes, she kept quiet about them when she wrote the note to the poem for her collected edition. There she alludes to the poem's "brilliant imagery" and its "fantastic ideas," but can do no better with its sources than to suggest that they were borrowed "from sunrise or sunset, from the yellow moonshine, or the paly twilight" which Shelley had observed during his ramblings through "the sunny land he so much loved." Either Mary was filling editorial space or intentionally spreading yellow moonshine, for *The Witch of Atlas* is not a nature-poem at all. It is the most completely and obviously literary poem Shelley ever wrote. The sunny land he loved even more than Italy was the land Keats called the realms of gold. Not only Vergil, but also Ovid, Herodotus, Pliny, Diodorus Siculus, Shakespeare, Spenser, and Milton are made to collaborate in the fabrication of this "visionary rhyme."

Shelley's immediate model for *The Witch of Atlas* was the Homeric Hymn to Mercury, which he had freely rendered into *ottava rima* (the stanza of *The Witch*) in mid-July, 1820, some five weeks before he wrote his own poem.[12] This merry and fantastic hymn undoubtedly helped to determine the tone of Shelley's poem. It is an account of the infant Hermes' exploit in stealing and devouring the prize oxen of Apollo, in being apprehended and brought to Jove for a hearing, in guilefully talking his way out of his predicament, and in effecting a reconciliation with the sun-god.

When he pleads not guilty at the court of Jove, Hermes swears by the glorious portals

> Through which the multitude of the Immortals
> Pass and repass forever, day and night,
> Devising schemes for the affairs of mortals.[13]

In the closing stanza we are told that

> Hermes with Gods and men even from that day
> Mingled, and wrought the latter much annoy,
> And little profit, going far astray
> Through the dun night.[14]

---

[12] *Letters*, x, 187. Cf. Bush, *op. cit.*, p. 140.
[13] Shelley's *Hymn to Mercury*, Stanza LXV.   [14] *Ibid.*, Stanza XCVII.

Shelley's witch is just such a prankish creature as Hermes in the Homeric Hymn. Being messenger to the gods, Hermes passes continually back and forth through the portals of heaven, devising schemes for the affairs of mortals and causing mankind, as he has caused Apollo, "much annoy." For his own witch, Shelley wanted a similar being, full of quips and cranks and mischief, and periodically taking leave of her cavern on Atlas to mingle with the souls of men, as the infant Hermes had left his lofty Arcadian cavern to steal and eat Apollo's cattle. It is clear, once one has read Shelley's translation of the *Hymn to Mercury* and observed how close is its date to that of *The Witch*, that he meant his lady-witch to be a kind of female counterpart to Hermes.

But the poem is not simply an idea from Vergil's *Aeneid* projected through a conception of character derived from the older hymn. It is very literally an eclogue, a compendium of choice extracts, where Shelley's mind ranges up and down the ages, from Herodotus to Spenser, from Pliny to Shakespeare, and from Diodorus to Milton, culling whatever is pertinent to his semiserious purpose. *The Witch* originates in just such a state of mind as Shelley displayed only a week later in connecting the frogs of Aristophanes with the pigs of the San Giuliano street-fair. Shelley's insatiable literary curiosity, his wide reading in ancient and modern classics, his extraordinarily retentive memory, and his associative imagination all collaborated to produce in three days' time this gay and irresponsible little idyl.

Since it was written in three days, the story is patchy and episodic, and it would be quite without form were it not that Shelley has characteristically gathered his images under the roof of a ruling idea: the harmonizing power of love. Like Dido's nameless priestess, the Witch of Atlas can set free the hearts of whomsoever she wishes; she is, like Hermes, a past master in all sorts of subtle sleights. She can befuddle evil-doers, or divert the energies of those engaged in evil practices to constructive ends, or prankishly grant the unvoiced wishes of simple and innocent creatures.

Very little, in a dramatic sense, happens in *The Witch of Atlas*. Of the seventy-eight *ottava rima* stanzas, roughly the first third are expository in nature, and it is evident that Shelley is here leaning heavily on two old favorites of his, Spenser and Milton. The witch, we are told, was sired by Apollo, who enveloped her mother with the *aura seminalis* in a clear reminiscence of Spenser's account of the sun-inspired birth of Belphoebe and Amoret. Diana from *Comus* and Eve with her gentle menagerie from *Paradise Lost* combine with Spenser's Una to give Shelley his picture of the animals who tamely respond to the witch's sovereign power. Among her mythological votaries are a number of those pleasant sylvan creatures whom Spenser assembles to pay tribute to Una, and a number of others drawn from the crowded pages of Herodotus and Pliny. The witch's library is stored with manuscripts, "the works of some Saturnian Archimage"—Spenser's villainous Archimage made over into a literary magician and translated back to the Golden Age of Cronos.[15] Here may be found ancient "scrolls of strange device" (very like those in the care of Eumnestes in the stately turret of Spenser's Alma) whence the lady-witch derives her knowledge of the literature of love. Since, like her predecessor Asia, the witch is warmly luminescent (a feature which she shares also with Spenser's Una), she weaves herself a shielding veil of dawn-light, star-beams, and mist (diffused light and atmospheric shrouding) through which to mask the splendor of her love.[16]

Yet like Asia before the reunion with Prometheus, the witch is a lonely being, aloof because uncourted, and for the most part companionless because she is immortal. Her aloneness is emphasized by means of the first real dramatic interlude in the poem. All the Oreads, Naiads, and Hamadryads of the earth beg leave to become her familiars. But she sadly denies them the privilege because they are not immortal: they will vanish when their streams and rivers and oceans go dry, or perish when their trees or mountains fall. If they were allowed to become her satellites, she

---

[15] Shelley is evidently remembering that Spenser's Archimage (*Faerie Queene*, I, i, 36) at one point goes to his study where, amidst

> His magicke bookes and artes of sundry kindes,
> He seekes out mighty charmes, to trouble sleepy mindes.

Some of these magic books, or comparable volumes, have been handed down to the Witch of Atlas. Her study of them teaches her the "mighty charmes" with which she presently goes among mankind, troubling "sleepy mindes."

[16] The documentation of these remarks is readily available outside the pages of this volume, and has been done with sufficient thoroughness not to require repetition here. The curious reader is referred to Douglas Bush, *op. cit.*, to K. Koller, "A Source for Portions of *The Witch of Atlas*," *MLN* 52 (March, 1937), 157-161; to D. L. Clark, "What Was Shelley's Indebtedness to Keats?" *PMLA* 56 (June, 1941), 479-494; and to "A Note on Shelley and Milton," *MLN* (December, 1940), 585-589, and "Spenser and *The Witch of Atlas*," *PMLA* 56 (June, 1941), 472-479.

herself (the everlasting love) would have to weep for them, and she is much too tenderhearted. The sobbing forms depart, and the witch is left alone.

The fountain-symbol provides one of the most important clues to what is perhaps the very obvious meaning of *The Witch of Atlas*. Within the boundaries of her secret paradise (another of those "Elysian, windless, fortunate abodes" mentioned by Demogorgon in the fourth act of *Prometheus*)[17] the witch is safe from the perpetual war of the elements, and it is her custom to hibernate in a magical well of mingled water and fire. The well, which Shelley describes as very active and ebullient, appears to be the equivalent of the burning fountain of love mentioned in *Adonais*,

> A portion of the Eternal, which must glow
> Through time and change, unquenchably the same.

The apparently mixed image in *Adonais*, the "fire for which all thirst," suggests that Shelley was then still thinking of love in terms of an inextinguishable fountain of fire and water.[18] The conception is not, perhaps, uncommon; but a modern scholar believes that Shelley probably found an analogy for it in one of the Greek Romances (by Achilles Tatius), where the author describes a Sicilian fountain "whose waters are mingled with fire." The flame is not extinguished by the water, nor is the "water ignited by the flame, but a mutual truce exists between the elements." Whatever its literary origin, this idea exerted a particular fascination upon Shelley because it connoted the ability of love to unify such diverse elements.

Love is the ruling passion of this poem as it was in Shelley's life. Even the witch's boat, moored upon the glowing surface of the fountain, has been fabricated among the deities of love. Like Homer or Vergil or Ovid, for whom helmets and swords and ships must have a genealogy, Shelley provides the fragile craft with a fantastic history. Either it was fashioned by Vulcan as a gift for Venus and thereafter sold to the witch's father, Apollo; or else it grew like a gourd upon some sensitive plant, tended by "the first-born Love" until it had attained a sufficient size to be scooped out, Indian-fashion, to serve as a coracle.

[17] *Prometheus Unbound*, IV, 531. [18] *Adonais*, Stanzas 38 and 54.

That the witch's trance-like immersion in the well of love has equipped her, as has also her reading, with the harmonizing power is proved by her manufacture of the Hermaphrodite. To assuage her loneliness, she creates a being more beautiful than Pygmalion's image. The allusion to Pygmalion suggests that Shelley was thinking of the Hermaphroditus whom Ovid displays under amorous attack in the fountain of Salmacis.[19] But if this is the truth of the matter, he combined the idea with one from Spenser, where another witch creates False Florimell using snow as a principal ingredient. Shelley is not only imagining that love is capable of blending opposite sexes (as one of the speakers points out in Plato's *Symposium*); he is also fancifully supposing that the witchery of love can effect a combination of fire and snow. The witch tempers the "repugnant mass" with "liquid love," for, as Shelley says,

> All things together grow
> Through which the harmony of love can pass.

The idea is of course a favorite with Spenser. By love's power, says Colin Clout, the world was made of yore.

> For how should else things so far from attone
> And so great enemies as of them bee,
> Be ever drawne together into one,
> And taught in such accordance to agree?
> Through him the cold began to covet heat,
> And water fire; the light to mount on hie,
> And th' heavie downe to peize; the hungry t'eat
> And voydnesse to seeke full satietie.[20]

So creative a being as the Witch of Atlas cannot, however, reach "full satietie" by such expedients as the fashioning of Hermaphrodite. Love is not passive but active. Thus it is probably in Shelley's view inevitable (since she has in her boat a means of transportation and in the Hermaphrodite a suitable companion) that she should descend from her lofty and lonely citadel into the world of men.

[19] As Douglas Bush points out, Ovid's figure is said to be a scion of Atlas. *Metamorphoses*, IV, 368. See Bush, *op. cit.*, p. 142, note 33.
[20] Spenser, *Colin Clout*, 841-850.

The witch does not, however, move directly into the minds and hearts of mankind. Her route is as devious as that of Milton's Satan before he finally fixed upon the serpent as the most convenient means of gaining acceptance in Eden.[21] Her first move, after she leaves her private Ethiopian paradise, is to another paradise in the vicinity of the South Pole. Shelley was evidently aware of the tradition, to which Milton alludes in *Paradise Lost*, that "True Paradise" lies under the "Ethiop Line" by "Nilus Head," and is enclosed by a wall of shining rock "A whole day's journey high."[22] But he had also developed in *The Revolt of Islam* the conception of an antarctic Paradise. It is to this region that the witch first descends. "Beyond the fabulous Thamandocana" (Timbuctoo) she possesses an Austral lake paved with constellations, just such a calm and flower-surrounded south polar sea as the Spirit of Good in *The Revolt of Islam* chose as the site of his temple. Here enormous armies of ministering spirits construct her imperial tent, which Shelley describes in imagery borrowed from the account of the construction of Pandemonium in the first book of *Paradise Lost*.[23] If Shelley needed any justification for the borrowing of this imagery, he doubtless found it in the fact that this antarctic retreat is also a pandemonium—though a concourse of the daemons of love in place of the *omnium gatherum* of hateful demons in Milton's nether world.

When she was not listening to the latest reports on the state of the cosmos beside her Austral Lake, or ascending to the level of the stratospheric spirits to help control the weather, the witch's choicest sport was quietly to change the habits and attitudes of men through the use of visions. Her nocturnal expeditions followed "old Nilus" from its headwaters in the vicinity of her Ethiopian mountain to the river's broader reaches in ancient Egypt. There, going ashore, the wizard-maiden "passed through the peopled haunts of humankind," sowing "sweet visions" in the minds of sleeping mortals. To the most beautiful among them she gave "strange panacea in a crystal bowl," and these lived afterwards as if they had submitted to a new control even more powerful than

---

[21] Satan spends a week in darkness, thrice encircling the equinoctial line, and four times encircling the earth longitudinally from pole to pole. *Paradise Lost*, IX, 63-83.

[22] *Paradise Lost*, IV, 282-284.   [23] *Paradise Lost*, I, 710-730.

life itself. Reluctant lovers were encouraged with innocently erotic thoughts and were appropriately astonished to discover that they had collaborated in the production of young; broken friendships were knitted up in the interests of fraternal understanding among men. Upon the brains of the "less beautiful" the wizard-maiden wrote "strange dreams": misers, liars, priests, and kings felt the impress of her practical jocularity. Soldiers beat their swords to ploughshares, and jailers released "those of the liberal schism" to stride through the streets of Memphis and to disturb the complacency of King Amasis.

Were it not that the witch indulges in certain bawdy political antics, the over-all tone of the poem would seem rather kittenish. Shelley had, for the time being, let his political perseverance out to play in fields of asphodel and Egyptian catnip. If his tone is kittenish, his manner relaxed, and his powers of moral persuasion disappointingly clawless, his excuse for the lapse can be found in the dedicatory poem addressed to his wife Mary and prefixed to *The Witch*:

> What, though no mice are caught by a young kitten,
> May it not leap and play as grown cats do,
> Till its claws come?

Shelley's original claws had been blunted by long use in the arenas of political reform, and he may have felt compelled to revert to kittenhood in order to grow another set. The *Oedipus Tyrannus*, begun a week later, shows that the new claws grew fast.

To explain the meaning of the Witch of Atlas requires no abstruse neo-Platonics. Grabo compares her to Asia before the reunion with Prometheus: she is "the spirit of love and beauty in nature, Venus, the earthly incarnation of the divine love . . . [and] Minerva, goddess of intellectual beauty."[24] Bush succinctly describes her as Asia "on a holiday."[25] But she is also a female counterpart of the prankish Hermes of the Homeric Hymn; she is Vergil's Massylian priestess; she is Una, and she is Alma; she is the joyous nymph of *L'Allegro* bidding loathed melancholy an impolite adieu, and bringing quips and cranks (and even wanton jollity) into the vacated place; she is a female Archimage without evil

---

[24] Grabo, *The Magic Plant*, pp. 334-335.   [25] Bush, *op. cit.*, pp. 139-140.

intent, and she is Eve before the Fall. In short, the witch is a composite portrait of all the womanly grace, wisdom, beauty, and sympathy that Shelley could conceive of, and she would resemble the visionary maiden of *Alastor* in this and other respects if she were not as chaste and sexless as "holy Dian" before "she stooped to kiss Endymion." As such, she takes her place beside Asia and the Lady of *The Sensitive Plant* in the hierarchy of Shelley heroines. But the most interesting aspect of the witch is her variety of ancestors; she is a literary hybrid of more complex genealogy than any other among those which Shelley nurtured and brought to final flower.

Peacock once told Shelley that his poetry was of two sorts: daydreams and nightmares. The visionary rhymes of 1820 are all daydreams, though a nightmare of mildew and mold, of cold and damp, fearfully intrudes upon the radiant warmth of the garden in *The Sensitive Plant*. Day-dreaming was not new to Shelley. What was new with him was that breach in the wall of his perseverance, that rather touching determination to take refuge in the future—either the future life, or the predictable future in which his name and the doctrines he had preached would take a firmer root in the consciousness of society than they had done in his lifetime. His day-dreaming, in short, was directed towards two kinds of immortality. In such day-dreaming there is a strong suggestion of quietism. Shelley no longer emphasizes, as he did in *Prometheus Unbound*, the necessity of moral action in the here and now. His mood is not that of the self-steeling Beatrice Cenci when she cries, "Something must be done. What, yet I know not." His small community of true friends is a partial compensation for that stark loneliness which would otherwise confound him. But there is in him now, more markedly than ever before, a deep heliotropic drive, a hunger after the immortal state, which makes him turn his face away from the "error, ignorance, and strife" of this world, and up to the unfailing light of the supernal sun.

8

COR CORDIUM: *EPIPSYCHIDION*

The distorted notions of invisible things which Dante and his rival Milton have idealized, are merely the mask and mantle in which these great poets walk through eternity enveloped and disguised.

—SHELLEY IN *A Defence of Poetry*

What the . . . visionary hails as his ideal will be no picture of his destiny or that of the world. It will be, and will always remain, merely a picture of his heart. This picture, indestructible in its ideal essence, will mirror also the hearts of those who may share, or may have shared, the nature of the poet who drew it. So purely ideal and so deeply human are the visions of Shelley. So truly does he deserve the epitaph which a clear-sighted friend wrote upon his tomb: *cor cordium*, the heart of hearts.

—SANTAYANA IN *The Winds of Doctrine*

· I ·

IN the single decade of his poetic career Shelley completed three poems of a very considerable magnitude.[1] Each of them represents a dynamic synthesis of themes and images with which he had been experimenting in prior poems, and all of them stand as landmarks in his writing life. These poems are *Prometheus Unbound, Epipsychidion,* and *Adonais.* Like *Alastor, Prometheus Unbound* is a study of a state of mind, though for dramatic effect that state must be shadowed forth in visual images. Like *The Revolt, Prometheus* is a study of revolution, though one which occurs within the human consciousness rather than a political effort within the body of society. The synthesis achieved is dynamic and many-layered because, when the poet brings into collocation the elements which he

[1] *The Triumph of Life,* a poem of at least equal magnitude, was not completed. Its implications are considered in the Epilogue of this book.

has treated separately, or differently, in the two preceding poems, he produces a quite new and different order of values, and likewise an internal organic harmony where hitherto disparate and even unlike elements are made to supplement and complement one another, so that the life-blood of each informs and revivifies the tissues of the others. The instrument of articulation which is largely responsible for maintaining balance and symmetry in the new collocation is a ready-made armature of myth, derived from Aeschylus' *Prometheus Bound*, but of course shaped and bent, clipped and fitted, until it can do the supporting work which is newly required of it.

What the *Prometheus* is to Shelley's poetry in the period 1815-1818, *Epipsychidion* and *Adonais* are to the poetry of 1818-1821. His sense of the vast conspiracy of human society and what might be called the worldly life against the sensitive individual soul, his overwhelming experience of that heartless persecution to which the innocent and free are continually subjected by the obtuse and the unscrupulous, had been set forth in the conversation-pieces of 1818-1819, in *The Masque of Anarchy* during the fall of 1819, and in *The Sensitive Plant* during the spring of 1820. His dream-like consciousness of a supernal region of light, harmony, liberty, beauty, and love (these concepts being used almost interchangeably by Shelley) had reached its fullest expression before 1821 in the third and fourth acts of *Prometheus*. By the use of nature-images he had tried to suggest and embody the Idea in *The Sensitive Plant* and the *Letter to Maria Gisborne*; in *The Witch* he had tried once again by using symbolism derived from classical and renaissance mythology. *Epipsychidion* and *Adonais* brought into collocation the themes of earthly discord and heavenly concord not, it is true, for the first time, but as if through his experiments with *The Sensitive Plant* and *The Witch*, Shelley had reached an even sharper realization of the real disparity between his heavenly vision and his view of the worldly life. As in the first of his master-poems he sustained the whole with a modification of Aeschylean myth, so now he fixed respectively upon Dante's *Vita Nuova* and *Paradiso*, and the Adonis-myth from Bion and Moschus, as the new *modus dicendi*.[2] These "sources," as in *Prometheus*, determine the

---

[2] One may notice here the remark Shelley made in the *Defence* (*Prose*, VII, 130): "*The Divina Commedia* and *Paradise Lost* have conferred upon modern mythology

formal approach and provide the means whereby antecedent themes can be brought into a new synthesis.

The close imaginative rapport between *Epipsychidion* and *Adonais* on the one hand, and *A Defence of Poetry* on the other, makes Shelley's greatest critical essay a useful gloss upon his intention in the two difficult poems now to be considered. *Epipsychidion* was completed and sent off to publication by mid-February, the *Defence* by March 20, and the privately printed copy of *Adonais* was sent to London soon after the completion of the elegy on June 8. All three thus belong to the first half of 1821. All three spring from the conviction that poetry—broadly defined to include all great thinking of an idealistic kind, whatever its form—is man's highest calling. All three deal in various ways with the actualities of the creative process. All three examine the poet's relation to his own inmost self, to the divine fire which informs all great poetry, to the world of nature and human society. In all three there are representations and symbolic descriptions of the corrupting forces, both inside and outside the poet, which constantly threaten his integrity and limit his chances of being understood. There is, in short, a deep inner coherence among these three documents which must be taken into account by one who would deal fairly and fully with them.

This coherence has not been sufficiently marked by critics of Shelley. But what seems hardly to have been observed at all is that *Epipsychidion, Adonais*, the *Defence*, and the fragmentary *Triumph of Life* have a common frame of reference and to a certain extent share in the complex inner symbolic structure which was present to Shelley's mind when they were composed, but which cannot be understood until they are studied together. To have evolved this structure was an imaginative achievement of the first order; Shelley's success with these poems is limited chiefly by the fact that, unlike Dante, he lacked the architectonic skill to order it solidly and to anchor it firmly within the compass of a single work of art. The difficulty for Shelley was to confine and discipline his image-making power, and more than that his image-fusing power, so that what was made or what was fused would stand firm long enough to be comprehended by those who sought to follow in his

a systematic form." Where it suited him, Shelley borrowed elements from Dante's system.

train. There was a continuous expansiveness in Shelley's imagination; there was a protean shiftiness to his images, for which cloud-shapes as they change form, or sunset-colors as they merge and brighten and fade, provide a kind of illustration. The fault in these poems is not a fault of vision except in a secondary sense; the real fault is in the multiplicity of the ways in which that vision is projected, a fault, let us say, of re-presentation. This fault matters, of course, but not so greatly as one might at first suppose. The very complexity and magnitude of the conception, Shelley's sense of the interrelation and ultimate unity of the cosmos, requires that he fight shy of oversimplification, because any oversimplification is, *ipso facto*, a kind of lie, and he is desperately determined, if he can, to communicate his vision of the truth in all its manifold, shifting, interrelated, expanding complexity.

· II ·

"FEW poets of the highest class," wrote Shelley in the spring of 1821, "have chosen to exhibit the beauty of their conceptions in its naked truth and splendour; and it is doubtful whether the alloy of costume, habit, etc., be not necessary to temper this planetary music for mortal ears."[3] This remark, like several others in *The Defence of Poetry*, had a strongly empirical basis. Only a few weeks earlier Shelley had completed and sent to London a poem in which the splendor of his conception of heavenly love had been presented in semilocalized terminology. Ostensibly, *Epipsychidion* was a love-poem in praise of the nineteen-year-old Italian beauty whom the Shelleys had discovered in the latter part of 1820, a virtual prisoner in the obscure convent of St. Anna at Pisa: "the only Italian," said Shelley, "for whom I ever felt any interest."[4] Actually, though Shelley's adoption of the name of a particular woman as the focal point of his poem has deceived some literalists into supposing that *Epipsychidion* is an invitation to adulterous elopement, Emilia is only, or mainly, one more metaphor of the Shelleyan epipsyche. Those of the "most delicate sensibility and the most enlarged imagination," he wrote in the *Defence*, are often aware of "evanescent visitations of thought and feeling" comparable in their effects to "the interpenetration of a diviner nature

---

[3] *Defence, Prose*, VII, 117. [4] *Letters*, x, 249.

through our own." Being by definition persons of the "most refined [nervous] organization," poets are both subject to such semi-
mystical experiences and sufficiently articulate to arrest the "vanishing apparitions which haunt the interlunations of life," to veil
them "in language or in form," and to send them forth from "the
caverns of the spirit" into the world of men. Poetry, said Shelley,
"redeems from decay the visitations of the divinity in man."[5] *Epipsychidion* was not in its deeper movements a love-poem to a particular Italian girl, though it masqueraded as one. It was Shelley's
attempt to arrest and to project an apparition with which his
imagination had always been haunted.

This elusive concept assumed, in the course of Shelley's lifetime, many more shapes than the "Carpathian wizard," Proteus.
In his periodic attempts to "veil" the phantom "in language or in
form," which usually meant the fusion of its substance in a particular image, he had always felt a measure of defeat. This is very
likely why he translated the conception into so many different
terms; but it is also why all of these terms bear a generic resemblance one to another. Asia, Emilia, Urania—these were names. It
was what these names ultimately signified which was important to
Shelley.

The Idea which bears the name of Emilia in *Epipsychidion* may
be defined as that part of the inmost soul which participates in the
world-soul. Shelley had attempted an exposition of this mystical
idea in the prose fragment, "On Love." Here Shelley defines the
epipsyche (the "soul within our soul" which gave him the title of
his poem) as a miniature of the inmost self. It is, however, a self
so purified of "all that we condemn or despise" that it is in fact the
"ideal prototype of every thing excellent and lovely that we are
capable of conceiving as belonging to the nature of man." It is in
itself as sexless as an angel, for on the spiritual plane where Shelley is standing, sexual distinctions are of no consequence. He indicates its completely ideal character by comparing it to a special
kind of selective mirror which "reflects only the forms of purity
and brightness."[6] This is the Idea behind the figure of Emilia in
Epipsychidion.

The perception of the pure Idea carried with it an overpowering
desire "to arrest the faintest shadow" of the conception which

[5] *Defence, Prose,* vii, 137.   [6] *Prose,* vi, 202.

ruled his mind, and hence to seek exemplifications of it wherever and whenever he thought they could be found. He was early impelled by this consuming *eros* to try to discover in some human creature "an understanding capable of clearly estimating" his own; an "imagination which should enter into and seize upon the subtle and delicate peculiarities" which he "delighted to cherish and unfold in secret"; and a "frame" whose nerves would "vibrate with the vibrations" of his own. This ideal was, he said, "the invisible and unattainable point to which Love tends."[7]

If the intensity of Shelley's desire was such that he sometimes believed that he had found the living antetype of his conception, it may be that when he first saw the ardent Italian brunette with the classic face and the voluptuous eyes he really imagined that he had found at last his true epipsyche. On the other hand he was perfectly familiar, as his notes to *Hellas* show, with that state of mind "in which ideas . . . assume the force of sensations through the confusion of thought with the objects of thought" and in which "excess of passion" animates "the creations of imagination." It is worth remembering that Shelley had recently been reading Dante, where he had had occasion to watch with awe the apotheosis of another Italian girl, not only into the most famous figure in the literature of the Italian Renaissance, but also into an emblem of Dante's highest religious aspirations.

On the whole it was unfortunate for the future reputation of his poem that Shelley found it impossible to exhibit his conception in "its naked truth and splendour." In one of the cancelled passages of *Epipsychidion* he had come closer to defining it:

> There is a Power, a Love, a Joy, a God
> Which makes in mortal hearts its brief abode
> A Pythian exhalation which inspires
> Love, only love.

Metaphorical language was always necessary: the power produces "a mood which language faints beneath." Its effect is like that of a wind across the wires "of the soul's giant harp." It was this power,

---

[7] *Idem.* The "vibrations" metaphor may be drawn from music, most likely the conception of a chord. Cf. *Epipsychidion* (142-145):

> Are we not formed, as notes of music are,
> For one another, though dissimilar;
> Such difference without discord, as can make
> Those sweetest sounds. . . .

this joy, this emanation from the regions of the sun, this wind across the taut responsive wires of the soul, which he was really trying to define. The love inspired was like the consuming *eros* which filled the Sensitive Plant from its root to its topmost leaf. But the love which did the inspiring, love as goal rather than love as *eros*, often took, so high was Shelley's reverence for womankind, the shape and quality of a woman when he attempted to define it metaphorically.

Although care should be exercised not to overemphasize the influence Dante's poetry exerted upon the composition of *Epipsychidion*, Shelley's estimate of Dante's worth was very high. He had formed an acquaintance with parts of the *Divine Comedy* late in 1817, and there was a corner of the Milan Cathedral to which, during the following spring, he used to retire with a copy of Dante.[8] In the summer of 1819 he and Mary read a number of cantos together.[9] In 1820 he translated a *canzone* from the *Convito*, and in the early months of 1821, while the *Epipsychidion* was being composed, the Shelleys read the *Vita Nuova*.[10]

Shelley's own *Vita Nuova* was probably though not certainly composed during the first six weeks of 1821, and the manuscript was sent off to Charles Ollier on February 16 to be issued without the author's name. "It is to be published," said Shelley, "simply for the esoteric few; and I make its author a secret, to avoid the malignity of those who turn sweet food into poison." The edition was to be strictly limited to a hundred copies, and Shelley ventured the guess that even so small an edition might be too large, since "those who are capable of judging and feeling rightly with respect to a composition of so abstruse a nature certainly do not arrive at that number."[11]

[8] *Letters*, IX, 257 and 298. On Dec. 7, 1817, Shelley ordered H. F. Cary's translation of the *Purgatorio* and the *Paradiso*.

[9] F. L. Jones, *Letters of Mary W. Shelley*, I, 77. In the winter of 1819-1820, Shelley and Mary viewed with amused alarm Medwin's attempts to render Dante into English. *Ibid.*, I, 129. Jan. 14, 1821.

[10] *Shelley and Mary*, III, 582. The learned and enthusiastic Dantean, John Taaffe, came to their house in the evening of Dec. 3, 1820, and was thereafter a frequent visitor. *Shelley and Mary*, III, 548 *et seq.*, *passim*. Taaffe had made a translation of Dante, with a 2-volume commentary which Shelley admired and tried to have published by Ollier. One volume of the commentary appeared in 1822 under John Murray's aegis. See *Letters*, X, 260, 276 and note, and Helen Angeli, *Shelley and his Friends in Italy* (London, 1911), p. 179.

[11] *Letters*, X, 236. The editors of the Julian edition make an odd error in their footnote on this page in saying that Shelley had completed *Epipsychidion* before

Shelley's insistence on the abstruseness of the poem's essential doctrine, its esoteric nature, its purity and sweetness which "the vulgar" could easily corrupt through misunderstanding, is especially noteworthy in view of the remarks he was shortly to make about Dante in *A Defence of Poetry*. Shelley wished the poem to be accepted and read as "a mystery."[12] It is as an explorer of the mysteries of love that Dante is praised in the *Defence*, where we are told that he "understood the secret things of love even more than Petrarch," and where the *Vita Nuova* is called "an inexhaustible fountain of purity of sentiment and language." There also the *Paradiso* is said to be "a perpetual hymn of everlasting love"; Dante's "apotheosis of Beatrice in Paradise, and the gradations of his own love and her loveliness, by which as by steps he feigns himself to have ascended to the throne of the Supreme Cause" seem to Shelley "the most glorious imagination of modern poetry."[13] The *Epipsychidion* was likewise a hymn in honor of everlasting love, a monument along the path of Dante.

Perhaps Shelley did little enough to make this intention clear, even to the more serious and attentive reader. But the advertisement contains a hint or two for the sapient. *Epipsychidion* is said to resemble the *Vita Nuova* in being "sufficiently intelligible to a certain class of readers." Others, says the poet, will miss the point because of a defect in their organs of intellectual perception. Shelley also throws in a quotation from the end of section xxv of *Vita Nuova*, whose implication is that he could, if he chose, provide the true explanation for what the poem sets forth with high "rhetorical coloring" under the "garb of a figure."[14] More to the point would have been the remark with which Dante opens the same section of the *Vita Nuova*: "It may be that some person . . . [will] be perplexed at my speaking of Love as if it were a thing in itself, and

---

the close of 1820. The evidence cited is Mary's letter to Hunt, Dec. 29, 1820, which alludes to "a long poem." But the long poem was by Rosini. See Jones, *Letters of Mary W. Shelley*, I, 124.

[12] *Letters*, x, 333.   [13] *Defence, Prose*, VII, 128.

[14] The quotation, which Shelley gives in Italian, reads as follows in English: "It would be a great disgrace to him who should rhyme anything under the garb of a figure or of rhetorical coloring, if afterwards, being asked, he should not be able to denude his words of this garb, in such wise that they should have a true meaning." See *The New Life of Dante Alighieri*, trans. C. E. Norton (Boston, 1895), p. 59. Several cancelled passages in *Epipsychidion* broadly hint that Shelley was not writing about flesh and blood—as do several letters also.

not only an intellectual substance, but as if it were a corporal substance."[15]

Shelley's second hint to the esoteric was another quotation from Dante: the final stanza of a *canzone* from the *Convito* which he had translated in 1820. Those sufficiently curious to examine the second book of the *Convito* (where this *Canzone* stands at the core of the discussion) could find Dante explaining that books can be understood, and ought to be explained, in four principal senses: the literal sense ("the simple narration of the thing of which you treat"); the allegorical ("truth concealed beneath a fair fiction"); the moral (i.e. how to live best); and the anagogical (referring to "supernal things of the eternal glory").[16]

Whether or not Shelley had in mind Dante's four modes, they are all applicable to *Epipsychidion*. Literally speaking, the poem is the story of the advent of a beautiful and responsive woman named Emilia into the life of one who had hitherto searched in vain for such a paragon as she. The narrator concludes with a lengthy account of his retirement with his lady to a fortunate island in the Aegean sea, where the two live thereafter a life of divine simplicity.[17] The allegorical meaning of the poem, the truth concealed beneath this "fair fiction," is that the search for a special kind of complementary being is the dominant motive in the lives of all sensitive, idealistic, and creative men. The moral meaning, largely comprised in Shelley's definition of "True Love," is abstrusely stated at the close of the first section of the poem and will presently be examined in detail. Anagogically, as Shelley said of Dante's *Paradiso*, the poem is a "perpetual hymn" to that love which activates in man the higher forms of creativity.

Except for several verbal echoes, *Epipsychidion* does not follow the scheme of the *Vita Nuova* in any particularized way.[18] But

[15] *The New Life*, p. 56.

[16] *The Banquet of Dante Alighieri*, tr. Katharine Hillard (London, 1889), pp. 51-53.

[17] Shelley sought to give his poem the aspect of a realistic narrative by pretending in his advertisement that its author had died at Florence while "preparing for a voyage to one of the wildest of the Sporades . . . where it was his hope to have realized a scheme of life, suited perhaps to that happier and better world of which he is now an inhabitant, but hardly practicable in this."

[18] Ackermann, Woodberry, and Locock have noticed these verbal echoes. The last of these editors provides the fullest list. See his edition of the complete poems (London, 1911) II, 453-458.

Shelley's characterization of his own poem and of Dante's work are strikingly similar. The *Vita Nuova*, said Shelley in the *Defence*, "is the idealized history of that period and those intervals of [Dante's] life which were dedicated to love." The *Epipsychidion*, he told John Gisborne, was "an idealized history" of his own "life and feelings." One was "always in love with something or other." The real difficulty, he added, consisted in "seeking in a mortal image the likeness of what is perhaps eternal."[19] When Shelley read Dante's description of his first meeting with "the glorious Lady of my mind, who was called Beatrice by many who knew not what to call her,"[20] he had, in effect, a striking analogue for his own first meeting with that glorious "Lady" who had so long sat enthroned in the highest circle of his thoughts.

In coming to the poem itself, two further observations should be made about Emilia Viviani's relation to it. Although it is dedicated to her, and although her name is twice used in the text, the actual circumstances of her life have nothing to do with the conduct of the piece. The first twenty lines, where the imprisoned Emilia is addressed under the apt figure of a caged nightingale, and where veiled compliments are paid to her skill as a purveyor of "music," are in effect a dedicatory lyric. With these out of the way, Shelley proceeds to the real business at hand. The second point is that in one form or another most of the elements of *Epipsychidion* can be located with ease in Shelley's earlier "ideal" poetry. Emilia is another manifestation of Intellectual Beauty, of Asia the "light of life," and of the radiant lady whom the Sensitive Plant adores. *Alastor* provides an earlier example of the central movement of the poem, the history of the search for an epipsyche, while the Laon-Cythna, Lionel-Helen, and Prometheus-Asia relationships have all involved, with certain variations, a similar story. The island, or its equivalent, is to be found in *The Revolt*, the *Lines Written Among the Euganean Hills*, the *Prometheus*, and *The Witch of Atlas*. Without the immediate "inspiration" which Emilia provided, the particular poem called *Epipsychidion* might not have been committed to paper. But its leading ideas are all foreshadowed in the prior poems.

[19] *Letters*, x, 401.   [20] *Vita Nuova*, section 2.

· III ·

THE poem is perhaps best described as an extended psychological and philosophical lyric with some narrative elements. It contains three formal movements, each of approximately equal length, and each rising at some point to a climactic passage. The first of these (lines 1-189) is a prolonged semidescriptive invocation, replete with clusters of imagery, and bearing also the burden of the poem's philosophic statement. The second movement (lines 190-387) contains the "idealized history" of Shelley's "life and feelings," though it should be pointed out at once that the "life" (as almost invariably in Shelley's poetry) is that of the mind rather than veiled autobiography. The third movement (lines 388-604) describes the voyage to, and the ideal life within, the island paradise. This section culminates in what is clearly intended to be the climax of the poem, a passage which employs sexual imagery to symbolize the absolute and permanent union, on a spiritual plane, of the human spirit (the creative soul) and the divine power it requires.

Through most of Part I, Shelley strives with epithets to suggest the magnitude of his conception. The first group of images in the invocation all share in a single conception: that the "seraph of heaven" who is being addressed gathers and veils in her radiant woman's form the light of that realm which lies above the dark chaos of mortal life. She is a benediction in the eternal curse, the glory of the lampless universe, a moon beyond the clouds, a star above the storm, a harmonizer (like the sun) of all nature, and finally—in Platonic terms, a living "Form" among the walking dead who inhabit this nether world. The second group of images coheres around the notion of solace: a soul formed to be blessed and to bless, a well of "secret" (this adjective should be observed) happiness whose waters banish gloom, a smile amid frowns, a lute whose music lulls grief asleep. Shelley vainly searches the world of fancy for an adequate summarizing image. Failing in the attempt, he next tries to describe the effect of a meeting with her. But the visual images with which he commences presently dissolve in light and she becomes "one serene Omnipresence," gathered into that beauty "which penetrates and clasps and fills the world," or as Shelley called it in *Adonais*, the One Spirit of the plastic stress. Here the poet draws up once more, conscious of the inade-

quacy of his language, and begins again the search for the summarizing phrase:

> See where she stands! a mortal shape indued
> With love and life and light and deity,
> And motion which may change but cannot die;
> An image of some bright Eternity;
> A shadow of some golden dream; a Splendour
> Leaving the third sphere pilotless; a tender
> Reflection of the eternal Moon of Love,
> Under whose motions life's dull billows move;
> A metaphor of Spring and Youth and Morning;
> A Vision like incarnate April, warning,
> With smiles and tears, Frost the Anatomy
> Into his summer grave.

Most remarkable here is the Protean variety of the images. For
that variety betokens Shelley's hovering sense of failure to make
language penetrate to the core of the mystery. We have not Eternity but an *image* of it; not the golden dream but the *shadow* of it;
not the Moon of love but the *reflection* of it; not Spring, and
Youth, and Morning but only their *metaphor*. Yet the lines, like
the shape on whom they focus, display uninterrupted motion, the
inward stir of all that grows or rises towards the light. As Shelley
earlier introduced a Platonic image, he now quietly derives one
from the *canzone* of Dante of which he has quoted a stanza in his
advertisement. This *canzone* opens with an invocation: "Ye who
intelligent the Third Heaven move." The Third Heaven is the
sphere of Venus, guided by supreme intelligences or "Splendours,"
and Shelley's goddess is compared to one of these.[21]

The attempt to define "true love" concludes this opening section
of the poem and is possibly the most abstruse passage in the whole
of the mystery. The fundamental notion is the limitlessness of love;
it is an enormous unused potential in life. Since it is an indestructible essence coeternal with the universe, rather than a tangible substance like gold or clay, there is no limit to the number of times it
may be subdivided by all sentient and even inanimate beings,
whether consciously or not, according to their respective capabili-

[21] A few months later Shelley made an extended application of the image. See
the discussion of *Adonais*, stanzas 44-46, in the following chapter.

ties. For human beings the great instrument for its apprehension is imaginative thought, and the inevitable result of its apprehension is pleasure.[22] A further refinement of the matter is that both thought and pleasure resemble love: however many times they are subdivided, they are still inexhaustible. The limitless power of love is described at the deep well of truth from which sages draw the sustenance of hope; it is likewise the "eternal law" which guides all those to whom the mundane life is like a ravaged garden which they are working to recreate.[23] The conclusion is that since love is an inexhaustible source of power and pleasure, any attempt to confine it within narrow limits is morally wrong. Shelley therefore asserts that he has never joined that great modern "sect," each of whose members singles out one other person as the sole recipient of his love. Whoever loves in his heart, contemplates in his brain, or creates in his spirit only one "Form" is in effect confining eternity in a sepulcher of his own devising, and is so far contradicting the law of the universe—as Diotima told Socrates.

This romantic expansiveness, this centrifugality, implies another characteristic of true love. As Shelley describes it in a later passage, love is the enemy of all constraint whatsoever: it overleaps all boundaries; it pierces "its continents" with an invisible but lightning-like violence; it can no more be grasped than the free winds of heaven; its incursions are as unavoidable as those of death. Yet love is stronger than lightning or wind or death. For with love the human spirit can burst free from the charnel, the chain, the agony, the dust, and the chaos of this life.[24]

Shelley compares love also to the liberating agencies of the mind. It resembles understanding, which grows bright by "gazing on many truths" instead of confining itself to one. Chiefly it resembles the imagination, which is at once the strongest instrument for the apprehension of love, and the best weapon for the extirpation of human error. Shelley's reason for associating love with

[22] Cf. the *Defence*: "There are two kinds of pleasure, one durable, universal, and permanent; the other transitory or particular." In the passage above Shelley seems to be speaking of both.

[23] This image should be noticed in connection with *The Sensitive Plant*, where the ravaged garden at the end of the poem symbolizes life when love is absent.

[24] Lines 397-407. By the same token, as the fragment "On Love" asserts, man without love is as good as dead. "So soon as this want or power is dead, man becomes the living sepulchre of himself, and what yet survives is the mere husk." (*Prose*, vi, 202.)

imagination is more explicitly stated in the *Defence* than in the *Epipsychidion*. Since the two passages were probably composed only a few months apart, the *Defence* provides a useful gloss to Shelley's meaning. "The great secret of morals is love," says Shelley, and he defines love, as we have seen, as "a going out of our own nature, and an identification of ourselves with the beautiful which exists in thought, action, or person, not our own." Imagination is the instrument by which our nature is enabled to "go out," to identify itself with the beautiful outside the imaginer. "A man, to be greatly good, must imagine intensely and comprehensively; he must put himself in the place of another and of many others." Hence "the great instrument of moral good is the imagination," as the great source of moral good is love.[25]

In the ultimate refinement of Shelley's thought, love is conceived of both as that supreme essence which is loved and that *eros* which impels the soul to love. For it is the nature of the supreme essence to "interpenetrate"—Shelley often describes its movement as an "effluence"—and as soon as interpenetration occurs, the soul is impelled to unite with the essence whose effluence it feels. Whoever has grasped this conception has arrived at the philosophic center of *Epipsychidion*.

The second section of the poem is the idealized history of Shelley's life and feelings, presented under the image of a quest.

> There was a Being whom my spirit oft
> Met on its visioned wanderings, far aloft
> In the clear golden prime of my youth's dawn.[26]

But as he sprang from the dream-filled caverns of his youth and rose like a moth towards "the lodestar of [his] one desire" the Being vanished under the "dreary cone of our life's shade." He would have followed, even across the gulf of the grave, except that he heard a voice beside him saying:

[25] *Defence, Prose,* vii, 118. Shelley's fragment "On Love" defines love as "the bond or sanction which connects not only man with man, but with everything which exists." He is evidently using *sanction* in its ethical sense: an influence which impels towards moral action.

[26] Cf. the *Canzone* in Dante's *Convito* (Shelley's translation), stanza ii:

> A sweet thought, which was once the life within
> This heavy heart, many a time and oft
> Went up before our Father's feet, and there
> It saw a glorious Lady throned aloft.

"O thou of hearts the weakest,
The Phantom is beside thee whom thou seekest."
Then I—"Where?"—the world's echo answered "Where?"[27]
And in that silence, and in my despair,
I questioned every tongueless wind that flew
Over my tower of mourning, if it knew
Whither 'twas fled, this soul out of my soul.

The night that had closed upon his epipsyche could not be dissipated either by prayer or by verse. On the other hand, neither prayer nor verse could "uncreate"

That world within this Chaos, mine and me,
Of which she was the veiled Divinity,
The world I say of thoughts that worshipped her.[28]

In this dilemma (inability to dissolve the cone of shade which concealed his epipsyche, and inability to dissipate the *eros* which made him yearn towards her) he set out upon his quest.

In many mortal forms I rashly sought
The shadow of that idol of my thought.[29]

His experiences were at first disastrous. He found a False Florimell whose "touch was as electric poison," whose glances sent flame into his vitals, and whose bosom emanated a killing air which pierced to the core of his green heart and lay upon its leaves until, withering, they hid its unblown prime "with ruins of unseasonable

[27] A similar passage occurs in Dante's *Canzone* (Shelley's translation), stanza iv:
"Thou are not dead, but thou hast wanderèd,
Thou Soul of ours, who thyself dost fret,"
A Spirit of gentle Love beside me said.
For that fair Lady, whom thou dost regret,
Hath so transformed the life which thou hast led,
Thou scornest it, so worthless art thou made.

[28] Lines 243-245. The syntax of this passage is difficult. Shelley is making a distinction between the chaos (the *not-me* or that which lies outside the epicenter of the soul) and the *me* (the central firm microcosm within the chaos, "the world of thoughts that worshipped her"). The idea recurs in lines 345-346, where Shelley addresses the "Twin spheres of light who rule this passive Earth, This world of love, this *me*." The italicization here is Shelley's own.

[29] Cf. Dante's *Canzone* (Shelley's translation), stanza iv: "And still call thou her Woman in thy thought."

time."[30] There were other forms, as well—fair, wise, or true—but none of them conformed to his vision.

At last, when he stood at desperate bay like a hunted deer, deliverance came in a form "as like the glorious shape" which he had dreamed of as the moon is like the sun. She calmed, concealed, and protected him, and for a long time he lay within "a chaste cold bed" like a sensitive plant in moonlight—neither alive nor dead. His status was indeed so indeterminate that both Death and Life, coming to look upon him, cried in chorus, "Away, he is not of our crew."

When the Moon had run through her several phases and begun to shrink "as in the sickness of eclipse," his soul was left like a lampless sea. At this point, a tempest shook the ocean of his sleep, a storm in the spirit apparently induced by the proximity of the fiery "Planet of that hour." This Planet, however, was soon "quenched."[31] Then frost crept across the moving waters, sealing all in a death of ice, which gaped and split through the force of internal (emotional) earthquakes, while over all the white moon smiled powerlessly down.

At this juncture, itself nearly as desperate as that from which the Moon had saved him, there arrived at long last the Vision he had "sought through grief and shame"—radiant as spring, "soft as an incarnation of the Sun," paving and roofing her way with flowers, "dissolving the dull cold in the frore air," and calling to his reborn spirit, which rose now in the living light. The section concludes, after an invocation presently to be discussed in connection with the total pattern, with a direct address to the epipsyche:

> Lady mine,
> Scorn not these flowers of thought, the fading birth,

[30] Cf. Dante's *Canzone* (Shelley's translation), stanza III:
> This lovely Thought, which once would talk with me
> Of a bright seraph sitting crowned on high,
> Found such a cruel foe it died.

Cf. also *Epipsychidion* (307) "I wept, and though it be a dream, I weep" and the *Canzone* (Shelley's translation), "My spirit wept, the grief is hot even now." Through most of this passage, the speaker employs a metaphor of the destruction of a plant. The inevitable comparison is to *The Sensitive Plant*.

[31] Shelley does not call this Planet fiery but implies this notion by saying that it was "quenched." The argument below is based in part upon the assumption that the Comet (line 368) which is urged to "float into our azure heaven again" (line 373) is the equivalent of the Planet above-mentioned.

Which from its heart of hearts that plant puts forth,
Whose fruit, made perfect by thy sunny eyes,
Will be as of the trees of Paradise.[32]

· IV ·

IN interpreting this "idealized history" of Shelley's "life and feelings," the editors (reluctantly) and the biographers (with mixed
feelings) have ordinarily read it as slightly allegorized autobiography. The widely accepted interpretation of the moon and sun
imagery is that the moon stands for Mary (as she herself seems to
have supposed) and the sun for Emilia Viviani. The supposition is
that Shelley is presenting in fairly strict chronological order—not
forgetting to allude symbolically to each of his ladies from Harriet
Grove to Claire Clairmont—the history of his earthly love-life.
Since Shelley chose to label his sublime Idea with the name Emilia,
the rest of the argument logically and literally follows, and Mary
is ticketed forever as the "chaste cold moon" smiling down upon
the ice which locked poor Shelley's heart until Emilia warmed it
with her sun-like smiles.

Such an interpretation is obviously possible, and to an extent
Shelley invited future critics to take such a view by the particular
"alloy" of localized nomenclature which he used. Yet this interpretation is too obvious, too literalistic, and—if one thinks it over
carefully in the Dantean context in which the poem was written—
too ridiculous to be entirely credible. Has not Shelley, after all,
been victimized by the literalists beyond his just deserts? Has not
criticism, charmed or disgusted by the romantic vicissitudes of

[32] The trees of Paradise would be that of life, and that of the knowledge of
good and evil. It may be noted here that Shelley described his fictional protagonist
in a cancelled draft of his "Advertisement" to *Epipsychidion* as one whose "fate
is an additional proof that 'the Tree of Knowledge is not that of Life.' " The
quotation is from Byron's *Manfred*. It may be further noted that the "heart of
hearts" phrase was made over by Hunt into the Latin epitaph, "Cor Cordium," for
Shelley's grave. Finally, the phrase "fading birth" should be set beside its analogue
in the *Defence*: "The mind in creation is as a fading coal, which some invisible
influence, like an inconstant wind, awakens to transitory brightness; this power
arises from within, like the colour of a flower which fades and changes as it is
developed. . . . Could this influence be durable in its purity and force, it is impossible to predict the greatness of its results." The idea of the union described
at the close of the poem is, of course, to make the influence perdurable in all its
purity and force.

Shelley's life, been wrongly disposed to consider him as much of a fool in his twenty-ninth year as in some respects he was in his nineteenth? Is the interest in states of mind and conditions of the soul which he had earlier displayed in *Alastor,* the *Hymn to Intellectual Beauty, Prometheus Unbound, Julian and Maddalo, The Cenci, The Sensitive Plant,* and dozens of great and lesser lyrics, to be forgotten or de-emphasized when one takes up a mystery like *Epipsychidion?* Are his guileful subtlety, his electric sensibility, his superactive speculative imagination, and his habitual preoccupation with abstract thought to be taken so little into account in estimating the depth of this later poem? A considered appraisal of the end of his poetic career would indicate rather, perhaps, that he was too nervously responsive to multiple stimuli, too imaginative, too subtle, and too abstract in what he wrote ever to have the right to suppose that such a poem as *Epipsychidion* would be widely understood.

The meaning of the central section of the poem is sufficiently esoteric, but not so much so that the lines cannot be made to surrender, under close examination, the essentials of that meaning. It is, precisely as Shelley said it was, the "idealized history" of his "life and feelings"—but the deep inner "life and feelings" of the spirit rather than the outer events of the man's career. "Idealized" for Shelley meant "taken out of the time-space dimension and rendered as an abstraction." "Feelings" for Shelley meant "excitations of the intellectual imagination." A poet, he said in the *Defence,* "participates in the eternal, the infinite, the one. As far as relates to his conceptions, time and place and number are not." It is in the context of remarks like this that Shelley's own characterization of *Epipsychidion* must be accepted; and it is in the spirit of this remark that the central section of the poem must be read.

One discovers, then, in this complex poem, the odyssey of a creative soul, which in the beginning dimly conceived the possibility of its fullest development through the establishment of contact with divine power. This power was the Being whom the ascendant spirit first "met on its visioned wanderings." Presently (though such adverbs as *presently* have no real significance in the timeless sequence of the poem) this vision passed "into the dreary cone of our life's shade."[33] Like "a man with mighty loss dismayed," the spirit set out upon its great quest, seeking among the "untaught foresters" for

> One form resembling hers
> In which she might have masked herself from me.

The searching spirit did not find the Power he sought. Instead, he came first upon "One whose voice was venomed melody." The language is of course highly metaphorical. Shelley is perhaps referring to false imaginations, like those of which Beatrice accuses Dante in the first canto of the *Paradiso*: "With false imagining dost thou so dull thyself that thou perceivest not what else thou wouldst perceive, if thou hadst thrown it off."[34] Shelley is also referring to that partial social corruption which in the *Defence* he connects with the erotic poets of the Hellenistic period. This corruption "begins at the imagination and intellect as at the core, and distributes itself thence as a paralysing venom, through the affections into the very appetites, until all become a torpid mass in which hardly sense survives." At such times, poetry's "voice is heard, like the footsteps of Astraea, departing from the world."[35] In the face of this corruption and other analogous influences, Shelley's creative soul stood at bay before his thoughts.[36] It was then that a kind of rescue arrived. One stood upon his path who was "as like the glorious shape" which he had dreamed, as the moon is like the sun.

Since we are now in that part of the "idealized history" which employs the Comet, the Moon, and the Sun as symbolic of states of the soul, it is necessary to examine briefly their respective meanings. The clue, like so many others in connection with *Epipsy-*

[33] The "dreary cone of our life's shade" is the Shelleyan equivalent of Wordsworth's "light of common day" in the great *Ode*. For Shelley at this period, the figure for life is usually darkness, shadow, or some other substantive by way of contrast with the "white radiance of eternity."

[34] *Paradiso*, I, 88-90. The translation is Courtney Langdon's. See his edition of *The Divine Comedy* (Cambridge, Mass., 1921), III, 9. Shelley greatly admired the opening of the *Paradiso* as "a neglected piece of excellence." See *Letters*, x, 404.

[35] *Defence*, *Prose*, VII, 124. The figure is the same in both instances: that of a venomous paralyzing force which pierces to the center and then moves outward through the whole *corpus*, whether of the individual or of society. Cf. "The contagion of the world's slow stain" in *Adonais*.

[36] The figure is repeated in *Adonais*, stanza XXXI, where it is developed in terms of the Actaeon-myth. See below, Chapter Nine.

chidion and *Adonais*, is provided by a passage in the *Defence*. "At a certain period," writes Shelley, "the three forms into which Plato had distributed the faculties of mind underwent a sort of apotheosis, and became the object of the worship of the civilized world."[37] The source of Shelley's notion is apparently the *Timaeus*, with which he had long been familiar, and the clearest explanation of Plato's "three forms" is that of Jowett, who says, "The soul of man is divided by [Plato] into three parts. . . . First, there is the immortal part which is seated in the brain, and is alone divine, and akin to the soul of the universe. This alone thinks and knows and is the ruler of the whole. Secondly, there is the higher mortal soul which, though liable to perturbations of her own, takes the side of reason against the lower appetites. . . . There is also a third or appetitive soul, which receives the commands of the immortal part, not immediately but mediately, through the higher mortal nature."[38]

Shelley made over this conception according to his own particular lights, as he always did with any conception he borrowed. For the purposes of clarity it may be well to set down the equation at which Shelley arrived, with the caution that the equivalences are only approximate.

1. Plato's immortal soul, "akin to the soul of the universe" >< Shelley's Epipsyche >< Shelley's concept of Imagination >< Shelley's Sun-symbol.
2. Plato's higher mortal soul >< Shelley's concept of Reason >< Shelley's Moon-symbol.
3. Plato's appetitive soul >< Shelley's concept of unruly Emotion (perhaps desire) >< Shelley's Comet-symbol.

Behind the first two rough equations lie Shelley's definitions (both in the *Epipsychidion* and the *Defence*) of "True Love." But there is also a letter which Shelley composed (probably in March, 1821), relative to Peacock's *Four Ages of Poetry*. In the letter the idea is that Peacock's essay has failed to grasp the significance of poetry in its highest reaches. "He would extinguish Imagination which is the Sun of life," wrote Shelley, "and grope his way by the cold and uncertain and borrowed light of that moon which he calls

---

[37] *Defence, Prose*, vii, 126. The reference is apparently to the Christian Trinity.
[38] Jowett, iii, 582. Quoted by A. S. Cook in his edition of *A Defence of Poetry* (Boston, 1890), p. 72.

Reason, stumbling over the interlunar chasms of time where she deserts us, and [like] an owl, rather than an eagle, stare with dazzled eyes on the watery orb which is the Queen of his pale Heaven."[39]

Some such conception as that just quoted informs the Moon-episode in *Epipsychidion*. The soul is rescued from "false imaginings" by "the cold chaste Moon" of Reason, which "warms not but illumines." Under the influence of the Moon, the soul in a creative sense is neither alive nor dead, but occupies some middle purgatory.[40] When the power of Reason goes temporarily dark, the soul is "as a lampless sea" torn by storms caused by the proximity of its appetitive part (the Comet symbol) and when the influences of this "Planet" are quenched, the soul is sealed in a "death of ice." The climactic moment is the advent of the long-lost Vision, the immortal soul, the epipsyche, the reawakened imagination, the sun-symbol, the vernal dawn after the winter's night of the soul. Then the Spirit rises free and clear to merge for the first time with light, as Dante in Paradise gazes up towards the transfigured Beatrice. When one reads the following invocation to the Sun of Imagination and the Moon of Reason with the Shelleyan equations in mind, its significance in relation to the creative soul becomes plain:

> Twin Spheres of light who rule this passive Earth,
> This world of love, this *me*; and into birth
> Awaken all its fruits and flowers, and dart
> Magnetic might into its central heart;
> And lift its billows and its mists, and guide
> By everlasting laws each wind and tide
> To its fit cloud, and its appointed cave;
> And lull its storms, each in the craggy grave
> Which was its cradle, luring to faint bowers
> The armies of the rainbow-wingèd showers;

[39] *Letters*, x, 246. Cf. the reference in the *Defence* to the "vanishing apparitions which haunt the interlunations of life." The visitations evidently occur while the moon of Reason is down.

[40] Cf. Shelley's letter of Jan. 20, 1821, written about the time he was engaged with the *Epipsychidion*: "I could be content either with the Hell or the Paradise of poetry; but the torments of its purgatory vex me, without exciting my power sufficiently to put an end to the vexation." *Letters*, x, 232. The figurative connection with Dante's *Divine Comedy* should be noticed.

And, as those married lights, which from the towers
Of Heaven look forth and fold the wandering globe
In liquid sleep and splendor, as a robe;
And all their many-mingled influence blend,
If equal, yet unlike, to one sweet end—
So ye, bright regents, with alternate sway,
Govern my sphere of being, night and day!
Thou, not disdaining even a borrowed might;
Thou, not eclipsing a remoter light;
And, through the shadow of the seasons three,
From Spring to Autumn's sere maturity,
Light it into the Winter of the tomb,
Where it may ripen to a brighter bloom.

This extraordinary invocation continues with an address to the appetitive soul, not now to be feared as a brewer of tempests or as the author of internal convulsions, but as a power which, though "fierce" in itself, can be controlled and accommodated in the "azure heaven" where the immortal and higher mortal parts of the soul now perfectly cooperate.

Thou, too, O Comet, beautiful and fierce,
Who drew the heart of this frail Universe
Towards thine own; till, wrecked in that convulsion,
Alternating attraction and repulsion,
Thine went astray, and that was rent in twain;
Oh, float into our azure heaven again!
Be there love's folding-star at thy return;
The living Sun will feed thee from its urn
Of golden fire; the Moon will veil her horn
In thy last smiles. . . .

The conception of the three parts of the soul or three ascending aspects of love, which in *Epipyschidion* are imaged forth as the Comet, the Moon, and the Sun, was not any greater novelty in Shelley's poetry than the quest for the epipsyche (*Alastor*); the separation-reunion device (*Revolt, Prometheus Unbound*); the intrusion of the false lady (*Prince Athanase*); the bodying-forth of an Ideal Form in a woman-symbol (Asia, the Lady of the garden in *The Sensitive Plant, The Witch of Atlas*); the use of sun, earth and moon images (*Prometheus Unbound*, Acts II-IV); or sundry other organizational or symbolic devices which are used in *Epipsychidion*. A good partial analogue for the ascending aspects of love in the soul is to be found in the three sisters of *Prometheus Unbound*: Ione, Panthea, and Asia. But even that conception is made over, broadened, and deepened in *Epipsychidion*, which, as was suggested in the beginning of the present chapter, is a synthesis of many ideas and themes derived from Shelley's earlier poetry. In setting forth this "idealized history" of his imaginative inner life and feelings, Shelley ranged back through his whole poetic experience for whatever might be of use to him.

The third part of the poem is largely descriptive of the wonderful island to which, now that the great reunion has been effected, the soul will retire with its "bride."[41]

> To the intense, the deep, the imperishable,
> Not mine but me, henceforth be thou united
> Even as a bride, delighting and delighted.

Shelley again makes concessions to his audience by providing his island, though in terms intentionally vague, with a geographical location and a pastoral population. But the spot is obviously an elysium for the creative soul, and perhaps an allegorical representation of the realm of ideal poetry, where the creative soul merges with the world-soul at the highest possible level. There at the climax of this section of the poem, Shelley sets forth the merger and the soul's transfiguration under a metaphor of marriage:

> We shall become the same, we shall be one
> Spirit within two frames, oh! wherefore two?
> One passion in twin-hearts, which grows and grew
> Till like two meteors of expanding flame,
> Those spheres instinct with it become the same,
> Touch, mingle, are transfigured. . . .
> One hope within two wills, one will beneath

[41] As Ackermann points out, this section of the poem evidently is related to the sonnet of Dante's (addressed to Guido) which Shelley had translated some years before and which was published in the *Alastor* volume. The poem's brief epilogue echoes a line or two from the sonnet. But there are echoes of Spenser's *Hymne of Love* (280-293) in the epilogue, and the conception of the island is indebted also to Ovid (*Metamorphosis*, xv, 39-40), and probably to Shakespeare's *Tempest*, as Woodberry and Locock have suggested.

Two overshadowing minds, one life, one death,
One Heaven, one Hell, one immortality,
And one annihilation.

There will be those who will protest that this interpretation is too complicated, and who will wish to see in *Epipsychidion* only a febrile extravaganza about Shelley's relations (real or hoped-for) with earthly women. To such protestations it may be answered that the full appreciation of the tortuous subtleties and the high imaginative reaches of Shelley's mind have rarely been fully appreciated, though most of his friends and associates recognized and commented in no uncertain terms upon his extreme love of abstraction, his consuming nervous sensibility, and his great imaginative powers. For Shelley really meant what he said in quoting Dante's words:

My song, I fear that thou wilt find but few
Who fitly shall conceive thy reasoning,
Of such hard matter dost thou entertain.

The hard matter is the relation of the poet's inward and immortal soul to the undiminished fountain of intellectual might and pleasure (or blessedness) which the poet apprehends through the activity of a kind of religious imagination. This conception is re-expressed in the *Adonais*.

9

THE EVENING STAR: *ADONAIS*

Sing out the song, sing to the end, and sing
The strange reward of all that discipline.
—W. B. YEATS IN *The Phases of the Moon*

Does Shelley go on telling strange Stories of the Death of Kings? Tell
him there are strange Stories of the Death of Poets.
—KEATS TO HUNT, 1817

· I ·

THE ADONIS legend is one of the two which intrude between the
actualities of Keats' life and the conception of that life which informs *Adonais*. The other is more or less adventitious, for Shelley
appears to have been taken in by that false though widespread and
long-lived fairy tale that Keats' death had been hastened if not
caused by the malevolent and anonymous attack on *Endymion* in
the *Quarterly Review* for April, 1818. Shelley embraced this legend
(with a willingness that would otherwise have seemed naïve) for
two reasons: he had himself felt the bite of adverse criticism in the
contemporary journals, and his mind was naturally predisposed
both to pity and in some degree to apotheosize a fellow-poet who
had been similarly wounded. Secondly, his estimate of Keats'
character had been formed less through personal acquaintance
than through a perusal of works like *Endymion* and "I stood tip-
toe," and he had therefore conceived the stereotype of a superlatively gentle, sensitive, and rather fragile Keats which had very
little to do with the sturdy, courageous, and stoical little poet who
had died in Rome. The Adonis legend was of course equally effec-

tive in modifying Shelley's story away from historical actuality. Having chosen Adonis as the prototype of his poetic conception of Keats, he had a partial inclination to follow the limited characterization of Adonis as he found it in Bion's *Lament*, though he altered the original Greek story wherever it suited his pseudo-biographical purpose.

What must have pleased Shelley was that the *Quarterly Review* legend and the Adonis legend coincided to a degree which made sweeping modifications unnecessary. The fundamental conception—a goddess mourning the untimely death of a gifted mortal in whom her hopes had been concentrated—was well suited to Shelley's own purposes, just as Milton, in mourning the death of Edward King, had thought proper despite King's limited poetic skills, to introduce an allusion to the Epic Muse Calliope sorrowing for the death of her son Orpheus.

The point has long since been established that it was characteristic of Shelley's mythopoetic approach to accept for his "ideal" poems only such mythological situations as could be, like Spenser's, "clowdily enwrapped in allegorical devices." Both by the use of a variant of the name of Adonis and by the application to the Venus-figure of only one of her innumerable Greek surnames, Shelley partially concealed his source-myth. But in modified form all the elements of the original story are present: Venus' temporary absence from the side of her beloved, Adonis' daring the boar, the beast's attack, Adonis' death, the arrival of mourners, the gentle ministrations of subdeities, Venus' attempt to revive her lover, and finally, though this is merely suggested as one of the possible fates of Adonais, the victim's metamorphosis into a flower. The place of the boar in *Adonais* is of course occupied by the reviewer whom Shelley blamed for Keats' death. But the original boar (no matter how spelled) did not suit the degree of Shelley's anger, the depth of his sympathy with Keats, or his desire to infuse the original myth with allegorical devices. In the place of the boar, therefore, the reader finds an array of vituperative images: the reviewer is a cowardly archer, a killing frost, a venomous snake, an unpastured dragon, a wolf, a hound, a raven, a vulture, and a carrion kite.[1]

---

[1] E. B. Hungerford's chapter on *Adonais* in *Shores of Darkness* (New York, 1941), pp. 216-239, provides a very useful comparison between Shelley's poem

Urania herself is scarcely less complex in her origins than the Witch of Atlas, and it is only through a consideration of her meaning that Shelley's total conception emerges. She is first of all what she is in the original fable, a goddess enamored of a mortal youth. But the epithet "Urania" immediately indicates that she is not the lower or Cyprian Aphrodite of Bion and Moschus. She is rather a spiritual counterpart at a much higher level, a goddess of heavenly love, like Asia. The obvious reason for presenting this goddess as enamored of Keats is that his poems had helped, as Shelley saw them, to spread the doctrine of love of which he was himself so ardent a champion. In the *Defence* (which has much in common with *Adonais*) he had been at pains to list the great "poets" from Plato to Rousseau who had celebrated the divinity of love and thus planted "as it were trophies in the human mind of that sublimest victory over sensuality and force." Shelley there groups his contemporaries together as "the great writers of our own age" without naming particular names; but his growing admiration for Keats' poetry suggests, at least, that if he had prepared a list of divine love's votaries among the living poets, the name of Keats would have been included.

Shelley was not content merely to elevate the Cyprian Venus of Moschus and Bion to a heavenly status and thereby to de-emphasize the element of concupiscence implicit in the original fable. His purpose was served better by changing Urania from a bereaved lover to a mother bereft of her son. For Urania is both a symbol of heavenly love and, as her name would suggest to students of Milton, a muse who has in her charge the most sublime poetry.[2] Among the nine muses of classical mythology Urania is the muse of astronomy. Shelley retained this conception in *Adonais* through careful development of a Lucifer-Hesper star-image derived from Plato. But he was fully aware that Milton, in the

---

and the source-myth. The Rossetti-Prickard edition of the poem (Oxford, 1903) had earlier done the same task in somewhat less detail. One wishes that Shelley might have contented himself with a single image for the reviewer, developing his remarks in terms of it.

[2] Woodberry follows Rossetti in pointing out that Urania is primarily the heavenly Aphrodite. Rossetti considered but rejected the opinion that she was in some manner connected with Milton's Urania, though he suggested that since Keats' *Endymion* and *Hyperion* had dealt respectively with the moon and the sun, the muse of astronomy would do very well as the mother of Adonais.

proem to the seventh book of *Paradise Lost*, had invoked her as the guide of his highest poetic effort, the astronomical task of describing the creation. In making Keats the "nursling" of this most noble muse, Shelley was paying him a very high compliment.

But Urania was also the Platonic Idea which he had mystically celebrated under the name of Emilia in the *Epipsychidion*. There, as we have seen, he had developed to the highest point his conception of the force of *Divine Love* as the ultimate inspiration of great poetry, and had employed the marriage-symbol as a sign of the hoped-for permanent union of his creative soul with this supernal power. The *Defence* had extended the notion by applying it historically; Shelley is unequivocal in his belief that all great "poets" from Plato through Dante to Milton and the great writers of the modern period have somehow shared in a sublime vision comparable to his own. At some time in the winter of 1820-1821 (or possibly earlier) he evidently made the imaginative connection between his own concept and the muse Urania. The day before he sent *Epipsychidion* to Ollier (and only a week before he began his *Defence*) he half playfully told Peacock that the *Four Ages* essay in which the latter had inveighed against poetry had excited him "to a sacred rage, or *caloëthes scribendi* of vindicating the insulted Muses," adding that he had "the greatest possible desire" to answer Peacock's arguments with an argumentative essay "in honour of my mistress Urania."[3] The letter to Peacock shows clearly enough that even then (February 15) Shelley was thinking of Urania as the name of the Muse who had inspired his own best poetry. As he worked the matter out in the *Defence*, it is evident that he connected this same concept (though not by name) with the inspiration of the greatest poetry and philosophic prose of the western tradition. It is therefore of the utmost importance to an understanding of the richness of the Urania-concept in *Adonais* to recognize that in it Shelley was summing up the view of divine inspiration which he had symbolized at the conclusion of *Epipsychidion* and rendered into the eloquent prose of the *Defence*.

[3] *Letters*, x, 234. Feb. 15, 1821. On Feb. 22, Shelley wrote Ollier that the "paper" (the *Defence*) would be sent as soon as written, "which will be in a very few days." *Ibid.*, 242. It took longer than he expected and was sent March 20.

BESIDES Urania, Adonais has several mortal mourners, among them Byron, Moore, Hunt, and Shelley—who appear in the thin disguise of mountain shepherds. The apt conceit previously applied to Adonais (i.e. a shepherd whose sheep were his thoughts) is further developed here, and the mountain which these shepherds all inhabit might well be Helicon, the domain of the Muses, on one of whose peaks lies the "secret paradise" from which Urania-as-muse has first descended in her effort to reanimate the mortally wounded Adonais. Out of deference to the memory of their fellow-poet, their magic mantles (signifying, as Prospero's cloak perhaps signifies, the poetic imagination) are rent in mourning, and the leaves of their garlands are sere and yellow.[4]

Although Shelley's dramatization of himself as chief mourner has often struck readers as mere sentimental egotism, the portrait (like that of the Witch of Atlas) is actually an extraordinary complex of ethical attitudes, literary and mythological images, and semiprivate symbolism. When its origins are understood, the self-portrait appears to be less sicklied over with self-pity than involved, as in *Epipsychidion*, with a kind of self-analysis on an ideal plane. In the first place, the conviction that Keats was done to death by the vindictiveness of the reviewers had for Shelley a profoundly personal application. As the consideration of *Hellas* indicated, Shelley in 1821 was both convinced of and depressed by his own failure to have gained a sympathetic public hearing— a failure in which, as he had good reason to suppose, the reviewers had played a significant role. One strong resemblance between his own career and that of Keats was therefore apparent to him. His own loneliness and separateness from the other mourners are emphasized because of his feeling (no doubt partly real and partly feigned for dramatic effect) that whereas there had been, until

---

[4] It is of little consequence that only one of this quartet (Leigh Hunt) had a real personal friendship with Keats. Shelley is merely suggesting that the loss of any promising poet from the ranks of modern literature is a sufficient reason for mourning among his contemporaries. All poets of the "liberal schism" have a common cause. Since Rossetti was puzzled by the "magic mantles" it may be worth pointing out that in one of the canceled passages of *Adonais*, the mantle belonging to the Shelleyan figure was made of chameleon-skin, signifying the adaptability of poets. This may have been Shelley's modification of the fawn-skins customarily worn by the bacchanals. See below, note 9.

recently, two poets whose efforts went unappreciated, he alone survived. Of the four mourners, Shelley was the only one "who in another's fate now wept his own."

The loneliness, the frailty, and the completed or imminent defeat—the grounds on which, in Shelley's opinion, his career parallels that of Keats—are only part of the complex pattern of self-analysis. The Actaeon figure from Ovid is given, as frequently happened in Elizabethan poetry, a symbolic turn, and brought to bear upon the predicament of the philosophical and psychological poet in the early nineteenth century. The hunter Actaeon, having burst by chance upon the naked Diana in a sylvan pool, was transformed into a stag and pursued to his death by his own hounds. In Shakespeare's *Twelfth Night* Orsino had used the hound-figure to describe the intensity of his own amatory desires.[5] The Shelleyan poet, indefatigable hunter after philosophical truth, has penetrated to the secret fountain and "gazed on nature's naked loveliness." Thereafter he has taken flight across the barren wilderness of the world, torn to anguish by the very intensity of his thoughts, as Actaeon by his raging hounds.

The semiprivate symbolism of the thirty-third and thirty-fourth stanzas is partly explained by a parallel passage in the concluding stanza of Shelley's ode to the beleaguered Spaniards in 1819. The chief mourner's head is bound with a coronal of "pansies overblown" and "faded violets,"[6] and he carries a light spear tipped with a cypress cone and wreathed in ivy. When Urania murmurs, "Who art thou?" he silently bares his forehead to reveal a bloody brand "like Cain's or Christ's." The concluding stanza of the ode on the martyred Spaniards probably indicates Shelley's meaning:

> Bind, bind every brow
> With crownals of violet, ivy, and pine!
> Hide the bloodstains now
> With hues which sweet nature has made divine—
> Green strength, azure hope, and eternity;
> But let not the pansy among them be—
> Ye were injured, and that means memory.

[5] *Twelfth Night*, I, i, 15-23.
[6] Cf. the "garlands sere" of the other mourners.

The overblown pansies and the faded violets would seem therefore to signify old memories and faded hopes,[7] while the bloody
brow, as in the ode on the Spaniards, signifies the injury he has
sustained at the hands of his oppressors. The symbolic connection
with Christ's passion and the crown of thorns is obvious and has
struck some readers as impious; the allusion to Cain was doubtless
intended to suggest, not that Shelley was not his brother's keeper,
but that in the attempt to guide his brothers he had succeeded
only in becoming, like Cain, an outcast and a wanderer in the
world's wilderness.[8]

Finally one may discern, like underpainting below the surface
of Shelley's self-portrait, a sketch of the particular attributes of
the swift-footed and beneficent Greek hill-god, Dionysus or Bacchus—not that Hellenistic figure who has come to stand as the
type of sybaritic self-indulgence, but that almost Promethean
benefactor of savage tribes who taught his way eastward to India, a beautiful swift spirit drawn in his conquering chariot by
leopards, and bearing, as the Shelleyan poet bears, a cone-tipped
ivy-wreathed thyrsus in his hand.[9]

[7] With perhaps a reminiscence of Ophelia's violets which "withered all" when
her father died, and her pansies (*pensées*): for thoughts. Rossetti, and subsequent
editors, cite the lyric *Remembrance*: "Pansies let my flowers be."

[8] In connection with Shelley's view of himself as a misunderstood poet, one may
notice the line in stanza 34 in which he is said to sing new sorrow "in the accents
of an unknown land." This has puzzled Shelley's editors: Rossetti, Woodberry, and
more lately Mr. Barnard have identified the unknown land as England. The best
gloss on this line, however, is probably a sentence from the fragment "On Love."
Shelley says that when he has sought to appeal to other men and to unburden his
inmost soul to them, he has found his "language misunderstood, like one in a distant
and savage land." *Prose*, VI, 201.

[9] The reminiscence of Bacchus in Shelley's self-portrait was suggested by Professor Charles G. Osgood to Professor Stephen A. Larrabee, in whose *English Bards
and Grecian Marbles* (New York, 1943), pp. 197-199, occurs an illuminating discussion of Shelley's admiration for various statues of Bacchus. The Ampelus-Bacchus
group which he saw at Florence precisely fitted his conception of the Grecian deity,
not as a decadent wine-god, but as "one who walks through the world untouched
by . . . its corrupting cares," showing a countenance of "divine and supernatural
beauty." As Professor Larrabee points out, he "condemned a Bacchus by Michel-
angelo" as not in accord with his idea of Bacchus' essential nobility.

Shelley had probably formed his conception of the ideal character of Bacchus
some time before 1819, when he wrote his notes on the sculptures in the Florentine
galleries. He had read, for example, Euripides' *The Bacchae* with its sympathetic
portrait of Dionysus' conflict with a tyrannical King Pentheus; he probably knew
the allusions to Dionysus in Vergil's *Georgics* (II, 113 and III, 264); he knew Ar-
rian's account (*Historia Indica*, VIII, 5.8-10) of Dionysus' conquest of India; he and
Peacock had both read the *Dionysiaca* of Nonnus, on the basis of which Peacock

· III ·

THE first two-thirds of the elegy, therefore, is developed in terms of the Adonis myth, though Shelley has broadened and deepened the significance of Aphrodite, built up the importance of the shepherd mourners, and charged the whole with angry vilification of the boorish reviewer whose attack precipitated the tragedy. The web of ancient story provides the pattern into which Shelley weaves his multiple meanings.

When one turns to the final third of the poem, a question of the unity of *Adonais* arises. As commonly analyzed, the elegy consists of two parts: thirty-seven stanzas of mythological narrative, and eighteen stanzas in which the narrative element is apparently abandoned in favor of philosophic consolations. It has therefore been supposed, upon occasion, that Shelley destroyed the unity of *Adonais* through his failure to sustain the mythological device until the end. A recent critic has argued, however, that the myth is not abandoned but carried along, at least by implication, to the conclusion. When Adonais enters the realm of the immortals, he is permanently reunited with Urania who, in the meantime, has been dissolved in light and transformed from an incarnated goddess into the mystical "One," or the World-Soul.[10]

The argument is only slightly weakened by the fact that Shelley makes no recognizable allusion to the sustaining myth in the final third of his poem. For there is a wealth of precedent in Shel-

had planned a narrative poem about a Bacchic prince whose love for a nymph caused his destruction. See Shelley's letter to Ollier, Dec. 7, 1817, and his letter to Peacock of Aug. 16, 1818. See also Brett-Smith and Jones, *Works of Thomas Love Peacock*, Halliford ed., I, lxxix-lxxx. There are some twenty allusions to Bacchus and Bacchic revels in Euripides' *The Cyclops*, which Shelley translated in 1819. Dionysus was widely supposed to be a hill-god (his birthplace, Nysa, was sometimes thought of as a mountain), while one of his noteworthy characteristics was his great swiftness. See G. M. N. Davis, *The Asiatic Dionysos* (London, 1914), pp. 154 and 182-183. He was, in short, a very handsome figure, lithe as the leopards (or pards) which drew his chariot, and an ideal antetype for a poet of Shelley's inclinations. Other reminiscences than those of Dionysus are doubtless merged in the self-portrait. In Vergil's tenth Eclogue (19-30) one meets a situation resembling the mourner's scene in *Adonais*. As Gallus pines with love for his sweetheart Lycoris, and Adonis is mentioned feeding sheep beside a stream, shepherds come to console the empty-handed lover. Apollo comes, Silvanus arrives "with rustic ornaments on his brow, waving his fennel flowers and long-stalked lilies." Pan comes, "god of Arcady . . . crimson with vermilion and blood-red elderberries." The situation, except that Gallus is only dying of love, not dead, is very like that in *Adonais*.

[10] Hungerford, *op. cit.*, pp. 236-237.

ley's poetry for such a transformation as is here alleged. Although the visionary maiden of *Alastor* takes on bodily attributes during the visionary experience of the poet, she has become, in the end, nothing but a kind of light: "two starry eyes hung in the gloom of thought." The ineffable brightness of Asia at the hour of her second birth (which is the hour of her reunion with Prometheus) is a comparable representation of an Idea which has been incarnated but whose real essence is supernal light. Many of the epithets used to describe "Emilia" in *Epipsychidion* share in this notion: in fact they anticipate the epithets applied to the "One" of the third part of *Adonais*. The argument for the unity of the whole poem gains further support from the intrinsic meaning of Urania. We have seen that she is the heavenly muse under whose aegis the most sublime poetry is written; at the same time she is the Uranian Aphrodite, goddess of spiritual love. She has thus been both the inspiration for Keats and the goal of his aspiration, a goal which he has now attained. The two concepts, though they can be arbitrarily separated for examination, are actually merged in Shelley's complex conception. According to the *Defence*, the highest kind of poetry has always been that in which love's dominion is celebrated. One of the ways in which the plastic stress manifests itself in earthly affairs is through the agency of divinely inspired poetry. Thus the muse of heavenly poetry is the goddess of heavenly love viewed in another aspect, and it is entirely fitting that Adonais, in entering the immortal state, should be reunited with that divine light which informed his poetry during his earthly career.

The narrative of the first two-thirds and the implied narrative of the last third of *Adonais* would thus seem to be of a piece. Of equal or even greater subtlety is Shelley's use of star-symbolism as a device of unification. In the *Adonais*, as at many points in the *Defence of Poetry*, Shelley is preoccupied with the notion of an astronomical hierarchy of dead poets. The clue to his intention in the elegy for Keats is provided by the Platonic epigram which he uses as a headnote, and which he subsequently rendered into English as follows:

> Thou wert a morning star among the living,
> Ere thy fair light had fled;

Now, having died, thou art as Hesperus, giving
New splendor to the dead.

The star here alluded to is the planet Venus, which is both the morning-star (Lucifer: light-bearer) and the evening star (Hesperus or Vesper). The over-all conception is that when great poets pass away they become as stars fixed in the firmament of time, stars whose light (the poets' works) continues to shine down upon the benighted earth. This happened to Milton, whose "clear Sprite" still reigns over the earth along with Homer's and Dante's. Shelley now supposes that the same wonderful translation has occurred with Keats. As a "morning-star among the living," Keats was a bringer-of-light through his poetry. But when he entered the immortal state, he continued to shed light. He is now one of the "splendors" of the "firmament of time"; he has climbed like a star to his "appointed height"; once there, he is greeted by his fellow-immortals, the poets, as "thou Vesper of our throng." And it is as Vesper (Hesperus or the evening star) that he shines as beacon-light for Shelley's aspiring spirit in the closing stanza of the poem. Hence the star-symbol of the Platonic epigram is an important device of unification in the poem.

Shelley's morning-star symbolism has also a connection with Dante which requires explanation. *Adonais* contains no mention of Dante by name, but the allusion to Milton as "the third among the sons of light"[11] is also an allusion by implication to Dante. As the *Defence* shows, Dante was the second of the great epic poets in Shelley's calendar of immortals. Even more to the point, however, is another passage in the *Defence* where Dante is called "the Lucifer of that starry flock which in the thirteenth century shone forth from republican Italy, as from a heaven, into the darkness of the benighted world."[12] But this is not all. One of the symbolic statements made about Emilia, the Urania of *Epipsychidion*, is that she is "a Splendour" who has descended to earth, "leaving the third sphere pilotless."[13] The conception, as we have observed, is Dantean, since the third sphere is that of the planet Venus. Be-

[11] *Adonais*, stanza IV.
[12] *Defence, Prose*, VII, 131. Like many other Shelleyan symbols, that of the morning-star was not new. It had been used to symbolize the Spirit of Good in *The Revolt*, while the helmet of Liberty, in *The Masque of Anarchy* (XXIX) was adorned with "a planet, like the Morning's."
[13] *Epipsychidion*, 116-117.

cause it is also in Dante's cosmology, the sphere of Rhetoric, it is a fitting location for the souls of great poets, who in *Adonais* are called "the splendours of the firmament of time."[14] If Shelley has in mind any specific location for the region to which Adonais has risen, it is the third heaven of Dante's *Paradiso.*

Thus the consolatory argument is developed in terms of the re-union of the lesser with the greater light and is based upon the belief that poets are the Lucifers, or light-bearers, for the earth. The final third of the poem is filled with verbs ordinarily asso-ciated with fire and light: dazzling, burning, beaming, beneficently smiling, glowing, kindling, beaconing, and cold-consuming. The spirit of Adonais has returned to the burning fountain whence it came; it has become a portion rather than now an earthly instru-ment of that fire which unquenchably glows through time and change. This wonderful change from instrument to agent is the mystical aspect of Adonais' translation. As one merged in the di-vine fire he now bears his part in the "plastic stress" which forces the unwilling dross of the temporal world towards (though, as in the *Timaeus* myth, never quite *to*) the condition and likeness of the eternal world. Such is the double nature of immortality, how-ever, that Adonais, while functioning as agent, still continues to function as instrument through the powerful survival of his works. The great poets, "the splendors of the firmament of time," may be temporarily eclipsed, but their light cannot be extinguished. When the youthful aspirant elevates his thought to the level required to comprehend great poetry, he will find that the great dead live and move like winds of light above the storm-winds of the mind.[15] Nor will the "transmitted effluence" of these poets die out on earth, for it is a manifestation of the cosmic light whose smile forever kindles the universe. The great poets are the "kings of thought" who strove against "their time's decay." They are the only parts of the past which cannot pass away. All men, as indeed all living things, are in some sort, however, the instruments of cosmic power. For the idea of eternity is woven, as light is diffused, through the whole web of being. Yet it shines bright or dim precisely in proportion as

---

[14] *Adonais,* stanza XLIV.

[15] Cf., as an excellent gloss on this passage, Shelley's letter to Claire, written just as he finished *Adonais:* "The only relief I find springs from the composition of poetry, which necessitates contemplations that lift me above the stormy mist of sen-sations which are my habitual place of abode." *Letters,* x, 272. June 8, 1821.

each of its earthly instruments is capable of serving as its mirror. Of all earthly instruments, great poets are the clearest mirrors, and it is they who best reflect the cosmic fire. They are the Lucifers, earthly bearers of supernal light. But in their heavenly status they become as evening stars, not only adding new splendor to the company of the immortals, but serving (like the soul of Adonais in the concluding stanza) as manifestations of that great light to which every man aspires according to his degree.

The comprehension of this dual scheme enables the reader to see that what look like philosophic contradictions in the poem are really not contradictions at all. Thus stanzas 41-43 develop the idea that Adonais yet lives in the forms and essences of phenomenal nature. Earth, Air, and Sky are admonished against mourning, for "he is made one with Nature." His voice still speaks in the roll of thunder or in the chant of the nightingale; he is a part of the natural loveliness which once he made more lovely through the enhancements of his verse. The development given to this notion in stanzas 42 and 43 indicates that Shelley did not have in mind the survival of the material atoms of Adonais' dust, so much as the survival of the poet as a spiritual essence merged in the world-soul. His pure spirit or immortal part had returned to the burning fountain whence it originated, and therefore became a part of the One Spirit which moves everywhere through nature, sustaining it beneath (through the principles of fertility and growth) and kindling it from above (through emanations like those of the sun). Under the sign of eternity, the soul loses its personal identity after death, and undergoes a merger with the *Weltseele*. This is one way of looking at immortality. In terms of the temporal world, however, man's immortality is a matter of degree, and is measured by the quality of his creative achievement, as, in Plato's *Phaedrus*, creativeness of several sorts is distinguished as a guarantor of immortality. From the point of view of the earthling, immersed as as he is in mundane affairs, immortality may be defined as undying earthly fame, and it is from this point of view that Adonais is said to have taken his place among those literary immortals, splendors of the firmament of *time*, who are thrown across the dark skies like a galaxy of stars.

Although it has required many pages to demonstrate the details of the symbolism of the poem, the substance of the informing vision can be briefly summarized. The world we know is spiritually a Cimmerian desert, dark, storm-ridden, suffused with mist. Far above it, arched beyond mortal sight, is the Primum Mobile, the Divine light of the World-Soul, the white radiance of Eternity, a burning fountain like a spiritual sun. Its effluence is felt everywhere in nature and in man, and its effectiveness corresponds precisely to the sensitiveness of that which receives it. As a vitalizing force, it impels all things in their degree to aspire towards the condition of immortality: in Shelley's very exact phrase, it "tortures the unwilling dross" towards "heaven's light." Idealistic poets are the most sensitive receivers of this light, and in them the driving force, the *eros* or aspirational principle, is almost unendurably strong. In a very real sense, psychologically speaking, they are "tortured" by the desire to clarify and to spread among mankind the wonder of their vision of Eternity. As "splendours of the firmament of time," they occupy after death the third sphere of heaven, where they reign immortal in the memories of man. But their souls, like those of all men after death, rejoin the World-Soul and thus carry, as it were, a joyous double burden in the enlightenment of the world.

· IV ·

THIS, then, is the metaphysic by which Shelley supplemented the moral conclusion he had reached in *Prometheus Unbound*. There he had concluded that the human mind, if it could destroy through an act of internal reform the awful burden of hate and despair with which it was weighed down, could rise to unexpected heights of self-realization. For in casting down its burden it could rise free of the Promethean chains to reunite with the Asia-principle of divine love. Then the sole "clogs" upon its ability to transcend "the loftiest star of unascended heaven" would be chance, death, and mutability—those three survivors of the materialist necessitarianism with which Shelley had started in *Queen Mab*. If man could achieve the great act of self-reform, Demogorgon, enigmatic law of the universe, could be enlisted on his side, and the Jupiter-principle of hate would be cast down for as long as man was joined to the Asia-principle of love.

Shelley did not combine Love (Asia) and Eternity (Demogorgon) in *Prometheus Unbound*. Perhaps that was one of his reasons for calling his masterpiece, as he once did, "a very imperfect poem."[16] For he had, in the meantime, evolved a new metaphysical conception in which Love and Eternity together became the "One" which remains while the many change and pass. He had worked out to his own satisfaction the relationship of that One to earthly life and to the monumental poetry of the western world, and reached the conclusion which informs the two poems and the great idealistic essay which he wrote between January and June, 1821. If the old concept of Necessity still remained, it had paled to minor consequence by the side of the new concept of the One. It does not seem quite accurate to say, as many commentators have, that the old Necessity "became" the new Love or Intellectual Beauty. A more exact statement of the case would be that Demogorgon was already a new conception: Necessity-as-amoral-law, beside which the old materialistic Necessity of the *Queen Mab* days still survived as a fag-end. Sometime after 1819, "Demogorgon" was metamorphosed from an essentially passive principle to an active or informing principle by fusion with the principle of Love.

One possible designation for the metaphysical position of the mature Shelley is the term, "panpsychism," which Mr. Santayana proposes as more nearly exact than the much-abused "pantheism." Shelley, says Santayana, "did not surrender the authority of moral ideals in the face of physical necessity, which is properly the essence of pantheism."[17] His final position was the "exact opposite"— a forthright insistence upon the sovereignty of moral ideals, and a relegation of physical necessity to a distinctly inferior position. The *Defence of Poetry* is above all a profession of faith in the morally regenerative value of "that great poem, which all poets, like the co-operating thoughts of one great mind, have built up since the beginning of the world."[18]

The monistic conception at which Shelley finally arrived had been adumbrated a decade earlier in what the author of *Queen Mab* had had to say about the daemon of the world. But the intervening years had been devoted, with that purposiveness and sense

[16] *Letters*, x, 266. May 4, 1821.
[17] George Santayana, *The Winds of Doctrine* (New York, 1913), p. 180.
[18] *Defence, Prose*, vii, 124.

of self-dedication to which Shelley's biographers often allude, to the ordering and clarification of the conception. By 1821-1822, through a series of intuitive syntheses, Shelley was able to associate, under the sovereignty of this ruling Idea, all of the principles —aesthetic, moral, and metaphysical—to which his life had been devoted. The One included Intellectual Beauty, Intellectual Love, and Intellectual Freedom. Shelley's worshipful devotion to this Great Principle was as strong as his opposition to the Old Testament God of Wrath, and to what he regarded as the perpetuation of that principle through the persecutions sanctioned by the Church. To the end of his life he condemned the crimes which, in his view, had been committed in the name of Christianity. But he spoke with awe of Jesus Christ's "sublime human character," called him the "most just, wise, and benevolent of men," and placed him at the top of his line of the world's great poets. He did not accept the doctrine of the Trinity, though he suggested that it was derived ultimately from Plato, and (at least for poetic purposes) accepted the Platonic doctrine of the three parts of the soul. That theology which identified Jesus Christ with "a Power who tempted, betrayed, and punished the innocent beings who were called into existence by His sole will" made no sense to him, and he rejected it as unequivocally at the close of his life as he had done in his nineteenth year. He preferred to think of Jesus Christ as one who had been preeminently in contact with the "One" of his own private theology, and the purity of Jesus' doctrines had been, he felt, sullied by generations of self-appointed theological commentators.

The "One Spirit" which Shelley worshiped seems to have connections with St. Augustine's concept of *Caritas* in being available to the aspiring spirit according, as Shelley put it in his notes to *Hellas*, "to the degree of perfection to which every distinct intelligence may have attained." At the same time, the notion of the "inextinguishable thirst for immortality" by which, he thought, all men were impelled in varying degrees, seems to have been derived from Plato. "Until better arguments can be produced than sophisms which disgrace the cause," said he in the same set of notes, "this desire itself must remain the strongest and the only presumption that eternity is the inheritance of every thinking being."

For human society as a whole Shelley had no very high regard in his last years. "My firm persuasion is," he wrote in 1822, "that the mass of mankind, as things are arranged at present, are cruel, deceitful and selfish, and always on the watch to surprize those few who are not"[19]—a remark as close to Swift as Shelley ever came. One of his reasons for admiring *Don Juan* was that Byron unveiled "in its true deformity what is worst in human nature." Since we are damned to the knowledge of good and evil, he added, "it is well for us to know what we should avoid no less than what we should seek."[20] His real heroes in human society were those poets who taught men to know what they ought to seek, and the best of these were the "sacred few" who resisted absolutely the temptations of the worldly life. In his final judgment, Jesus Christ and Socrates were the only heroes who passed the severest of all tests.[21]

In the last analysis Shelley saw evil as ubiquitous and unlikely to be extirpated. Although it was largely the result of a blindness, a hardness, and a lethargy of the human spirit, he admitted that "ill-health is one of the evils that is not a dream,"[22] and his view of the problem may be presumed to have included chance, death, and mutability among the nonmental evils with which men have to contend. While he held it to be the duty of poets to prophesy "periods of regeneration and happiness" in order to awaken men to an awareness of their unused potentialities, he was not, he said, so presumptuous as to suppose that "the Gordian knot of the origin of evil can be disentangled" by any idealistic assertions which the poet may make.[23] Yet he claimed the right, with Isaiah and Vergil, to overleap "the actual reign of evil which we endure and bewail" and to see "the possible and perhaps approaching state of society in which the *'lion shall lie down with the lamb'* and 'omnis feret omnia tellus.'" Without the ministrations of such poets, the world would be a Cimmerian desert indeed.

---

[19] *Letters*, x, 351. Jan. 25, 1822.
[21] *Triumph of Life*. See the epilogue, below.
[23] Cf. Shelley's notes to *Hellas*.

[20] *Ibid.*, x, 331. Oct. 21, 1821.
[22] *Letters*, x, 368. April 2, 1822.

EPILOGUE:

THE TRIUMPH OF LIFE

> For what is poesy but to create
> From overfeeling good and ill; and aim
> At an external life beyond our fate,
> And be the new Prometheus of new men,
> Bestowing fire from heaven, and then, too late,
> Finding the pleasure given repaid with pain
> And vultures to the heart of the bestower,
> Who, having launchèd his high gift in vain,
> Lies chained to his lone rock by the sea-shore?
> —BYRON IN *The Prophecy of Dante*

THE long poem on which Shelley was at work when he was drowned was called *The Triumph of Life,* and the likelihood is that, if he had been able to finish what he had begun, the result would have been a fourth great poem to add to the *Prometheus,* the *Epipsychidion,* and the *Adonais.*[1] *The Triumph* is filled with

[1] In concentrating upon *The Triumph of Life,* a fragment sufficiently complete in itself to make judgment practicable, it has seemed advisable to omit detailed consideration of two other fragments of which the same cannot be said. The history play, *Charles the First,* sporadically engaged Shelley's attention between 1818-1822, and was finally laid aside in the last month of his life. The fragment totals nearly 800 lines of competent and at times very effective blank verse, and parts of five scenes have been attempted. The longest is an apparently complete unit of nearly 500 lines involving Charles, his queen, his arrogant court retainers, and the fool, Archy, who might have become, under Shelley's hands, an honest and fearless opponent of kingly oppression. Even in the fragment Archy emerges as a character of some depth—a kind of blend of the melancholy Jacques, and of Kent and the Fool in *Lear.* The character of the king suggests Shelley's growing appreciation of the complexities of the monarch's life, and although the king has comparatively little to say in the surviving fragment, he displays a mixture of motives which suggests that Shelley's abilities as a realizer of dramatic character might in time have developed considerably beyond the point reached in *The Cenci.* But Shelley found the drama, particularly as a piece of construction, a hard nut to crack, and never gained an interest in it sufficient to carry it anywhere near its probable conclusion: the beheading of Charles in Whitehall. Beside this fragment may be placed another, far removed from the actualities of political history. It might have borne some such title as *The Enchanted Island* and, from what Mary reveals of Shelley's plans, would have shown some points of resemblance to *The Tempest* (with a female Prospero), to the Dido episode from Vergil, and perhaps to some one of the "starry autos" of Calderón. Both fragments can be studied with profit.

solemn music, charged with deep melancholy, more nearly mature in its inward control and majestically dignified in its quiet outward demeanor than anything Shelley had done before. The movement is *andante*; the language is intentionally subdued. There is no avid searching after the proper epithet as there was in the *Epipsychidion*; the word that Shelley wants, or something near it, is the word most frequently chosen. Once chosen, it is placed with a precision about which he had never cared quite so much until at least the time of *Adonais*.

Because it is melancholy, solemn, quiet, muted, controlled and majestic—because it is, so to speak, a return from paradise to purgatory, a fashion has arisen which looks upon *The Triumph of Life* as the first work of Shelley's second, and greater, maturity, or as the commencement of something to which he had gradually grown up through years of experimentation with "ideal" poems— something in itself fundamentally new. This stress on the newness has led in turn to the frequent implication that *The Triumph of Life* is in some sort a palinode to many of Shelley's previous philosophic affirmations.

But *The Triumph of Life* is rather a reaffirmation than a palinode. In it Shelley reexamines, from a slightly different point of view than was usual in his "ideal" poems, two connected problems which had engaged his attention in *The Sensitive Plant*, *Epipsychidion*, *A Defence of Poetry*, and *Adonais*: the poet's relation to the worldly life around him, and his relation to the divine light which, in Shelley's view, informs the highest efforts of the best poets. Though the fragment breaks off before the reexamination has been completed, it provides, as it stands, a quiet corroboration of the position endorsed in Shelley's most recent work.

Putting aside for the moment the difference in tone already mentioned, there appear to be three major differences between this last poem and those which precede it. The first is that *The Triumph* focuses on worldly life almost to the exclusion of the eternal life, though the values implicit in the latter are everywhere assumed, and in a strange way are visible *through* the unlovely but awesome and pitiable vision which Shelley is at pains to keep in immediate focus. Both *Epipsychidion* and *Adonais* had pointed a similar contrast between the temporal and the eternal, though not by means of this oddly effective device of the double vision.

The second major difference is that Shelley (if we may identify him with the Dantean narrator) is spectator rather than protagonist. In *Epipsychidion*, Shelley (or his creative soul) was a direct participant; in *Adonais* he had moved a little to one side in order to give Keats the center of the stage, but his idealized self-portrait had a prominent place in the poem, and it was his own aspiration of which he spoke in its closing stanzas. There is a new objectivity in *The Triumph of Life*, and Shelley is the curious questioning bystander trying to understand the complexity of the vision. Aside from the central allegorical procession, the center of interest is Rousseau and his psychomachia, rather than Shelley and his own struggle with the world.

The third major change from antecedent poems is a shift of the image by which the scene of worldly life is presented. The "dreary cone of our life's shade" (*Epipsychidion*) and the lowering mist, charnel-house gloom, and night-shadow (*Adonais*) have now become an ice-cold brassy glare "intenser than the noon"— light so harsh that it "obscures" the supernal sun. This new figure is preferable to the Cimmerian desert figure of *Adonais* or the "cone of shade" figure of *Epipsychidion* because it is in closer conformity with natural fact. But it had been anticipated at the close of *Adonais* in the dome of many-colored glass, which refracted, diffused, distorted, and stained the white radiance of eternity without excluding all supernal light. It will be seen that none of these differences from preceding poems is complete— most of Shelley's poems feed into one another—but the over-all difference is marked enough to give *The Triumph of Life* a complexion and a tone which are different from those of any earlier production.

Those who have previously examined this poem have thrown valuable light on its literary analogues and on some aspects of its allegorical significance. But *The Triumph* has never been viewed as a whole in the full perspective of Shelley's theory of the relation of the poet to society and to the cosmos. To accomplish this task, one must first answer the question: What happens in the poem?

The theme of *The Triumph of Life* is partly summarized in Wordsworth's lines about the light of heaven in the *Ode on Intimations of Immortality*.

> At length the Man perceives it die away,
> And fade into the light of common day.

For the ice-cold glare which emanates from the Chariot of Life in Shelley's poem is a more intensely felt version of Wordsworth's "light of common day" which intercedes against and eventually supersedes the "vision splendid" which the youth has known. Another aspect of the same theme is expressed in Byron's *The Prophecy of Dante*, which Shelley read with great admiration in the fall of 1821.[2] Especially in the third and fourth cantos of this poem, Byron put into Dante's mouth an impassioned statement of a problem which troubled Shelley increasingly in his last years: the corrupting forces in human society which destroy the artist's integrity.

> They shall sing
> Many of love, and some of liberty,
> But few shall soar upon that eagle's wing,
> And look in the sun's face with eagle's gaze
> All free and fearless as the feather'd king,
> But fly more near the earth; how many a phrase
> Sublime shall lavish'd be on some small prince
> In all the prodigality of praise!
> And language, eloquently false, evince
> The harlotry of genius, which, like beauty,
> Too oft forgets its own self-reverence
> And looks on prostitution as a duty.[3]

The dramatic method employed in *The Triumph of Life* is analogous to that of the *Inferno*, with Shelley and Rousseau in the place of Dante and Vergil, although instead of moving from place to place like the observer and the commentator of the *Inferno* and the *Purgatorio*, Shelley and Rousseau stand in one place to watch the approach, the passage, and the departure of the swiftly moving

---

[2] *Letters*, x, 322. Sept. 14, 1821. "The subject," said Shelley, "is addressed to the few, and . . . will only be *fully* appreciated by the select readers of many generations."

[3] *The Prophecy of Dante*, Canto III.

car of worldly life. The idea of the pageant is derived from Petrarch's *Trionfi*, with clear reminiscences of the procession of Lucifera in Spenser's *Faerie Queene*.

The fragment consists of a prologue, three unnumbered sections, and a final question. The prologue (1-40) is an extraordinarily beautiful description of the physical setting (the seer lies under a chestnut tree on a slope of the Apennines, facing westward to the sea, with sunrise behind him) in which transpires the waking trance which overspreads his mind as the advancing light overspreads matutinal earth. Part the first (41-175) is a detailed and graphic description of the visionary pageant, the advancing *triumphus* of the car of Worldly Life and its victims. Part the second (176-300) discovers the commentator Rousseau, who, like Vergil in the *Inferno*, first identifies himself and then helps the spectator to identify certain historical characters among Worldly Life's countless victims. Part the third (300-543) is Rousseau's "idealized history" of his "life and feelings" and occupies all the rest of the fragment except the final question of line 544 (which is probably Shelley's): "Then, what is life?"

The vision opens with the picture of a dusty and sterile public highway on which millions of aimless people hurry to and fro, pursuing "their serious folly as of old" and unaware of the contiguous forests, fountains, caverns, and banks of violets which lie beyond their beaten track. Heralded by an ice-cold glare which wildly activates the madding crowd now comes swiftly the triumphal chariot with the deformed, caped and hooded figure of Worldly Life as its passenger, "wonder-wingèd" hours as its steeds,[4] and a "Janus-visaged Shadow" with four faces and four pairs of eyes (all blindfolded) as the highly inefficient charioteer. The nearer approach of the car stirs the crowd to frenzy. The vanguard of the procession is made up of youths and maidens wild as bacchanals and maenads, convulsed in "agonizing pleasure" of insane mutual attraction, commingling and falling senseless to be rolled over by the chariot of "her who dims the sun" with her icy glare. The rear is brought up by obscene "old men and women foully disarrayed" who vainly strive to keep up with

---

[4] That these are hours may be conjectured from Shelley's statement (lines 97-98)

> I heard alone on the air's soft stream
> The music of their ever-moving wings.

the car and the cold light which emanates from it, and who wheel about "with impotence of will" until "ghastly shadows" close round them and they sink in hopeless corruption.[5] The allegorical significance of this pageant will be obvious to anyone who has read the Lucifera passage in *The Faerie Queene* on which this section of the poem is chiefly founded. The car of Worldly Life with its deformed occupant attracts the millions who blindly follow its cold light or run ahead in breathless haste, torn by wild passions. The vanguard and the rearguard represent respectively passionate love and spiritual impotence, and the fierce Spirit whose "unholy leisure" the youths and maidens serve is evidently the lower Venus.[6]

Somewhat more difficult, however, is the identification of the "Janus-visaged Shadow" with blindfolded eyes who serves as charioteer.[7] One who has read through Rousseau's account of his own life (where he makes it plain that his failure was a failure of vision as poet, so that he plunged too soon into the cold light of common day) will return to the Janus-figure with a stronger sense of what it stands for: it is the type of the poet who has been hoodwinked by the worldly life, and does not therefore own the skill —which for Shelley was the true use of great poetry—to guide

[5] A similar wildness is discernible in the throngs which surround the coach of Lucifera (Worldly Pride), one of whose ministers is Lust, in *The Faerie Queene*. Also comparable are Shelley's "public way, thick-strewn with summer dust" where "flowers never grew" and Spenser's "broad high way" which leads to Lucifera's House of Pride, and is "all bare through people's feet, which thither traveiled." (*F.Q.*, I, iv, 2.) The old obscene people in Shelley who fall behind the chariot of Worldly Life are paralleled in Spenser by those who have gone to Lucifera's castle and come out badly. They lie "by the hedges" along the highway in "balefull beggerie or foule disgrace" like "loathsome lazars." (*F.Q.*, I, iv, 3.) Lucifera, who puts up a resplendent front, is of course a quite different figure from the hooded, shrouded, and misshapen creature who occupies Shelley's car of Worldly Life. But she produces similar victims, for under the feet of the "huge routs of people" who follow her train lie scattered "dead souls and bones of men, whose life had gone astray." (*F.Q.*, I, iv, 36.) It is significant that Shelley finds Worldly Life a huddled and distorted creature. Spenser emphasizes rather her false shows. "Her glorious glitter and light" says Spenser (*Ibid.*, stanza 16) "doth all men's eyes amaze." With Shelley men's eyes are "amazed" by the cold bright sheen. But, as is usual with Shelley, like has blended with like. Bradley lists nineteen parallels between Petrarch's *Trionfi* (Amore, Morte, Fama, chiefly) and Shelley's poem. See *MLR* 9 (1914), p. 442 note.

[6] Cf. the "Comet beautiful and fierce" of *Epipsychidion*, 368.

[7] On the basis of lines 103-104 editors have conjectured that the four faces of this double Janus look toward past, present, future and the fourth time-dimension— eternity. This is entirely acceptable to the identification offered. The ideal poet can see in all these directions; the imperfect poet is blinded to them.

aright the chariot of worldly life.[8] Shelley's conception of ideal poets, as outlined in the *Defence*, included not only the progenitors of all the arts but also "institutors of laws . . . founders of civil society . . . inventors of the arts of life, and the teachers, who draw into a certain propinquity with the beautiful and the true, that partial apprehension of the agencies of the invisible world which is called religion." Hence, Shelley added, "all original religions are allegorical . . . and, like Janus, have a double face of false and true." The ideal poets, "those who imagine and express" the "indestructible order" are both legislators and prophets, and can "behold intensely the present as it is" as well as see "the future in the present."[9] Suppose that these ideal poets are corrupted by the false shows of worldly life into losing contact with the "indestructible order" of things. They are, in effect, putting blindfolds on their great visionary powers; they can neither "behold intensely the present as it is," nor see "the future in the present." It is the generic type of the blindfolded poet who has "assumed the guidance" of the wonder-wingèd team of hours which draws the chariot of Worldly Life.[10]

[8] Shelley says that the car was guided "ill" (line 105), and Locock noted (though without following out the suggestion) that *The Faerie Queene* also contains an ill-guided car (I, iv, 19):

> May seeme the wayne was very evill led
> When such an one had guiding of the way,
> That knew not, whether right he went, or else astray.

The evil-led wayne (wagon) of Spenser is Lucifera's chariot (see notes above) and the outrider here alluded to is Idleness. He is not blindfolded but "drownd in sleepe," which perhaps comes to much the same thing, since he can scarcely hold up his head to see whether it is day or night. But the charioteer in Spenser is Satan, who sits upon "the wagon beame" cracking a whip over his team. (*Ibid.*, stanza 36.) Shelley's charioteer likewise occupies the "chariot-beam" (line 94). It is not necessary to suppose that Idleness and Satan entered into the picture of Shelley's blindfolded charioteer, though neither is far from his meaning.

[9] *Defence, Prose*, VII, 112.

[10] This identification of the charioteer is not widely different from that proposed by Mr. Barnard in his Odyssey Press edition of Shelley, New York, 1944, p. 492. It is easy to concur in his rejection of the idea that the charioteer represents destiny— a suggestion based on an allusion in *Hellas* (711) to "the world's eyeless charioteer, Destiny" and followed by most editors through Locock. "The point," says Mr. Barnard, "seems to be that the charioteer is possessed of powers which he cannot or does not use. And this makes questionable the identification of this figure with Destiny; an identification which is dubious on other grounds as well, since Shelley at no time in his life regarded the universe as a chaos ruled by blind Destiny." Mr. Barnard's identification of the figure as "the human soul, blinded by evil desires and by the careless or cowardly acceptance of base superstition, corrupt institutions, and degrading customs and conventions (in short all that is personified by the

Besides the bacchic rout of youth and age who are crushed beneath or fall behind the chariot are another "captive multitude" who include all those grown old in power or misery, all the men of action and martyrs who subdued their respective worlds, and all those known to worldly fame or infamy. The reminiscence of Petrarch's *Triumph of Fame* is clear enough in this group. But the captives of the worldly life do not include the "sacred few" of Athens and Jerusalem

> who could not tame
> Their spirits to the conqueror—but, as soon
> As they had touched the world with living flame,
> Fled back like eagles to their native noon.[11]

The "sacred few" were those who established contact with the "living flame" of heavenly light and did not lose it by taming their spirits to the cold glare of the worldly life. Evidently Christ and Socrates are foremost among the sacred few.

When the first part of the vision has been enacted, and the spectator wonders, half aloud, about the meaning of the pageant, and the identity of the shape within the car, a voice answers, "Life!" Out of the near hillside rises then the owner of the voice, who identifies himself as the corrupt and half-destroyed shade of Rousseau. "Who are those chained to the car?" asks the spectator. Rousseau answers that they are the great and famous who established "thought's empire over thought" but never learned to know themselves. Among them is the giant Napoleon

> Whose grasp had left the giant world so weak
> That every pigmy kicked it as it lay.

And as the phantasm of Napoleon passes, the spectator falls to grieving that the opposition of power and will is the badge of

---

figure of Life) and hence unable to see any meaning in the past or present, to say nothing of foreseeing or influencing the future or passing beyond time into Eternity" seems to me essentially right—if one adds that Shelley means a particular kind of man, the poet who has failed in his task of prophecy and legislation.

[11] This passage follows Rossetti, Locock, and Barnard in reading *conqueror* (i.e. life) instead of *conquerors*, as in Mary's edition. There seems to be no reason to doubt that Christ and Socrates are meant. But "few" would suggest more than two. Plato is not, it appears from lines 254-255, among this sacred few, for he soon appears, along with Aristotle, among the captives. The eagle-simile is found in Byron's *Prophecy of Dante*, Canto III.

mortal experience, and to wondering why God made "good and the means of good" irreconcilable. Others of Life's victims pass in heterogeneous array—Plato, whose heart Life conquered by earthly love, Aristotle and Alexander the Great; Catherine the Great and Frederick the Great; Gregory the Great and other institutionalizers of Christianity who, in Shelley's view, "rose like shadows between man and God," corrupted the purity of Christian doctrine, and thus produced a false idol which still prevails and is worshiped in place of "the true sun" it superseded. But the spectator soon sickens of the historic pageantry and turns to the commentator to learn how it came about that Rousseau should be here beside the highway of the worldly life.

The idealized history of Rousseau's life and feelings which ensues closely parallels the idealized history of Shelley's life and feelings in *Epipsychidion* up to the point at which the "Being" he had dreamed of in his youth passed "into the dreary cone of our life's shade." The difference between the two careers is that when Rousseau's supernal vision faded, he did not, like the creative soul of *Epipsychidion*, continue to search, but plunged instead into the worldly life and

> bared [his] bosom to the clime
> Of that cold light, whose airs too soon deform.[12]

This is the central doctrine to which the whole fragment of *The Triumph of Life* is directed: that the poet must not abandon his search for the "living flame" he has known in his youth, though, as he grows up, the Worldly Life does all she can with her icy glare "intenser than the noon" to amaze his eyes, like Spenser's Lucifera, and to draw him into the killing airs which "too soon deform" the creative spirit. It is noteworthy that Shelley does not, like Wordsworth in the "Ode on Intimations of Immortality" embrace, though with sadness, the "homely nurse" of common life who seeks to make her foster-child ("her inmate man") forget the glories he has known. He will not take stoical consolation in the thought that advancing years will bring the philosophic mind because he has observed too often in literary history the Worldly Life's corrupting force. Indeed, as he showed in *Peter Bell the*

---

[12] *Triumph of Life*, lines 467-468.

Third, he regarded Wordsworth as a conspicuous victim of that force. He knows what Wordsworth means by "the light that never was on sea or land" and by "the consecration and the poet's dream." He knows, out of his own experience, how that nascent glory passes away from the earth into the dreary cone. But he will seek it still. "I go on until I am stopped," said Shelley, "and I am never stopped." *The Triumph of Life* is not a palinode against his previous affirmations about the poet's aspirations towards divine fire, but rather a palinode against Wordsworth's reluctant acceptance of what Shelley (and even Wordsworth) would regard as a lesser substitute. With Keats, of course, it was otherwise. In *Adonais* he is represented as one who never surrendered, and as one who, for all his alleged frailty, dared "the unpastured dragon in his den." Shelley admired the *Hyperion,* fragmentary though it was, as a great poem in that idealistic mode to which he was devoting his own efforts in the year of Keats' death. "Poetry," he asserted in the *Defence,* "lifts the veil from the hidden beauty of the world, and makes familiar objects be as if they were not familiar; it re-produces all that it re-presents, and the impersonations clothed in its Elysian light stand thenceforward in the minds of those who have once contemplated them, as memorials of that gentle and exalted content which extends itself over all thoughts and actions with which it coexists."[13] The cold glare of the light around the triumphal car of worldly life was anathema to one whose eyes were trained upon the Elysian light. "Poetry," said he again, "defeats the curse which binds us to be subjected to the accident of surrounding impressions" and "creates for us a being within our being. It makes us the inhabitants of a world to which the familiar world is a chaos. It reproduces the common [i.e. shared] universe of which we are portions and percipients, and it purges from our inward sight the film of familiarity which obscures from us the wonder of our being."[14] The film of familiarity was a phrase of Coleridge's, and was another way of describing the cold light to which Rousseau and Wordsworth, and dozens of other great poets, had surrendered.

One last time, though objectively now in Rousseau's life-story, Shelley reincarnated in woman's shape his conception of the source

[13] *Defence, Prose,* vii, 117-118.   [14] *Defence, Prose,* vii, 137.

of true poetic power—this time as Iris, many-colored goddess of the rainbow, prismatic reflector of the rays of the supernal sun. On an April morning long past, says Rousseau, he was laid asleep under a mountain. Running through the base of the mountain was a high-roofed cavern[15] out of which flowed a limpid stream of water which filled the grove with pleasant sounds and "kept for ever wet" the stems of the flowers that grew nearby. Back beyond this sweet oblivious sleep Rousseau cannot remember:

> And whether life had been before that sleep
> The Heaven which I imagine, or a Hell
> Like this harsh world in which I wake to weep,
> I know not.[16]

The sleep-figure is a symbolic representation of Rousseau's birth.[17] "I arose," says he, and for a little while, though it was now broad day, the scene of woods and waters seemed to retain a gentle trace

> Of light diviner than the common sun
> Sheds on the common earth, and all the place
> Was filled with magic sounds woven into one
> Oblivious melody, confusing sense.

To put the matter in Wordsworthian terms, Rousseau after his birth retained intimations ("a gentle trace") of a previous immortal state.

Now comes Rousseau's vision of the supernal influence. Shelley has worked out the phenomenal aspects of this vision in such careful detail that one must place himself in full possession of the picture which was evidently in Shelley's mind. The hulking mountain (the great divide between the antenatal and postnatal condition) runs, as it were, on a north-south axis, blocking out the direct rays of the rising sun to the eastward. But the mountain is pierced straight through, on an east-west axis, by a cavern high

---

[15] Bradley, *MLR* (October, 1905) carefully examined this cavern, and concluded that it ran straight through the mountain.

[16] Cf. Wordsworth's "Ode on Intimations of Immortality" (line 59): "Our birth is but a sleep and a forgetting."

[17] The symbolism of the deep cavern *through* the mountain is that of the passageway to this life. Cf. "birth's orient portal" in *Hellas* (202). A. C. Bradley, *MLR* (October, 1905), and F. M. Stawell, *Essays and Studies*, 5 (1914), p. 124, both understand the passage as signifying birth, and Stawell says that "the conception is obviously influenced by the antenatal dreams of Plato and Wordsworth."

and deep, through which the soul, in the unconscious act of being born, has just come from the sun-filled regions of the east. Within the cavern is a well or fountain. From it flows the west-running stream beside which the soul has awakened after birth. But the rays of the eastern sun strike through the cavern, and the sun's image, "radiantly intense," burns on the waters of the well. It must be understood that the youthful soul is now on the western side of the mountain facing eastward toward the cavern where the sun's rays strike in upon the waters of the fountain. In the midst of this blaze is seen "on the vibrating floor of the fountain"

> A Shape all light, which with one hand did fling
> Dew on the earth, as if she were the dawn,
> And the invisible rain did ever sing
> A silver music on the mossy lawn;
> And still before me on the dusky grass
> Iris her many-colored scarf had drawn.[18]

The emanation from the "shape all light" is Iris, the rainbow, caused by the action of the sun's rays on the waters of the well. The same care which Shelley lavished on the setting for this phenomenon is applied in the development of the rainbow image. This vision is eventually to fade from Rousseau's sight and to lose itself in the light of common day just as a rainbow fades and vanishes. But for a while, as the youth Rousseau moves westward along the stream which flows from the cavern and the well, she remains visible to him, and all her actions and manifestations are such as would suggest, still, the rainbow.[19]

[18] During the masque in Shakespeare's *Tempest*, Iris calls herself the messenger of "the queen o' the sky." Ceres refers to Iris' "rich scarf," to the "refreshing showers" which are diffused from Iris' wings upon Ceres' flowers. The masque is performed to celebrate "a contract of true love." (IV, i, 64-84.)

[19] The whole episode, up to the time of Iris' disappearance, is a manifest reworking (with much more care for the detail of the vision and a far greater effort to compress and comprise it into the terms of a phenomenon which one could observe in nature) of the passage in *Epipsychidion* (190-228) in which Shelley describes the visionary "Being" who appeared to him in his own youth. It should be noticed also that Wordsworth's compass-pointing in the great ode is followed in *The Triumph of Life*. Wordsworth's youth daily travels "farther from the east." Like Rousseau, moving down the west running stream, Wordsworth's youth is attended on his way by the splendid vision. Bradley has argued convincingly that the general groundwork of the scene is based on Dante's *Purgatorio*, Cantos 28 and 29, a section with which Shelley was demonstrably familiar, since he translated the passage on Matilda gathering flowers (Canto 28). In both instances the narrator is following

It has sometimes been quite wrongly supposed that the Iris-figure is intended to be a creature with evil connotations. Thus she is said to blot out "the thoughts of him" who watches her swift movement, and one by one to trample them out, like sparks or embers, into "the dust of death." But from what follows it is plain that these are dark and evil thoughts, not thoughts in general, for her action is compared to that of day "upon the threshold of the east" treading out the lamps of night. Similarly, when Rousseau asks for some explanation of the mysteries of his origin and his present condition, the goddess offers him her cup of Nepenthe, the bright cordial of her own Elysium, with the invitation: "Quench thy thirst [for knowledge]." But even as he touches "with faint lips" the cup which she raises, his brain becomes as sand and a new vision (that of Worldly Life and the "cold bright car") bursts on his sight. The usual explanation is that as a result of drinking from Iris' cup, Rousseau's spiritual senses were overcome by the cold new vision. Actually, however, he is not said to drink, but only to touch his lips to the cup. Had he drunk the bright Nepenthe, he could have quenched his youthful thirst for knowledge of the mysteries. But at the crucial moment his courage failed, his brain became "as sand," his thirst remained unquenched, and the bright cold vision of worldly life burst in.[20]

Even in the severe excess of the cold light of the worldly life, Rousseau was sadly aware of the waning rainbow-vision, which still moved downstream by his side as he continued his journey through the wilderness. But it was dim now as

> A light of heaven, whose half-extinguished beam
> Through the sick day in which we wake to weep,
> Glimmers, for ever sought, for ever lost.

---

a flower-bordered stream in a kind of earthly paradise, when he sees a beautiful lady (Dante's Matilda, Shelley's Iris) across (or, in Shelley's poem, *upon*) the water. In Dante, the forest is suddenly lighted up and the car of the Church rushes in; in Shelley also with light as harbinger, it is the car of Worldly Life. Bradley, *MLR* 9 (1914), 442-443.

[20] This account agrees with both Stawell and Bradley in that it assumes that Iris is a beneficent spirit. Both of them assume, however, that Rousseau drank of the cup, while Stawell explains that the liquor was too powerful for him: only the "sacred few" could drink it without going astray. And Rousseau is not of these chosen few. *Op. cit.*, p. 126. This cup, like that of the Witch of Atlas, is out of Spenser. Cf. *Faerie Queene*, iv, iii, 42-45.

And turning his eyes to the triumphal procession of worldly life, Rousseau was swept up and borne along by the "loud million," baring his breast to the cold light "whose airs too soon deform."

As he closes the account of his great failure of nerve, Rousseau recalls one more phenomenon which he witnessed just after he had joined the "loud million." It was, he says, a wonder worthy to have been recorded by Dante. As the chariot of Worldly Life left the valley of the stream he had been following, he saw a convocation of fury-like phantoms filling the air along the chariot's tracks. And as he watched, all beauty, strength, and freshness slowly waned and fell from each of the human forms who followed the chariot, so that

> long before the day
> Was old, the joy which waked like heaven's glance
> The sleepers in the oblivious valley, died.

The situation here, as some commentators observe, is precisely the opposite of that which takes place at the end of *Prometheus Unbound*, after Prometheus has achieved his act of self-reform. At that time, the masks of ugliness fall from all created things. Now, in the procession of the Worldly Life, the masks are gradually assumed, and grow on. One who has observed the doffing of the masks in *Prometheus* and the assumption of them in *The Triumph*, might wish to use the observation as an argument that *The Triumph* is a palinode. But the argument would rest on a fundamental misconception of Shelley's intention in the two poems. The end of *Prometheus* is not intended as a picture of the actual, but only of what "ought to be." The beginning of the play, with Prometheus in chains, is Shelley's picture of the world as it is at present. The pageant of worldly life in *The Triumph* is, in effect, another vision of the conditions which obtain in the Prometheus up to the time of the hero's recantation. The voluntary or involuntary assumption of the loathsome masks is the equivalent of what happened to mankind when Prometheus granted sovereignty to Jupiter, god of hate and despair within the mind.

The fragmentary state of *The Triumph* leaves uncertain the identity of the asker of the final question, "What is life?" But whether the asker is Shelley or Rousseau, it is the answer which is important. If, as one strongly suspects, the "life" of the question is that which has been talked about through the greater part of the fragment, the answer to the question is clear, for worldly life is a corrupting force, a slow stain, a cold light whose effect is to deform. Shelley had discussed this question at some length in a passage of the *Defence* where he contrasted the Greek erotic poets (presumably those of the Hellenistic decadence) with Homer and Sophocles. The imperfection of the erotic poets, said he, consisted not in what they had but in what they had not. "It is not inasmuch as they were poets, but inasmuch as they were not poets, that they can be considered with any plausibility as connected with the corruption of their age." That corruption did not extinguish in them all sensibility to pleasure, passion, and natural scenery; had it done so, "the last triumph of evil would have been achieved."[21] For, as Shelley went on to say, "the end of social corruption is to destroy all sensibility to pleasure" and it spreads like a "paralysing venom" through imagination, intellect, affections, and even "into the very appetites," until the whole mind becomes "a torpid mass in which hardly sense survives."[22] But the true poetic principle is at perpetual war with social corruption, and a given age can corrupt a given poet only to the extent that the poet has cut himself off from his greatest source of power. The shade of Rousseau in *The Triumph*, a mere root or misshapen stump of a being, serves as the *exemplum*: one who turned his back on the visionary splendor and followed the millions who accompanied the chariot of life.[23]

To the poet who would avoid what Shelley called in *Adonais* "the contagion of the world's slow stain," death is one of three alternatives. Shelley outlined the other two in a letter to his wife, written while he was visiting Byron at Ravenna in August, 1821. One device "would be utterly to desert all human society," retiring with Mary and his son to a "solitary island in the sea" and shutting up "the floodgates of the world." On this plan, said Shelley, he would be alone, and "would devote either to oblivion or to future

---

[21] The phrase, "triumph of evil," and its context have close bearing on the theme of *The Triumph of Life*.

[22] *Defence, Prose*, vii, 123-124. Cf. Shelley's condemnation of the world's selfish and loveless dullards in the preface to *Alastor*.

[23] Shelley's remark on Lucretius (*Defence, Prose*, vii, 130) is pertinent here, for the author of *De Rerum Natura* "had limed the wings of his swift spirit in the dregs of the sensible world."

generations the overflowings of a mind which, *timely withdrawn from the contagion*, should be kept fit for no baser object." A more feasible alternative, said Shelley, would be "to form for ourselves a society of our own class, as much as possible in intellect, or in feelings; and to connect ourselves with the interests of that society."[24]

As it turned out, death by drowning in the Gulf of Spezzia was the alternative which preserved Shelley's spirit from the fate of those chained to the chariot of the Worldly Life. In the isolation of Lerici, on the shores of that gulf, he had been trying, surrounded by a little coterie, to put into practice the second plan. Without the solution chance forced upon him, Shelley might have succeeded in the great double task of preserving his integrity and maintaining, clear and unsullied before his mind's eye, the vision by which his best poetry was exalted. On the other hand, he sometimes felt, in the last year of his life, that his powers were beginning to wane. "I try to be what I might have been," he said of *Hellas*, the last major poem he was able to complete, "but am not successful." He summarized his feeling by quoting the first two lines of the following passage from Goethe's *Faust*:

> Over the noblest gift, the spirit's splendour.
> There floods an alien, ever alien stream;
> When this world's wealth is won, our souls surrender,
> The larger hope we call a lying dream.
> Our life of life, the visions grave and glorious,
> Fade, and the earthly welter is victorious.
> Imagination once, fire-winged with hope,
> Filled all eternity, and flamed to heaven;
> But now it dwindles to a petty scope,
> While joy on joy falls round us, wrecked and riven.[25]

This is the great problem to which Shelley addressed himself in *The Triumph of Life*: the impingement of the mundane and the meretricious upon the higher life of the mind. From the perhaps inevitable stain upon the spirit's splendor Shelley was saved, if he needed saving, in the late afternoon of July 8, 1822.

[24] *Letters*, x, 315. Aug. 16, 1821. Italics mine.
[25] *Letters*, x, 333. Miss Stawell (*op. cit.*, p. 125) was the first to call attention to the connection between this passage and Shelley's *Triumph*. I owe to her also the translation of the pertinent lines.

· II ·

"WE strive to grasp a Proteus as we read," said Stopford Brooke of Shelley in 1880. For his character as artist the metaphor is just, though no formula is capable of containing him. Yet one who penetrates the woven surface of his poetry finds deep inward coherence. As an artist, he is memorable and perhaps also culpable for the variety of his experimentation with a central object: it may be that he chose too many vantage-points from which to view and describe his revelation, or that the visionary splendor in which he frames his central ethic blinds the eye which would see through to the center. Yet one who is disconcerted, as Proteus' captors were, by the very changeability of the entity he seeks to hold to, may take comfort in the knowledge that there is a common denominator.

At the center stand a moralist exploring mind and a philosopher interpreting law. The close student discovers a growing sense that these are not peripheral issues with which Shelley is concerned and for which he provides the resolutions natural to the philosopher and director. The ultimately classic quality of his achievement is owing in part to his preoccupation with psychological experiences at once universal and primary, and in part also to his determination to reveal, and thus to make vitally significant to human life, his vision of the cosmic law. With something like religious devotion, Shelley spent his short life in formulating, clarifying, and applying the vision with which he began.

This is the vision of the soul's progress towards perfection, worked out through a set of inherited symbols modified by his own imaginative experience of the world. In 1815, Shelley might have said of his vision what Keats in 1819 said of his view of the world as a vale of "soul-making": "I can scarcely express what I but dimly perceive, and yet I think I perceive it." By 1818-1819, however, Shelley had succeeded in sharpening his vision and in achieving a symbolic structure suitable for its embodiment. By that time he was ready to act, not only as legislator but also as judge and as executive. His deepest interest was in the laws of mental growth, and in the necessary judicial action of that inward scale of values by which the degree of the mind's approach to self-realization is qualitatively measured. The desire to universalize this governing concept, to make the law prevail, is not unusual in a secular evangelical of Shelley's stamp. Seeing (like Mazzini) that complete self-realization for a moral and social end is man's highest duty, and understanding that there are multiple factors in human society which inhibit this enabling act, as well as others in human psychology which facilitate it, he works to destroy the first and to preserve and develop the second. Destruction and preservation are thus complementary forces in the central Shelleyan myth: the psyche's struggle for unification with the epipsyche. To read his account of that struggle literalistically, as gross autobiography, is in most instances to miss the spirit in the letter of his law. Shelley's laws are those of the soul.

Every poetic generation will frame its own laws with varying dependence upon the precedent of the past. Shelley's ethic offers a version of certain principles of the Enlightenment, reoriented towards a new center in the ethical imagination. Though he is far less sanguine than the author of *The Progress of the Human Mind* about the inevitability of progress, his end in view, like that of Condorcet, is mankind unlimited. With characteristic modifications he agrees with the opening sentence of Rousseau's *Social Contract*: man is born free, but he is everywhere in chains. As Rousseau is made to prove in *The Triumph of Life*, the chains are those which bind all men, except a sacred few, to the onrushing chariot of the worldly life, just as the cold light blinds all men, except a sacred few, to full recognition of their predicament and its causes. Shelley proclaims, therefore, his agreement with the ancient proverb that where vision is not, the people perish—of a sclerosis which leads inevitably to death in its truest sense, the corruption of spirit. For him the vision has been provided for all to see, though indirectly through symbolic means, in the world's greatest poetry, which he defines as all great thinking of an idealistic kind. It is for this reason that in the face of multiple personal discouragements Shelley can rise to the impassioned eloquence and conviction with which he asserts the importance of the poetic principle in human history. Altruism is for him the guarantor of social order and improvement, and genuine altruism, as he well knows, cannot be legislated. Yet through the unremitting exercise of the sympathetic imagination—the organ of man's moral nature—a predilection towards altruism can be inculcated. Even Descartes had suggested, what Bacon equally knew, that "the grace of fable stirs the mind." In Shelley's view, the tropes of poetry, the embodiment in art forms of the principles men ought to live by, are an imaginative means (Shelley's political pamphlets were his rationalistic means) to that inculcation. One must accept as an aberration Shelley's remarks against the probability of his continuing as poet and his implication that he yearned to be a moral philosopher. Both poetry and moral philosophy were inseparably mingled in him, and he could never have abandoned either while his powers remained. The central shape of the Protean artist is the Promethean thinker: they cannot stand dividually.

The present account of Shelley's development has shown that his moral idealism is infused with a strain of moral realism, although, because of his view of the function of the poet, it is ordinarily the former which is emphasized. Shelley learned empirically the dangers and despairs of living a moral life where his own convictions did not conform to those widely held by his British readers. He knew, both experientially and instinctively, the deep entanglement of evil with good, the "Gordian knot" which no words could cut, the paradox by which, as the last of the Furies told Prometheus, all best things may be confused to ill. The Shelleyan observer in *The Triumph of Life* turned away from the pageant of history in the grieved recognition that God had apparently made good irreconcilable with the means of good. Experience and observation rescued Shelley's dream from mere idyllicism even as he sought to show the Christian world the universal applicability of an impossible ethical ideal. Shelley knew, if he did not personally achieve, the shape of true virtue.

Through all his poetry runs the theme that true virtue consists in clarity of vision, discovery of the divine law's intent, and leadership in moral action. Up to 1818 Shelley explored and exemplified four views of the mind's relationship to outer and inner forces. The first was a materialistic necessitarianism, a conception of the inevitability of progress which Shelley inherited directly from the Enlightenment. The second was a form of psychological determinism, concerned with the idea of the inevitability of aspiration, the striving of the imperfect man towards self-realization. The third retained the deterministic bias to the extent that Shelley's myth was projected upon the broad screen of a cyclic theory of history; yet the stress fell upon the necessity for idealistic human leadership which despite, or perhaps because of, the inevitability of martyrdom for the principals, could point the way towards the moral conditions which ought to obtain in human society. The fourth returned to the psychological aspects of the problem, reaching the conclusion that the real key-concept was self-determinism: what is necessary to the clear vision, the discovery of law, and the assumption of moral leadership is the realization of the need for spiritual katharsis, followed at length by a willed rejection of all such dismal hatreds and fears as inhibit and corrupt the soul's receptivity. These wrestlings with the dark angel proved, in effect, that however the causes of evil be denominated—as the perpetuation of superstition through institutions, as the radical imperfection of man who has glimpsed but has abandoned the striving for perfection, as blind social resistance to needful historical change, or as the true hell of the unpurged mind—man ought theoretically to be able, through the proper appreciation and exercise of his potential strength, to vanquish his ancient adversary, who is himself Protean. But the plight of Tasso and the tragedy of Beatrice Cenci showed the strength of the chthonic forces in human society. Only a full realization of, and an absolute, universal, and unremitting conformity to, the law of love could thwart, at all entrances, the incursions of evil—a conformity manifestly impossible, yet not the less to be worked for on that account. Shelley came ultimately to a classification of individuals according to the relative degrees of their receptivity to the immanent power of love in the cosmos. He steadily opposed those forces in society which defeated the spread of the divine power, and reached the conclusion that poetry, which renders supple and active the moral organ in man, could accomplish its work of transformation by the conversion of individuals in sufficient numbers so that the effects would be broadly felt. If he felt doubts about the efficacy of such a program, and evidently he did, he nevertheless adhered to it as one means of resisting the perhaps otherwise inevitable triumph of life.

It is no accident that the title of Shelley's last poem should come so close to summarizing the central fear of his last years, or that the choice and arrangement of symbolic figures in *The Triumph of Life* should provide so exact an illustration of his own role as moralist and philosopher. He belongs neither among the sacred few nor among the many who follow the chariot in chains. From his place beside the roadway he points out to passersby the fields and forests which they might enter if they broke their chains. But he speaks in a language either objectionable or unfamiliar to a great part of the throng. Some few among them, pausing in passage, catch glimpses of the truth he would have them know: the spirit's splendor. Then they move on.

APPENDICES

APPENDIX I

AHASUERUS AND MILTON'S SATAN

SHELLEY's Ahasuerus, type of the eternal rebel, is closely modeled on the most famous example in Christian poetry, Milton's Satan. Called up by Mab's wand, the "strange and woe-worn" figure materializes:

> His port and mien bore mark of many years,
> And chronicles of untold ancientness
> Were legible within his beamless eye;
> Yet his cheek bore the mark of youth;
> Freshness and vigor knit his manly frame;
> The wisdom of old age was mingled there
> With youth's primeval dauntlessness;
> And inexpressible woe,
> Chastened by fearless resignation, gave
> An awful grace to his all-speaking brow.
>
> (VII, 73-82)

Milton's fallen Archangel, in a famous passage previously quoted by Shelley and Medwin in their "Wandering Jew" of 1810, shows a face which

> Deep scars of thunder had intrenched, and care
> Sat on his faded cheek, but under brows
> Of dauntless courage, and considerate pride
> Waiting revenge.　　(*Paradise Lost*, I, 601-604)

Satan is still in Shelley's mind when Ahasuerus tells of being cursed by the Saviour after taunting him:

> I fell
> And long lay tranced upon the charmèd soil.
> When I awoke, hell burned within my brain.
>
> (VII, 184-186)

This has no direct verbal parallel in Milton, but the connection between these sentences and Satan's fall is obvious. Some few lines later, Ahasuerus says that he learned to prefer "Hell's freedom to the servitude of Heaven" (VII, 195). As the editors of the Julian edition of Shelley's work have observed, this echoes Satan's remark, "Better to reign in Hell than serve in Heaven" (*Paradise Lost*, I, 263). Ahasuerus concludes by saying that he has withstood the tyrant's curse "with stubborn and unalterable will" (vii, 258). Satan proposes to his fallen comrades that they continue to oppose the tyrannous dictates of Heaven with "unconquerable will" (*Paradise Lost*, i, 106). Ahasuerus compares his staying powers with those of

> A giant oak, which heaven's fierce flame
> Had scathèd in the wilderness, to stand
> A monument of fadeless ruin there.
> (vii, 259-261)

Milton describes Satan's legions as standing, despite withered glory

> As when heaven's fire
> Hath scathed the forest oaks or mountain pines
> With singèd top their stately growth, though bare
> Stands on the blasted heath.
> (*Paradise Lost*, i, 612-615)

It would probably be fair to say that whatever grandeur Shelley's Ahasuerus shows is derived from Milton's Satan.

APPENDIX II

CYTHNA'S PROTOTYPES

CYTHNA in *The Revolt of Islam* may be to some extent an idealization of one of Shelley's real-life heroines: Mary Wollstonecraft, the mother of his second wife. His first wife Harriet thought, probably with some reason, that Shelley's admiration for Mary Wollstonecraft had something to do with his determination to elope with young Mary Wollstonecraft Godwin. "Mary was determined to seduce him," said Harriet bitterly in 1814. "She heated his imagination by talking of her mother, and going to her grave with him every day, till at last she told him she was dying in love with him."[1] In his dedicatory verses to *The Revolt*, Shelley gives every evidence that his earlier admiration for Mary Wollstonecraft, champion of the rights of woman, had continued unabated. What he says of her there amounts virtually to a deification, a kind of Shelleyan "Mariolatry." He does not wonder that young Mary should have been lovely from her birth:

> For One then left this earth
> Whose life was like a setting planet mild,
> Which clothed thee in the radiance undefiled
> Of its departing glory; still her fame
> Shines on thee, through the tempests dark and wild
> Which shake these latter days.[2]

[1] *Letters*, x, 420.
[2] Mary Wollstonecraft died in childbed, September, 1797.

In the second canto, Laon says that

> Cythna mourned with me the servitude
> In which the half of humankind were mewed,
> Victims of lust and hate, the slave of slaves.

"Consider," urged Mary Wollstonecraft, "whether . . . it be not inconsistent and unjust to subjugate women. . . . You *force* all women, by denying them civil and political rights, to remain immured in their families groping in the dark. . . . They may be convenient slaves, but slavery will have its constant effect, degrading the master and the abject dependent. . . . Reason loudly demands JUSTICE for one half of the human race."[3]

In the fourth canto, the hermit reports to Laon that "a maiden fair" has risen in the Golden City to acquaint her sex with "the law of truth and freedom," and to teach "equal laws and justice . . . to woman, outraged and polluted long."[4] Cythna's very lengthy exhortation to the mariners, which nearly fills Canto VIII, includes a strong plea for the rehabilitation of women, while in the following canto Cythna recalls that upon her entry into the Golden City, she was regarded as a kind of female messiah:

> Some said
> I was a child of God, sent down to save
> Woman from bonds and death. . . .

Her words elicited everywhere a sympathetic response:

> But chiefly women, whom my voice did waken
> From their cold, careless, willing slavery,
> Sought me; one truth their dreary prison has shaken,
> They looked around, and lo! they became free!

Mary Wollstonecraft produced no such miraculous effect upon the women of her day, yet it is conceivable that the author of *A Vindication of the Rights of Woman*, if sufficiently idealized, could have served as the model for Cythna. "Contending for the rights of women," said she, "my main argument is built on this simple principle, that if she be not prepared by education to become the companion of man, she will stop the progress of knowledge, for truth must be common to all, or it will be inefficacious with respect to its influence on general practice. And how can woman be expected to co-operate, unless she know why she ought to be virtuous? Unless freedom strengthen her reason till she comprehend her duty, and see in what manner it is connected with her real good?" Or again, "Liberty is the mother of virtue, and if women

[3] See Mary Wollstonecraft, *Rights of Woman*, dedication to M. Perigord.
[4] Canto IV, xviii-xxi.

are, by their very constitution, slaves . . . they must ever languish like exotics."[5]

It may be, therefore, that Cythna is an idealization of one of Shelley's real-life heroines. But in the process of idealization, it is probable that he invoked the shades of several heroines of literature, any one of which might have contributed to the total portrait. Astride her black horse, militant and sure, Cythna reminds Dr. Peck of the dashing lady from Lawrence's *Empire of the Nairs*, of which the subtitle, it may be noted, is *The Rights of Woman*. Seated in veiled majesty upon her throne among the thronging maidens, Cythna might be a lineal descendant of Spenser's Venus, while one is not unnaturally reminded of another Spenserian figure, Britomart, who combines fighting prowess with the chaste heart and unbreakable loyalty of a woman in love. Another possibility would be Zenobia, the warrior queen of Peacock's *Palmyra*, which Shelley had read with admiration in 1812.

> What countless charms around her rise!
> What dazzling splendour sparkles in her eyes!
> On her radiant brow enshrined,
> Minerva's beauty blends with Juno's grace;
> The matchless virtues of her godlike mind
> Are stamp'd conspicuous on her angel-face.

To these praises of Zenobia, Peacock adds some others in a learned footnote: "Zenobia is perhaps the only female whose superior genius broke through the servile indolence imposed on her sex by the climate and manners of Asia. She claimed descent from the Macedonian kings of Egypt, equalled in beauty her ancestor Cleopatra, and far surpassed that princess in chastity and valour. Zenobia was esteemed the most lovely, as well as the most heroic of her sex. She was of a dark complexion (for in speaking of a lady these trifles become important). Her teeth were of a pearly whiteness, and her large black eyes sparkled with uncommon fire, tempered by the most attractive sweetness." She was also, he goes on, a scholar and linguist of some skill. It is hardly necessary to point out that to a mind as open to suggestion as Shelley's, such a description would have been long remembered. In some other respects, but especially in her love-scenes with Laon, Cythna is an incarnation of the dream-maiden of *Alastor*. The available evidence makes it impossible to select among these heroines the most likely antetype for Cythna, and she may indeed be a composite likeness of several or all of them.[6]

---

[5] *Rights of Woman*, dedication to Perigord, and Chapter 2. These sentiments are developed at considerable length in the treatise, which is level-headed and completely unspectacular.

[6] Cythna's relation to *The Empire of the Nairs* is noted by Peck, *MLN* 40 (1925), 246-249. It may be added that Shelley had made a comparison between Lawrence's book and Mary Wollstonecraft's *Rights of Woman* in 1812 (*Letters,*

APPENDIX III

ADDENDA ON *PROMETHEUS UNBOUND*

1. The Father-Son Succession in Aeschylus' *Prometheia* and Shelley's *Prometheus Unbound*

SHELLEY has involved generations of interpreters in considerable difficulty by introducing a new concept (Demogorgon) into the father-son succession scheme which is implicit in the Aeschylean Prometheus trilogy so far as we know it. According to that scheme, Jupiter came to power by overthrowing his father, Kronos or Saturn. One of Jupiter's sons, in turn, is fated to succeed him, but he does not know which of them it is to be. Prometheus does know, however, and it is his refusal to divulge the secret which has caused Jupiter to torture him. Shelley conforms to the Aeschylean plan in making Jupiter the successor to his father Saturn (*Prometheus Unbound*, III, i, 54). But there is no justification in Aeschylus for Shelley's assertion that Prometheus "gave wisdom, which is strength, to Jupiter" (II, iv, 44), or for the logical corollary of this statement: namely, that Prometheus really put Jupiter on the throne. The original usurpation was Jupiter's own doing. Shelley's version of the myth would not allow him to retain this element.

Shelley's second change is an explicit rejection of the denouement of the *Prometheia*, the intention of which he seems, whether willfully or otherwise, to have misunderstood. In the lost *Prometheus Unbound* of Aeschylus, Jupiter and Prometheus were in effect reconciled and Prometheus set free. Aeschylus seems to have had in mind a symbolic reconciliation of the two virtues of justice and compassion. Shelley did not see the matter in this way. "I was averse," he says in his preface, "from a catastrophe so feeble as that of reconciling the Champion with the Oppressor of mankind." For him, Jupiter represented a force making for evil, as Prometheus represented a force making for good. Where Aeschylus was seeking some means of reconciling two cardinal virtues, Shelley was seeking to avoid the reconciliation of a cardinal virtue with a deadly vice. Thus the whole drive of this ethic is precisely the contrary of that of his Greek "source."

Shelley was compelled, therefore, to invent a catastrophe which would embody his new conception. He had heard that in the *Prometheus Unbound* of Aeschylus the reconciliation was achieved in the following way: Prometheus warned Jupiter not to consummate his marriage with Thetis because out of that union a son would be born who would destroy the father. Taking heed of this warning, Jupiter married Thetis to Peleus, and rewarded Prometheus by having Hercules release

---

IX, 17). With Cythna enthroned (V, xliii-lv) compare Spenser's Venus (*Faerie Queene*, IV, x, 37 *et seq.*). Shelley's comments on his reading of *Palmyra* appear in *Letters*, IX, 20.

him from the rock. Shelley retained the Jupiter-Thetis marriage device, but did not otherwise follow the Aeschylean pattern. In the third act, the marriage and the consummation have both taken place, and Jupiter supposes that the son he has begotten upon Thetis will utterly destroy the defiance of Prometheus, and thus enslave him forever. That son is as yet "unbodied," and floats between the bride and groom, "felt," although "unbeheld," awaiting incarnation, or as one might put it, actualization. Jupiter believes that a particular Hour is destined to arrive at Olympus

> Bearing from Demogorgon's vacant throne
> The dreadful might of ever-living limbs
> Which clothed that awful spirit unbeheld,
> To redescend and trample out the spark.

Although the passage is obscure, Jupiter appears to mean that Demogorgon will ascend to Olympus, enter into and thus produce an incarnation of Jupiter's as yet "unbodied" son, and that this son, clothed in "the might of ever-living limbs" will then descend from Olympus and trample out the "unextinguished fire" which originates in man and "burns towards heaven with fierce reproach." In this expectation, Jupiter is of course disappointed. Instead of extinguishing the defiance of mankind, Demogorgon casts Jupiter into the abyss, remarking as he does so:

> I am thy child, as thou wert Saturn's child;
> Mightier than thee; and we must dwell together
> Henceforth in darkness.

This statement, which has caused much difficulty, would seem to indicate that Shelley had in mind the general spirit of the father-son succession scheme as we find it implied in Aeschylus. Saturn was dethroned by his son Jupiter; now Jupiter is dethroned by his "son" Demogorgon. The knowledge that this would happen has been Prometheus' secret. The general conformity to the Aeschylean scheme is no doubt what led J. A. K. Thomson to remark that Shelley's Demogorgon, in this particular connection, is "imaginatively right."[1] It is imaginatively right in another way, also. For where Demogorgon, if looked at from the point of view of Prometheus and Asia, is a force for good and the right, the same figure, from Jupiter's point of view, turns out to be exactly the opposite. He is a doom. It is the doom of Prometheus to enter into the kingdom of heaven; it is the doom of Jupiter to sink to the depths of Tartaros. Shelley may have been trying to suggest that evil contains the seeds of its own destruction. The seeds are provided by Jupiter; the destruction is provided by Demogorgon. A further explanation of Shel-

[1] "The Religious Background of the *Prometheus Vinctus,*" *Harvard Studies in Classical Philology*, 31 (Cambridge, Mass., 1920), 6.

ley's meaning may be suggested by pointing out that the unbodied figure of his "son" probably exists only in Jupiter's imagination. He expects some change in the structure of the cosmos, and because he is so certain of his omnipotence, he imagines that it is Demogorgon's will to enter into this "son," bring it to life, and put it to work. But Demogorgon has no such intention. He is a son of Jupiter only in the ironic sense that he is the agent who will dethrone him. The speech of Demogorgon might then be paraphased, "You, Jupiter, were the son of Saturn, and mightier than he. Your relation to him was in one sense like mine to you: I am mightier than you are as you were mightier than he was when you cast him down. Come down with me."

It is evident that Shelley has completely reoriented the myth as he derived it from Aeschylus. He not only gives it a moral twist quite foreign to Aeschylus, but he also introduces from Boccaccio the figure of Demogorgon, substitutes that figure for the fateful son of Jupiter, avoids the reconciliation of Jupiter and Prometheus by causing the "son" to overthrow Jupiter, leaving Prometheus (the mind of man), "gentle and just and dreadless," as "the monarch of the world."

2. The Political and Scientific Interpretations of *Prometheus Unbound*

That Shelley intended *Prometheus Unbound* to partake of the nature of a moral allegory has been the consensus of scholarly opinion during the past century and a half. Two other interpretations, each of which proposes a much more particularized meaning for the symbols of the play, have been suggested, and it is the purpose of this note to examine them.

Professor K. N. Cameron, whose grasp of the political situation in England and on the Continent during the period 1789-1830 is enviable, has offered a detailed analysis of the poem in terms of what he calls its "political-historical content."[2] The most noticeable difficulty in his argument is that while he assumes a particularized symbolic political meaning for each of the major protagonists and antagonists, he is compelled, when he undertakes an *explication de texte*, to broaden this meaning until his interpretation becomes, in effect, the traditional moral interpretation with some political ornamentation.

He rightly asserts that Prometheus is something more than the Titan of Aeschylus and the Furies more than the Furies of the *Eumenides*. It is when he wishes to particularize them that he appears to take leave of Shelley's "ideal" purpose. Prometheus, he believes, represents the intelligentsia of the early nineteenth century who are aware of the need for political reform. The Furies are "those forces by means of which the governing aristocracy, the power of the Quadruple Alliance . . . kept

[2] K. N. Cameron, "The Political Symbolism of *Prometheus Unbound*," *PMLA* 58 (September, 1943), 728-753.

itself in power; its vast armies . . . its crooked judges, lawyers, and money-lenders . . . its bondholding parasites." Mercury symbolizes "those who carry out the will of the aristocratic class and despise themselves for so doing." In short, Prometheus, Mercury, and the Furies represent particular social groups or kinds of people: the rebellious, reform-minded intellectuals; the indecisive middle-class mugwumps; and the militarists, thieves, and parasites who subsist upon powers granted them by the aristocrats. According to this argument, Jupiter would typify the aristocratic ruling classes.

Thus far the statement of meanings is clear and explicit. But in applying these very particularized meanings to the action of the play, Professor Cameron is immediately compelled to hedge and to qualify. The first-act torture of Prometheus, he says, shows the intellectuals of Shelley's day "tormented by the thoughts of a Europe devastated by a quarter of a century of wars and oppression apparently never to rise again." Instead of being the forces by which the Quadruple alliance has kept itself in power—soldiers, lawyers, moneylenders, parasites—the Furies are now thoughts of devastation working on the mind of the intellectuals. Mercury, if he becomes anything under this dispensation, becomes the mind of the unrebellious oppressed, the in-between political mind harassed by a bad conscience. We are asked to believe, it appears, that this in-between political mind feels sorrow for the intellectuals who are tormented by thoughts of Europe's devastation; yet, if that is so, why is not Mercury tortured by the Furies? Having begun, almost against his will, to move from social-group symbols into mind-symbols, Cameron is compelled to abandon the social-group symbols previously assumed and to move over into a new position. A sign of his dilemma is his admission that "the Furies represent also, in a general ethical sense, tormenting thoughts of all kinds oppressing [the mind of] man." This is precisely what they do represent and, if this meaning is accepted, the meaning of the first act is plain. But if they represent "tormenting thoughts of all kinds," one is the less ready to suppose that they also stand for soldiers, lawyers, and parasites, or (in Cameron's second proposed meaning) that they represent thoughts of a Europe devastated by twenty-five years of war.

Cameron carries on his mind-symbols in interpreting the meanings of Ione (Memory) and Panthea (Hope). Again, his ideas would stand up in a general ethical sense were it not that he feels compelled to particularize them too much. The fact that Ione and Panthea dwell with Prometheus means, he suggests, that "the hope of a new order . . . and the memories of past struggles for liberty . . . live on in the hearts of mankind despite all the efforts of despotism to erase them." But it should be pointed out that Jupiter nowhere makes any visible attempt to "erase" Ione and Panthea. In accounting for Prometheus' first-act recantation of his curse on Jupiter, Cameron follows a similar pattern. The recantation means, he says, that "the intellectuals of the age are beginning to realize that they must erase all thought of revenge from their hearts in order to lead the coming revolution into peaceful channels, and, so, avoid anarchy." Yet this interpretation exists apart from the action of the play, for Prometheus expresses no fears that the coming revolution will be in any sense war-like, while a state of anarchy, in which the individual mind is self-sufficient and serene in self-dominance, appears to be the very goal which Prometheus seeks, achieves, and revels in.

Since Cameron agrees with other commentators in equating Asia with Love and Demogorgon with Necessity, the specific contribution of his political interpretation is the attempt to tie the *dramatis personae* to the particular social and political situation which Shelley found in Europe in 1818. Yet it is everywhere evident that in order to apply his social-group symbols to the interpretation of the play, he must in effect abandon them, or translate them into mind-symbols which in effect refute the social-group symbols. Insofar as he does so, he is undoubtedly moving in the right direction; but to the extent that he moves in the right direction he abandons his initial assumptions. That is, he abandons the specific socio-political context (in terms of which he wishes to view the play) in favor of a broader ethical context which is only tangentially related to the particularized meanings he alleges.

Because politics for Shelley was a branch of ethics, one may concede the view that he had in mind a general political idea. But no highly particularized interpretation using social-group symbols will stand alone, as is adequately shown by Cameron's respectable though abortive attempt to apply one to the play. What Cameron's argument proves, without his meaning to have it so, is that the more or less traditional ethical interpretation is probably the correct one.

Besides the political interpretation, another idea—namely, that the play occasionally moves on the plane of scientific meaning—has been suggested by Professor Carl Grabo. In his *A Newton Among Poets: Shelley's Use of Science in Prometheus Unbound*,[3] Grabo isolated and explained a sufficient number of scientific allusions in the play to make it evident that Shelley's interest in natural phenomena was of use to him in developing many of the images. A good example of Shelley's characteristic method (already alluded to in Chapter Four of this book) can be found in the fourth-act dialogue between the Earth and the Moon. But *Prometheus Unbound: An Interpretation*, published five years later by the same author, indicates (through the author's reluctance to assert that the play is exclusively a scientific allegory) that the scientific interpretation of the play fails to stand alone. This second book offers what Grabo calls a neo-Platonic interpretation of the action. On the whole, the argument is convincingly presented, except at those

[3] Published at Chapel Hill, N.C., 1930.

points where Professor Grabo, whose knowledge of neo-Platonic doctrine is both wide and deep, is led to apply to the interpretation of a given passage a concept either far from Shelley's customary views or not demonstrably known to the poet, who, though learned, was not so learned as Professor Grabo. The so-called neo-Platonic interpretation is, however, so deeply informed by ethical considerations that Grabo's is only a modification of the traditional view that the poem is a moral allegory. The unsatisfactory passages in the second of Grabo's books are those in which he tries to elevate the conclusions reached in the earlier study to a position of equal importance with the conclusions reached when the play is restudied in neo-Platonic terms. The formula under which Professor Grabo operates (that Shelley's symbols are often double-edged, being both "scientific and neo-Platonic in their import")[4] is strikingly parallel to the formula used by Professor Cameron. It serves Grabo well when applied to specific passages, but does not justify the inference that the drama as a whole is a scientific allegory any more than it is a political allegory. Fortunately, Professor Grabo does not protest too much. He appears to be much more deeply interested in the neo-Platonic than in the scientific aspects. It may not therefore be graceless to suggest that where Professor Grabo asserts or implies that the scientific aspects are of equal importance with the moralistic aspects, he is defending his own outworn thesis and is probably on unsafe ground; where he concentrates upon the exposition in moralistic terms, he produces one of the fullest and most searching, though not always the clearest, analyses of the poem which has been offered.

In concluding this note, one must enter a demurrer to the fashionable belief that Shelley's attainments in the field of nineteenth-century science were uncommon. That Shelley has rendered poetically, yet with a reasonable approximation of "scientific" exactness, a number of natural phenomena, is hardly a reason for supposing that he might have developed into a pioneer of modern physical science. Shelley was in fact an intelligent amateur. As a youth he showed commendable interest in test-tube chemistry, and as an adult he possessed more than usual curiosity about the functional aspects of the most common and easily observable natural forces. As a poet, Shelley displays interest in light, heat, elementary matter and energy, gravitation, vegetational changes, seeds and semination, winds, clouds, rain, snow, and the movements of the heavenly bodies. He often represents the results of his observations with telling effect, as in that *locus classicus*, "The Cloud." But his interest and curiosity in scientific problems is hardly such as to justify Professor A. N. Whitehead's remark that "if Shelley had been born a hundred years later, the twentieth century would have seen a Newton among chemists." Professor Grabo's error of judgment was not in accepting Professor Whitehead's implied "challenge" to English schol-

[4] *A Newton Among Poets*, preface, p. xi.

ars to explore Shelley's interest in science. His acceptance of the challenge has produced a heightened critical awareness of one of the sources of Shelley's imagery. The error consisted in Professor Grabo's quoting with tacit approval, and thus giving wide circulation to, Professor Whitehead's opinion on the probable course of Shelley's career if he had managed to postpone his birth until 1892. Of approximately equal worth would be the suggestion, based on Professor Spurgeon's researches in the iterative imagery of *Hamlet,* that if Shakespeare had been born 300 years later, the nineteenth century would have seen a pioneer in the study of carcinoma.

APPENDIX IV

THE DATE OF MARY'S DESPONDENCY

In one of the few vulnerable areas in his biography of Shelley Professor White has sought to establish the Este period, or that part of it succeeding Clara Shelley's death (i.e. late September, October, and early November, 1818) as a time when Shelley was extremely despondent. The constant implication is that his despondency was chiefly owing to his wife's physical and spiritual withdrawal, which in turn Professor White traces to the death of little Clara on September 24. The notion appears to be that, since Shelley had summoned Mary to join him at Este, and since the little girl fell ill en route, Mary held her husband in some measure responsible for the child's death, which occurred about two and a half weeks after the trip to Este had been completed.

This theory (which Professor White uses to support his argument that the story of the maniac in *Julian and Maddalo* is substantially an idealized representation of Shelley's own "hidden" feelings about his wife's coldness) is open to a great many objections. It is quite true that by Shelley's statement[1] the "unexpected stroke" of Clara's death "reduced Mary to a kind of despair." But it was a despair from which she soon recovered sufficiently to read, write, transcribe for Byron, enjoy (probably with some limitations) the sights and society of Venice, and to accompany her husband on a tour of historical spots. It need not be suggested that Mary took Clara's death callously. On the contrary, she was no doubt as heavily smitten by it as any other young mother would be. But she still had her son William and (sometimes) Claire's daughter Allegra to care for, and the presence of these children helped to fill the void Clara had left.

That Shelley accepted Clara's death with a degree of stoicism is indicated by the letter in which he tells the news to Peacock, a letter dated from Este in October. "I have not been without events to disturb and distract me," he says, "amongst which is the death of my little girl.

---

[1] *Letters,* IX, 333.

She died of a disorder peculiar to the climate. We have all had bad spirits enough, and I in addition, bad health. I *intend* to be better soon: there is no malady, bodily or mental, which does not either kill or be killed."[2]

In fairness to Professor White, it should be noticed that, by Shelley's statement, all of them had been in "bad spirits enough," during the two weeks following the child's death. But this is a very slight piece of evidence on which to base an argument to the effect that Mary had withdrawn spiritually from her husband at this time in the fall of 1818. What one must have is evidence that the "bad spirits" which would naturally ensue upon the death of a child were sufficiently powerful to cause a separation between Shelley and Mary. The letter to Peacock contains no such evidence. Bad spirits in a bereaved family at the end of the second week after a death occurs are natural and understandable; and the letter indicates nothing on the part of either Shelley or his wife which could be construed as abnormal.

The only other evidence that Mary was at all despondent in the period between the death of Clara and the death of William on June 7, 1819, is to be found in a letter of April 6, where she complains that she suffers from "ill spirits—God knows why but I have suffered more from them ten times over than I ever did before I came to Italy; evil thoughts will hang about me—but this is only now and then."[3] This would not seem to be part of a pattern of spiritual or physical withdrawal from her husband, but rather one of those sporadic attacks of sorrow which come to sensitive people. If, in her conscious recognition, the "ill spirits" of which she complains were connected with Clara's death, her statement that "God knows why" she has so suffered would be a peculiar way of indicating it. Moreover, as she concludes, the ill spirits and evil thoughts come only now and then. On April 26, she records that she is in "better health and spirits." It should be remarked in this connection that Mary had recently become pregnant (some time, at a rough guess, between late February and mid-March), a fact which in itself would help to explain her fluctuating moods. One should therefore view with grave doubts any implication that Mary's despondency was sufficiently marked in the fall of 1818 to occasion strained relations with her husband, with consequent despondency on his part.

The only poem of Shelley's which specifically belongs to the Este period (except, of course, the *Julian and Maddalo*) is the "Lines Written among the Euganean Hills," dated October, 1818. This is a sad poem, certainly, and one who chose to do so might connect it with Clara's death in the preceding month. But it is also, as Professor White appears also to believe, a fundamentally optimistic poem. There *are* green isles in the wide sea of misery; there *are* compensations for the

[2] *Letters*, IX, 334.
[3] *The Letters of Mary W. Shelley*, ed. F. L. Jones, I, 66-67.

agonies which human beings must endure. They consist in the beauties of nature, of poetry, of thoughts of liberty, and of dreams centering in some "healing paradise" for the writer and those he loves, where "the love which heals all strife" will encircle them "with its own mild brotherhood" so that soon "every sprite beneath the moon" would repent "its envy vain" and make the earth grow young again. In short, the "Lines" are of a piece with many other visionary poems from Shelley's pen; the fact that they were written in the month following his daughter's death may have had some bearing on their tone, but this is neither necessarily true, nor is there anything in the poem under consideration which would bear out such a conclusion. Unless and until some further evidence is forthcoming that Shelley had Clara or his own domestic situation prominently in mind when he wrote this poem, one is safest in the belief that he was trying to delineate sadness not in a specific but in a generalized sense. His prefatory remarks to this poem, though they do not prove anything in particular, might conceivably favor the interpretation just indicated. The poem was written, he says, after a day's excursion among the mountains where Petrarch's sepulcher lies. "If any one is inclined to condemn the insertion of the introductory lines, which image forth the sudden relief of a state of deep despondency by the radiant visions disclosed by the sudden burst of an Italian sunrise in autumn, on the highest peak of those delightful mountains, I can only offer as my excuse, that they were not erased at the request of a dear friend, with whom added years of intercourse only add to my apprehension of its value, and who would have had more right to complain, that she has not been able to extinguish in me the very power of delineating sadness."[4]

One may suppose that the "friend" was his wife, that despite her previous attempts to dissuade him from invoking his "power of delineating sadness" she urged him to retain the "introductory lines which image forth the sudden relief of deep despondency" by the sight of an Italian sunrise—primarily, one may suppose, because she liked the lines as poetry. One might also argue, with some reason, that the contemplation of the sepulcher of Petrarch, to which Shelley briefly alludes in a letter to Peacock on October 8, had something to do with the sadness of the "Lines." Yet this would fall into the area one wishes most to avoid, that of unprovable guesswork.

The death of William Shelley in June was clearly the blow Mary could not stand. Not only was her pregnancy further advanced, but also the searing realization that she was childless after four years of motherhood; the thought that the hateful climate of Italy had destroyed both her lovely children in less than a year; and the almost superstitious fear that the child she was coming to bear would constitute yet another risk, all combined to overlay her spirit with the deepest melancholy.

---

[4] The preface may be consulted in the *Rosalind and Helen* volume (1819) where Shelley inserted his poem.

"The hopes of my life are bound up in him," she had said while William lay on his deathbed.[5] A letter of June 27 shows how she sought to avoid mention of William's death three weeks after it happened, only to add before the letter was done, that she did not care how soon she died, and that she felt the loss more now than at Rome. "The thought never leaves me for a single moment—everything on earth has lost its interest to me." She is "childless and for ever miserable." Her hours are spent in tears; she is "not fit for anything and therefore not fit to live."[6]

In mid-September, as her lying-in approaches, she records: "My spirits suffer terribly—time is a weight to me"—a not unusual phenomenon among women in her condition. On September 24, however, she says piteously, "I am much changed, the world will never be to me again as it was . . . I ought to have died on the seventh of June last." She wishes for a dozen children—"anything but none," or one, which might be nearly as bad as none, for one child could (as she had with great suffering discovered) easily die, whereas of a dozen some might survive.[7]

Shelley, too, suffered deeply during that summer when he was writing *The Cenci.* His suffering was partly on his own but mostly on Mary's account. "It seems to me," he wrote on June 8, "that I should never recover my cheerfulness again," which was a much different remark from that which he had made to Peacock after Clara's death. "Our house is a melancholy one," he said in July. On July 25th he said that Mary bore their heavy misfortune worse than he.[8]

Mary resumed her diary on August 4, 1819, Shelley's twenty-seventh birthday. "We have now lived five years together," she wrote, "and if all the events of the five years were blotted out, I might be happy; but to have won, and then cruelly to have lost, the associations of four years is not an accident to which the human mind can bend without much suffering." The associations of four years were her dead children, of whom, rather than of her husband, she is clearly thinking. The next day Shelley recorded his own ill spirits and ill health, and said that "Mary's spirits still continue wretchedly depressed—more so than a stranger . . . could imagine." Ten days later he says that he is "surrounded by suffering and disquietude, and, latterly, almost overcome by our strange misfortunes."[9] While Mary was saying that she should have died with William on the seventh of June, Shelley was beginning to hope that Mary's confinement, which they expected towards the end of October, would be of help. "The birth of a child," he predicted, "will probably relieve her from some part of her present melancholy depression." Until that birth occurred, however, he wisely took no risks with Mary's state of mind. On the eve of her confinement he concealed a letter concerning William's gravestone, out of the "fear of agitating her on a subject which

[5] Jones, *op. cit.*, I, 72-73. June 3, 1819.   [6] Jones, *op. cit.*, I, 73, 74, 75.
[7] *Ibid.*, I, 79, 81.   [8] *Letters*, x, 53, 60, 64.
[9] *Ibid.*, x, 66-68.

has never until now [Nov. 18] ceased to be a source of perpetual grief to her."[10]

Shelley's prediction was sound. After the birth of the child Percy, Mary made rapid strides towards recovery, though her mind was still occupied with fear over the fact that all hope should be risked, perforce, in a single child. "Yet how much sweeter," she exclaimed, "than to be childless as I was for five hateful months."

The story is almost too full of horrors to be gone over. Yet the reader who has followed it thus far will see clearly that Mary's awful melancholy began in June and subsided in November, 1819. The evidence shows that, after the death of William Shelley, both Mary and her husband were perfectly explicit about their mutual woe and its cause. There is a reasonable supposition that if Mary's abnormal depression of spirits had begun in the fall of 1818, as Professor White implies, she or her husband would have given some expression to it. When it really came, they did not attempt to conceal it.

Mary's unpublished story, "Mathilda," which Professor Elizabeth Nitchie described at length in her valuable article in *Studies in Philology*, corroborates the view that an abnormal depression of spirits occurred in Mary sometime prior to August 4, 1819.[11] But it does not support Professor White's belief that an estrangement or a depression occurred in 1818. According to Professor Nitchie, the story "was probably written and copied between August 4 and September 12, 1819," though perhaps revised later. There is no good reason to suppose that Mary was here alluding to the events of the preceding September. In view of the evidence rehearsed above, however, there is some reason to think that she had in mind the events of June and July, 1819, when her abnormal depression was close to its nadir.

The facts, then, so far as they can be determined from Mary's journal and the letters of both Shelley and Mary, do not bear out Professor White's guess as to the date of the beginning of Mary's despondency. The conclusion is clear: The story of the maniac in *Julian and Maddalo* has nothing provable to do with Shelley's domestic affairs.

[10] *Ibid.*, x, 87, 127.   [11] *SP*, 40 (1943), 447-462.

SELECTED BIBLIOGRAPHY

I. WORKS AND LETTERS

Ingpen, Roger, and Peck, W. E., eds., *The Complete Works of Percy Bysshe Shelley*. Julian edition. 10 vols. London, 1926-1930.

> For Shelley's letters and prose works this is the best edition to date, although a number of letters are not included here. Unless otherwise indicated, references to Shelley's prose works and letters in the present volume are to this edition. Other letters are located by footnotes.

Jones, F. L., ed., *The Letters of Mary W. Shelley*. 2 vols. Norman, Oklahoma, 1944.

Jones, F. L., ed., *Mary Shelley's Journal*. Norman, Oklahoma, 1947.

Woodberry, G. E., ed., *The Complete Poetical Works of Percy Bysshe Shelley*. Cambridge edition. Boston, 1901.

> This excellent edition has here been preferred to the Julian edition for citations and quotations from Shelley's poetry.

II. BIOGRAPHICAL-CRITICAL STUDIES

Blunden, Edmund, *Shelley: A Life Story*. London, 1946.

> Sound and readable biography with fresh critical commentary on important poems.

Campbell, O. W., *Shelley and the Unromantics*. London, 1924.

> Usually sound and always concise and witty, this book offers a short biographical study and critiques of *Alastor, Prometheus Unbound*, and other poems.

Dowden, Edward, *The Life of Percy Bysshe Shelley*. 2 vols. London, 1886.

> The authorized life: a good Victorian biography.

Grabo, Carl, *The Magic Plant*. Chapel Hill, N.C., 1936.

> Shelley's life and thought in the light of the author's previous studies of neo-Platonic and scientific strains in Shelley. A judicious and valuable work, in which no attempt is made to cut the poet to a preconceived pattern.

Kurtz, B. P., *The Pursuit of Death*. New York, 1933.

> A thesis book, worth serious attention despite the exclusiveness of its concentration on certain phases of Shelley's thought.

Stovall, Floyd, *Desire and Restraint in Shelley.* Durham, N.C., 1931.
A useful and penetrating biographical study of the altruistic and egoistic aspects of Shelley. Concludes that Shelley eventually compromised his ideals in the face of continued opposition.

Weaver, Bennett, *Towards the Understanding of Shelley.* Ann Arbor, Michigan, 1932.
The prophetic strain in Shelley.

White, N. I., *Shelley.* 2 vols. New York, 1940.
The most thorough, painstaking, and factually authoritative biography to date. A revised, one-volume version of the larger work appeared as *Portrait of Shelley*, New York, 1945.

III. SPECIAL EDITIONS, ESSAYS, AND STUDIES

Barnard, Ellsworth, *Shelley's Religion.* Minneapolis, 1936.
A sympathetic and useful study, inclined to apologize for the young Shelley, who needs apology.

Barrell, Joseph, *Shelley and the Thought of His Time: A Study in the History of Ideas.* New Haven, 1947.
Contains a perceptive chapter on Shelley and Greek thought with special reference to Plato.

Bates, E. S., *A Study of Shelley's Drama, The Cenci.* New York, 1908.

Beach, J. W., *The Concept of Nature in Nineteenth-Century English Poetry.* New York, 1936.
Contains interesting chapters on Shelley's naturalism and idealism.

Bernbaum, Ernest, *Guide Through the Romantic Movement.* 5 vols. New York, 1938.

Böhme, Traugott, "Spenser's Literarisches Nachleben bis zu Shelley," in *Palaestra*, 93. Berlin, 1911.

Bradley, A. C., "Notes on Shelley's *Triumph of Life*," *Modern Language Review* 9 (1914), 441-456.

Brailsford, H. N., *Shelley, Godwin, and Their Circle.* New York, 1913.
Shelley as youthful radical.

Brinton, C. C., *The Political Ideas of the English Romanticists.* New York, 1926.
Stresses Shelleyan utopianism.

Bush, Douglas, *Mythology and the Romantic Tradition in English Poetry.* Cambridge, Mass., 1937.
The section on Shelley is excellent if perhaps unduly disparaging.

Cameron, K. N., "Shelley and *Ahrimanes*," *Modern Language Quarterly* 3 (1942), 287-296.

Follows up the business left unfinished by Peacock's editors, on the relation between Peacock's poem and *The Revolt of Islam*.

Cameron, K. N., "The Political Symbolism of *Prometheus Unbound*," *PMLA* 58 (1943), 728-753.

An important and already influential interpretation, which is considered in Appendix III of this book.

Cameron, K. N., and Frenz, Horst, "The Stage History of Shelley's *The Cenci*," *PMLA* 60 (1945), 1080-1105.

Clark, D. L., "Shelley and Shakespeare," *PMLA* 54 (1939), 261-287.

Cook, A. S., ed., *A Defence of Poetry*. Boston, 1890.

Eliot, T. S., "Shelley and Keats," in *The Use of Poetry and the Use of Criticism*. Cambridge, Mass., 1933.

Typical of and influential in much of the modern depreciation of Shelley. Eliot Ikonoklastes against the Idolaters.

Elton, Oliver, *A Survey of English Literature 1780-1830*. 4 vols. New York, 1920.

Contains a sane and illuminating study of Shelley.

Evans, F. B., "Shelley, Godwin, Hume, and the Doctrine of Necessity," *Studies in Philology* 37 (1940), 632-640.

Gates, E. J., "Shelley and Calderón," *Philological Quarterly* 16 (1937), 49-58.

Gingerich, S. F., *Essays in the Romantic Poets*. New York, 1924.

Shelley as necessitarian, with that philosophy considered as a steady force in Shelley's thought.

Havens, R. D., "Shelley's *Alastor*," *PMLA* 45 (1930), 1098-1115.

Included here as the best negativistic analysis of the poem, setting the problem of unity of intention.

Hoffman, H. L., *An Odyssey of the Soul: Shelley's Alastor*. New York, 1933.

A thorough investigation of the poem's sources, with an interpretation in terms of the Narcissus legend.

Hughes, A. M. D., "Shelley and Nature," *North American Review* 208 (1918), 350-358.

Hungerford, E. B., *Shores of Darkness*. New York, 1941.

The mythological aspects of *Prometheus Unbound* and *Adonais*.

Jones, F. L., "Shelley and Spenser," *Studies in Philology* 39 (1942), 662-670.

Kapstein, I. J., "The Meaning of Shelley's *Mont Blanc*," *PMLA* 62 (1947), 1046-1060.
> Shows the conflict in the poem between worship and defiance of the power of Necessity.

Larrabee, S. A., *English Bards and Grecian Marbles*. New York, 1943.
> Contains a valuable treatment of Shelley's interest in Greek sculpture.

Madariaga, Salvador de, *Shelley and Calderón, and Other Essays*. London, 1920.
> A graceful essay by the distinguished Spanish humanist.

More, Paul Elmer, "Shelley," in *Shelburne Essays: Seventh Series*. New York, 1910.
> Summarizes polemically the neo-humanist derogation of Shelley.

Rossetti, W. M., and Prickard, A. O., eds., *Adonais*. Oxford, 1903.

Santayana, George, "Shelley," in *Winds of Doctrine*. New York, 1913.
> A brilliant essay on Shelley's idealism.

Scott, W. S., ed., *Shelley at Oxford*. London, 1944.
> Like *The Athenians* (London, 1943) and *Harriet and Mary* (London, 1944), all under the editorship of Mr. Scott, *Shelley at Oxford* makes available in a very handsome format certain of the materials in the possession of the heirs of T. J. Hogg.

Solve, M. T., *Shelley: His Theory of Poetry*. Chicago, 1927.
> A fine study of a difficult subject.

Stawell, F. M., "Shelley's *Triumph of Life*," *Essays and Studies by Members of the English Association* 5 (1914), 104-131.

Stovall, Floyd, "Shelley's Doctrine of Love," *PMLA* 45 (1930), 283-303.

Walker, A. S., "Peterloo, Shelley, and Reform," *PMLA* 40 (1925), 128-164.
> The background of *The Masque of Anarchy*.

Watson, S. R., "A Comparison of *Othello* and *The Cenci*," *PMLA* 55 (1940), 611-614.
> A useful supplement to Professor Clark's article on Shelley and Shakespeare.

White, N. I., *The Unextinguished Hearth*. Durham, N.C., 1938.
> Reprints nearly all reviews and articles on Shelley, 1810-1822, with an introductory essay on the poet and his contemporary critics.

White, N. I., "Shelley's *Swellfoot the Tyrant* in Relation to Contemporary Political Satire," *PMLA* 36 (1921), 332-346.

BIBLIOGRAPHY

Woodberry, G. E., ed., *The Cenci, by Percy Bysshe Shelley.* Boston, 1909.

Includes the source manuscript of the play in Shelley's translation.

Yeats, William Butler, "The Philosophy of Shelley's Poetry," in *Ideas of Good and Evil.* London, 1903.

Shelley as philosophical symbolist, by a great poet who understood him perfectly in general though not always in particular.

INDEX

INDEX

Peter Bell (Wordsworth), 155, 164-
165, 168, 170-171, 173n
Peter Bell: A Lyrical Ballad (Reynolds), 164, 166
Peterloo, massacre at, 155, 155n, 157,
160, 162, 174, 193, see also Manchester
Petrarch, 16, 130n, 161, 161n, 222, 262,
289
Phaedrus (Plato), 53, 250
phantasm, in Alastor, 44; of Jupiter in
Prometheus Unbound, 97-98; of Leonora in Julian and Maddalo, 134; of
Liberty in Masque of Anarchy, 161-
162; of Liberty in Oedipus Tyrannus,
180; of Darius in Hellas, 184
Plato, 11, 16, 53, 93, 103n, 108n, 113,
186, 196, 211, 225-226, 234, 241-
242, 247-248, 250, 253, 262n, 263,
265n
Pliny, 207-209
Political Justice (Godwin), 22, 33, 82
Political Register (Cobbett's), 176,
176n
Pope, Alexander, 24-25, 29, 32-33
popularity, Shelley seeks, 138-139, 160n
Prelude, The (Wordsworth), 171n
Prickard, A. O., 241n
pride, in Prometheus Unbound, 97
priestess, of Atlas, 206-207, 213
priesthood, Shelley's attack on, 26
Primum Mobile, in Shelley, 251
Prince Regent (George IV), 155-156,
160-161
progress, idea of, 9, 36, 273
Prometheia (Aeschylus), 109n, 281-
283; Prometheus Bound, 90, 90n,
178n, 216; Prometheus Unbound,
184
Prometheus, Shelley's concept of, 90,
92; change in, 96-97; and Milton's
Satan, 97; and Jesus Christ, 98-99
Prophecy of Dante (Byron), 258, 262n
Prospero, 12-13, 18, 187, 243, 255n
Punch and Judy, 174, 177
Purgatorio (Dante), 221n, 258, 266n

Quadrio, 132
Quadruple Alliance, see Alliance
Quarterly Review, The, 167, 239-240
quest-motif, in Alastor, 43

radicalism, Shelley's political, 22-23, 80,
see also reform, revolution, etc.
realism, ethical, in Shelley, 273

reason, concept of, 234
reform, political and moral, 23, 39, 63,
78, 159; in Promethus Unbound, 96;
Reform Bill, 175, see also radicalism,
revolution, etc.
Reign of Terror, Shelley's revulsion at,
78
Republic (Plato), 113
republicanism, Shelley's, 34n
reputation, Shelley's, 11
resistance, passive, in Masque of An-
archy, 163
Revelation, Book of, 73, 161-162
Reveley, Henry, 203, 205
Revolution, "beau idéal" of, 39, 78,
184; bloodless, 8; French, 77, 183;
Greek, 156, 182; Neapolitan, 183;
Spanish, 182-183, see also Reign of
Terror
Reynolds, J. H., 164-165, 165n, 166
Richard III (Shakespeare), 150n
Richards, I. A., 90
Rinaldo Rinaldini, 79n
Rossetti, W. M., 112n, 241n, 243n,
245n, 262n
Rousseau, J. J., 36, 241, 257-260, 262-
269, 272
Royce, Josiah, 118n
Ruines of Time (Spenser), 72n

"Sacred few," Shelley's concept of, 40,
254, 262, 267n, 274
St. Anna, convent of (Pisa), 218
Salt, H. S., 112n
Santa Anna, hospital of, 130, 132, 149
Santayana, George, 252, 252n
Satan, Milton's, 24, 198-199, 261n, 277-
278
Scott, Sir Walter, 22, 65-66
Scott, W. S., 30n
Scudder, V., 103n
sculptures, Florentine, Shelley's interest
in, 245n
Seasons (Thomson), 26-28
Selden, 65
self-portrait, Shelley's in Adonais, 243
Serassi, biographer of Tasso, 128n, 129,
131, 133, 133n, 135
serpent, as symbol of good, 70-74, 77
Shakespeare, William, 12, 16, 23, 48,
96, 105, 139, 150, 150n, 187, 201,
207-208, 237n, 244, 245n, 266n, 287
Shaw, G. B., on Queen Mab, 38, 38n,
187

INDEX